PRAISE FOR *FUTURE MARKETING*

"Right now is the best time to 'future-proof' your marketing plan. There is a clear opportunity for those organizations to rethink how they've been communicating with consumers. Those that create better customer experiences will win...it's that simple. *Future Marketing* is the roadmap to help you get there."
—Joe Pulizzi, Founder, Content Marketing Institute

"In the past, we were all consumers. As technology evolves before us—we are all now prosumers. Every one of us is now researcher, reviewer, editor and expert on some topic. So, the lines between marketing, customer and influencer begin blurring substantially. Jon has artfully recognized this and constructed a pragmatic roadmap to help navigate us through this blur. An outstanding book."
—Robert Rose, Chief Strategy Advisor, Content Marketing Institute

"If you want to map a content marketing course to the future, settle in to Jon Wuebben's book and prepare for a wild ride to success."
—Michael Stelzner, Founder & CEO, Social Media Examiner

"Surviving the digital age as a business is tough. Surviving (and thriving) for the long term is even harder. But this exactly why Jon Wuebben's *Future Marketing* is so important. As businesses, we must do what it takes to stay ahead of the curve, and Jon gives you the steps, strategy, and plan to achieve just that."
—Marcus Sheridan, President, The Sales Lion

"Jon's been a popular speaker at Content Marketing Conference for years, and his third book, *Future Marketing*, is yet another well-documented journey where marketing possibility and probability collide. You'll find vision that's rooted with the greatest futurists of all time, and marketing predictions grounded by the content marketing revolutionaries. When you dive into the future, you'll surface with Jon's take on how consumers and promoters and providers all play together in the sandbox of the future,

with new tools, tactics and techniques that accelerate business growth in strange and mysterious ways."
—**Byron White**, Chair, Content Marketing Conference, CEO, WriterAccess

"Businesses are no longer completely in control of their products, brands and messages. The consumer, or 'prosumer' is now in control. Jon Wuebben knocked this book out of the park handing you a clear way to build a human business with the right influence, at the right time, and with the right people."
—**Bryan Kramer**, CEO, Pure Matter/Best Selling Author, TED Speaker

"*Future Marketing* helps you think and do differently from everyone else. This book can and should serve as a first step to expanding your content marketing practices. I don't think I have the guts to make predictions 5 years into the future, let alone 10+ years. But Jon does. And he might just be spot on. A highly recommended read for all marketers and business owners."
—**Arnie Kuenn**, President, Vertical Measures

"Want an express ride into the minds of today's consumers? Jon shows you how to prepare your marketing for the new digital age!"
—**Tim Ash**, CEO of SiteTuners, Bestselling Author of *Landing Page Optimization*, Chair of Conversion Conference

"Marketing is very exciting and fast moving, it's important not just to 'react' to the changes; we also need to step back and plan for future changes. Jon provides amazing insights into what is coming in marketing and is a must read for any marketer in the industry."
—**Ian Cleary**, Founder & CEO, Razor Social

"If you want to future-proof your brand's marketing and content strategy, read *Future Marketing*. And after you finish with Jon Wuebben's brilliant book, maybe you could read my book, *Digital Sense*? That's right, an ad in a book blurb. #nextlevel."
— **Travis Wright**, CMO/CTO, CCP Digital & Author of *Digital Sense*

"Most business books teach tactics or strategy for today's environment. But rarely do we journey into the future to think about what's possible—

which is exactly what *Future Marketing* does. This book should be the guiding light for all marketers, to help you think about your marketing and your company in new ways. It's grand in scope and deep on ideas, exactly what we need to be prepared for tomorrow."

–Carla Johnson, Chief Experience Officer, Type A Communications and Co-Author of *Experiences: The 7th Era of Marketing*

"The marketers that I admire most are the ones who are one step ahead of the current trends; the ones who take the timeless tactics of the past and mash them up with the present while embracing the uncertainty of the future. Jon Wuebben is two steps ahead with his latest book, *Future Marketing*. It's a field guide to not only future proofing your business, but also your career as a marketer."

–Jason Miller, Global Content Marketing Leader, LinkedIn

"If you want to read a book about what has and hasn't worked for marketers in the past, or today, you have roughly a million choices. However, if it's the future that intrigues you, Jon's book stands alone. It's a fascinating take on marketing. Bravo to Jon for having the vision–and huevos–to take us time traveling forward."

–Barry Feldman, President, Feldman Creative

"Jon Wuebben provides a comprehensive insight into the state of marketing through the lens of the past, the current and the next two decades. His insights are grounded in research, examples and intuition. His enthusiasm for the future of marketing is contagious."

–Bernie Borges, CEO, Find and Convert

"One of the many things I admire about Jon Wuebben is his ability to be forward thinking with ideas on business and marketing. *Future Marketing: Winning In The Prosumer Age* takes these ideas and provides a road map and real examples of how the future of marketing is happening right now. If you want to be a part of it, read this book!"

–Pamela Muldoon, President, Muldoon Media

"Marketers can often feel like they're running on a daily hamster wheel of change. With *Future Marketing*, Jon Wuebben gathers data and in-

sights to paint the exciting BIG picture of what's to come and how we'll get there. You'll be energized along the way with a vision that moves you well beyond the buzz!"
—**Deana Goldasich**, President, Well Planned Web, LLC

"No matter what the trend, those that get started sooner reap the biggest rewards. Business leaders should be in the habit of embracing what is coming and not wait for what has is fashionable. This book has given me the map I need to chart an early path into the minds of my prospects using content and smart marketing."
—**Brian Massey**, Founder & CEO, Conversion Sciences

"If you're gazing out over the futurescape of marketing and thinking it similar to a fumble on the one-yard line or driving in rush-hour traffic, *Future Marketing* provides a thought-provoking roadmap highlighting the many factors—customers, technology and culture—you'd be well advised to heed."
—**Jay Durgan**, Chief Content & Marketing Officer, Media Mobz

"Whether you're a startup or a small business veteran, Future Marketing is a must read! As an entrepreneur you don't just need to know what the trends are—you need to understand how to apply what's happening to your business so that you can bob and weave right along with it. *Future Marketing* is both a trend book and a guidepost that you can use to understand which trends will hit your business and how to leverage new technologies to support your business. If you're feeling overwhelmed by the speed of entrepreneurship, *Future Marketing* is for you."
—**Ivana Taylor**, CEO, Third Force Marketing, Publisher of DIY Marketers

"You are holding in your hands a clear-eyed vision of what is coming next in the marketing business. Lets face it, most marketers are several years behind the big trends. This book is a fast way to get caught up. In *Future Marketing*, Jon also provides a practical look at where we are today."
—**Andy Crestodina**, CEO, Orbit Media

FUTURE MARKETING

WINNING IN THE PROSUMER AGE

FUTURE MARKETING

Winning in the Prosumer Age

Jon Wuebben

Foreword by Robert Rose

content launch press
www.contentlaunch.com

Also by Jon Wuebben

Content is Currency: Developing Powerful Content for Web and Mobile

Content Rich: Writing Your Way to Wealth on the Web

FUTURE MARKETING: Winning in the Prosumer Age

Copyright © 2017 by Jon Wuebben

ISBN 978-0-692-77506-6

Table of Contents

CONTENTS ix

FOREWORD—Robert Rose xi

INTRODUCTION 1

MAKING THE CASE

1. The State of Marketing Nation 23

2. Mega-Trends: Cultural and Technological Shifts 32

3. Futurists' Predictions 42

4. Power of Content Marketing: Ushering in the New Age 52

5. Rise of Marketing Technology 66

THE CHANGING CUSTOMER

6. Power to the People 85

7. Prosumer and Peer-to-Peer Groups 110

8. The New Way to Engage: Experiences 121

THE CHANGING ECONOMIC SYSTEM

9. Post-Capitalism 128

MARKETING IN THE YEAR 2021

10. Overview: Five Years from Now 142

11. The Future Digital Marketing Agency 173

MARKETING IN THE YEAR 2030

12. Overview: 2030 Will Arrive Sooner than You Think 179

13. Marketing Beyond 2030 203

EVOLUTION OF MARKETING FUNDAMENTALS

14. The Future Marketing Mix Construct 215
15. The Future Marketing Department 228

CONCLUSIONS

16. Companies Showing the Way Now........................... 246
17. Wrap-Up and the Road Ahead 267

BIBLIOGRAPHY... 277
NOTES 278
INDEX 282

Welcome to the Future. You're Late.

Shakespeare once said that it is not in the stars that our destiny lies, but in ourselves. As marketers, as business strategists, our future is of our own making. Marketing has changed. Past tense. When you opened this book, you already recognized that. And so the only question that remains is, what are you going to do about it?

In our near past, we were all simply consumers. We consumed information provided by mass media. We consumed expert services that helped us communicate or optimally perform some task. And, we consumed products provided by companies that had the technical expertise to produce, promote, place and price them in places where we could be reached with frequency.

Yes. Marketing has changed.

As technology evolves before us, we are all now *prosumers*. Every single one of us is now researcher, product designer, reviewer, editor, and expert on some topic. So, the lines between marketing, customer, and influencer have begun to substantially blur.

As the need to reach and influence the prosumer increases, no function in the business has been as fundamentally revolutionized as marketing. The social and mobile Web has completely changed the speed, efficiency, and ease with which prosumers can engage with each other. New technologies on the horizon such as the Internet of Things, 3-D printing, virtual and augmented reality, and artificial intelligence will fundamentally disrupt the way we compete in new markets, reach people within them, and convince them our solution is the one they want or need.

This new engagement of customers—with keen awareness of their fragmented relationship with brands—now correlates to every single aspect of our business. Marketing now influences how our accountants account, researchers research, developers develop, service people service, and even how leaders lead.

Our ability to evolve will have the most profound impact on our business and our careers. Whether we build a subscriber base of evangelists (what we used to call loyal customers), or an audience that will buy from us with more intention or frequency (what we used to call leads and opportunities), the driver of building conversation with these prosumers about our product (as well as *why* our product) will revolve around one competency—content.

Welcome to *Future Marketing: Winning in the Prosumer Age*. What Jon has done in this book is to artfully recognize these seismic shifts. He has constructed a pragmatic roadmap to help navigate us through this fast-changing landscape. It's an outstanding book—and one that will help you thrive in this new age.

It is up to us, as marketers, to lead our businesses through this change. Focusing on the future brings it to our present, and creates the past that truly defines our experience. Shakespeare was right. It's not in the stars to hold our destiny. It's our responsibility, as well as our opportunity, to become the stars of our own future.

Are you ready? Then let's shine.

—**Robert Rose**
Chief Strategy Advisor
Content Marketing Institute

Introduction

The future: It is ours to create. We can plan for it and build it in whatever way we want to. We can dream and envision a world of unlimited possibility, where people everywhere experience a higher quality of life than they do now—or not. And as we look into the vast expanse of coming years and the opportunities they present, we should all be encouraged: there has never been a better time to be alive, a better time to be in business or...a better time to be a *marketer*. The next fifteen years will unleash a waterfall of unprecedented improvements in social connection, efficiency, and quality of life—for everyone, the world over. As marketers, we will have entirely new ways of operating. We will have new tools in our tool chest, new arrows in our quiver. Our role in our organizations, with our partners, our stakeholders, our agencies and as you will see, in *our world*, will take on new meaning, new importance and have an impact that will dramatically improve our customers lives.

Change: It is a constant. And the pace of it will, in fact, escalate. But we are conditioned to it now. We expect it. Back in the year 2000, at the dawn of our new century, that wasn't the case. But now we all know the constant evolution of technology, culture, processes, our work life, and the way we connect with customers; they're always in a perpetual state of *becoming*. This is important to keep in mind. If you are "status quo" in mindset, you will be at the back of the line in the future. You will be, in effect, marginalized.

As organizations and as marketers, we need to be open, flexible and forward thinking—*always* forward thinking. All ideas are on the table, all the time. This mindset, this approach, has really been a hallmark of the

1

Millennial Generation. What it has brought to bear over the last number of years has made a massive positive impact on our society. As a member of Generation X, I can see the differences, and I'm not sure our generation could have pulled it off. There is an energy, an enthusiasm and a confidence in the twenty- and thirty-something's of today that will continue to be very important as we usher in the future of marketing.

In addition, the Millennial Generation values connectedness and collaboration, which will be even more important skillsets in the future than they are today. Folks in their twenties and thirties have a unique type of impatience with things and have a need for constant feedback, other valuable traits. And, of course, their commitment to social justice, sustainability, and the civic good are all important distinctions as well. Oh, and by the way, Generation Z—those born between 1996 and 2011—shares these attributes. It's very inspiring to see.

In my last book, *Content is Currency: Developing Powerful Content for Web and Mobile*, in 2012, I taught the finer points of content marketing. It was a guidebook on how to use content to effectively connect with your audience. I'm very happy to say that the book did its job. It helped a lot of organizations and marketers all over the world. I was honored

and humbled by the positive response it received. Fast-forward four years and I'm ready to do this all over again! Except this time, I want to go in a new direction; I want to think bigger, I want to make *Future Marketing* more strategic and visionary and less tactical in its lessons. Teaching people how to do something is incredibly valuable, and I no doubt did that with *Content is Currency*. But with *Future Marketing*, I want to take you on a journey. I'd like to inspire some

thinking and planning. I want to offer you a possible roadmap or set of options. In short, I want you to be as excited about the future of marketing as I am. It's a positive story to tell.

A Beginning: May, 2016—Las Vegas

In May 2016 I spoke at the annual Content Marketing Conference (CMC) in Las Vegas. My topic was "Future Marketing: Tactics for the Peer-To-Peer Economy." In the session, I covered a very small portion of what I'm discussing in this book, but what was interesting was how engaged the audience was in the topic. There was a certain *magic* in the room, unlike other conference presentations I've given. In the last fifteen minutes of the session, lots of people started funneling into the room, as if they had heard from other conference attend- ees that something interesting was being presented. Indus- try thought leaders like Bryan Kramer and Drew Neisser were there; both came up to me af- terwards and thanked me for the information. I have to say, it was all a bit unexpected, but very nice to see.

Of course, I get it. It's the "crystal ball" thing or the "back to the future" effect—whatever you want to call it. Lots of people out there are enchanted by the idea of *what's coming next*. For the trailblazers and the optimists, the future always seems very exciting. I'm an optimist and I know the future will be amazing. Over the next couple of years, I plan to present this topic at dozens of conferences and events all over the world, but I'll always remem- ber that it all started at CMC in Vegas with that welcoming audience.

Cultural Changes Shifting the Business Paradigm

The sharing economy. The Internet of Things. Sound familiar? They wouldn't have just a few years ago. And that's because the technology didn't exist or people weren't ready. Of course, things have been chang- ing rapidly for the last twenty years or so. If you're over forty, you'll vividly recall a time before the Internet. For much of the 1970s through the 1990s, things in business really didn't change a whole lot. I know: I was there. There were no massive cultural changes in business or marketing. There were the standard business norms, the "way of doing things," and connecting with other people was done in a few limited ways: in person, over the phone, through mail, over television, on the radio, or through print. That was it. But that was *then*. Everything is different now. What else have we already witnessed in the changing culture? Here are a few more we've seen:

- The mobile revolution
- Crowdsourcing and crowdfunding
- The new connected home
- Voice recognition (like Siri)
- Gesture-controlled gaming

As someone who has lived four-and-a-half decades on Earth, I can confidently tell you, it's never been more exciting than it is right now! Things are about to get *really* interesting.

Rising Skillsets and Personal Traits—While the twentieth century was very much a "left-brain" century, where process, order, analytical thinking, memorization ability, and an orientation towards detail were important, the twenty-first century will be a "right-brain" century where "design" will be ascendant: design of objects, systems, ecosystems, mega-cities, and lives. We started seeing this in a big way at companies like Apple, where Steve Jobs and Tony Ive preached and practiced the design way of thinking every day of their working lives.

Creativity, which emanates in the right brain, is also a rising skillset across many industries. Essentially, anything that can't be easily duplicated by someone else will take on greater importance in coming years. Creating something unique and memorable is always difficult to duplicate. And even if the creation is duplicated, the original creator will always enjoy the greatest rewards. I discuss the importance of creativity throughout the book, especially in chapter fifteen, the future marketing department.

Rising Consciousness, Awareness and Spirituality–There is something all around us now, which has been growing over the past few years, something that's hard to put a finger on, but something that is truly different than what existed just ten to fifteen years ago: it's part consciousness, part spirituality, part intuitive knowledge and growth, part a "coming together." Whatever this is, it will rapidly expand over the next fifteen years and have deep and lasting implications for marketers everywhere. Again, this is another really exciting and positive part of the futurescape for my fellow optimists out there.

Perhaps it started with the Mayan Prophecy of 2012, which predicted a transformative change for humanity on 12/21/12. Perhaps it was ushered along by the likes of Oprah Winfrey, Deepak Chopra, Tony Robbins and others who have been at the center of the "peak performance" and "personal coaching" communities, groups that didn't even exist thirty years ago. Perhaps it's the globalization movement, the Internet, the smartphone, the impact of international trade. Perhaps it's a combination of all of these things and more.

David Houle, author of *Entering the Shift Age*, predicts that by the late 2020s our sense of the world on our electronic screens will move us beyond our "physical" reality and change our very consciousness. He writes, "This will be a significant separation, new to the human experience."[1]

Another leading mind puts it this way:

> *The people of the world have an "unfinishable mandate" to continually stretch, grow, propagate, and master not only the world around us, but also the entire universe. The human race has a genetic predisposition for pushing the envelope, coloring outside the lines, and reaching for things that will forever be unreachable. As individuals, there will be some who are content to find inner peace and live a minimalist lifestyle. But as a race, we are driven by the need to make a difference, be admired for our accomplishments, and create moments of triumph in our otherwise pale existence. We have only taken the first step in a trillion-mile journey. The next few steps, in my opinion, will be nothing short of spectacular.[2]*
>
> — Thomas Frey, futurist

The *Third Wave*—A Landmark Book

There was one person back in the 1970s and '80s who saw what today might be like. He peered into the future and came back with some incredible insights. He was what was called a "futurist," and his name was Alvin Toffler. In 1982, at the age of eleven, I read his groundbreaking book, *The Third Wave*. And I was totally mesmerized. In fact, I can still picture the scene, like it happened yesterday. When I picked it up at the Carlsbad Library, and started paging through it, it was a moment I'll never forget. He wrote of what life would be like in 2016. He explained how business—and marketing—might be done. He discussed how society would need to change. He based it on well-crafted research. He interviewed all the key players. He talked to the leading companies at the time. But mostly, he imparted some deep wisdom.

The Third Wave was so good that I read the first three chapters right there at the library, sitting on one of their beanbags in the children's section. I just couldn't put it down. The rest of the book I read at home in just four days. You see, what was true then, is still true for me now: *Thinking about the future is exciting!* Maybe you're the same. The possibilities, the potential, the improvements we can make—they're simply exhilarating to ponder. Couple it with my love of marketing (and writing), and it's a perfect match: "The Future" and "Marketing"—it's been a lifelong passion. Now I seek to bestow my ideas, my thoughts, others ideas and thoughts, and yes, my enthusiasm for the topic, on you. And likewise, I look forward to your thoughts and feedback. It will be a journey we will take together.

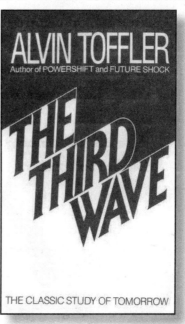

From Consumer to Prosumer

One of the key ideas that Toffler wrote about in *The Third Wave* was a revolutionary idea that he called the "Prosumer." He said, "in the future, the role of producers and consumers would begin to blur and merge." Toffler envisioned a post-capitalist world where people were serving themselves and serving each other. And isn't this exactly what Linux and the entire open-source software movement is about? And isn't Uber people helping other people? We are *there*, folks.

We can also see it in social media, where we post content and consume it as well. Additionally, "prosumer" can mean "product and brand advocate." Rather than simply "consuming" products, people are becoming the *voices* of those products and significantly impacting the success or failure of companies, products, and brands, particularly through their involvement on the social Web.

Of course, we can all agree that businesses are no longer completely in control of their products, brands, and messages. The consumer, or
prosumer, now has a hand in it. Prosumers are the online influencers that
business leaders and marketers must not just identify but also acknowledge, respect, and develop relationships with in order for their products
and brands to thrive. In fact, it's so important and so significant a change
from what we once had, that it really is a *movement*, a cultural shift. Ladies
and gentlemen, welcome to the Prosumer Age!

The Future of Tech

The early developers of the Web succeeded at making the Internet a
usable thing, but in one very big way, they chose the wrong construct: They
chose *space* over *time*. As we all know, the typical website is "space-orga-
nized," like a patterned quilt, for example. The alternative design would
have been to make it "time-organized," like a parade—first this band, three
minutes later this float, forty seconds later that band.[3] This "time construct"
is now making its way across the Internet and in the future, this setup will
be ubiquitous.

Internet as Flow—We go to the Internet for many reasons, but many times
it's to see what's happening *right now. Well, the only thing that can tell
us what is happening everywhere right now,* is obviously the Web. Today,
time-based structures, flowing data—in streams, feeds, blogs—increasingly
dominate the Web. *Flow* has become the basic organizing principle of the
cybersphere. We see it in the Facebook wall and many other feeds. But
most widely, we see it on Twitter.

The Web of the future will resemble an electric power network, with
information coming through at volume and speed, based on what we want
to see. As we'll see by 2030, flowing information will power your life. And
this change in delivery of information will dramatically impact the marketing practice.

Over the next fifteen years, Web pages and browsers will be far less important. It will be *all about* flows and streams. In addition to Twitter and Facebook, we stream photos, movies, and music and subscribe to YouTube channels and RSS feeds from blogs. The apps we use evolve in a flow of upgrades. Tags have replaced links. We tag and "like" and "favorite" moments in the streams. Some streams, like Snapchat, WeChat, and WhatsApp, operate totally in the present, with no past or future. They simply flow through the river of our digital life and if we see it and want to engage with

it, we can. If we don't, then we don't. Flows of this sort live in the online cloud, and along with tagging, they will be what futurist Kevin Kelly calls the "foundational units of this third digital regime."[4]

The Hyperconnected Internet of Humanity—Rohit Talwar notes that by 2030 mobile computing may mean that some five to seven billion people are linked to the Internet—some 50 to 250 billion devices and a trillion embedded sensors. The result, say companies like Cisco, will be more productive employees, more efficient supply chains, better asset deployment, happier customers, more innovative technology, and $19 trillion of value.[5]

Peter Diamandis's book *Abundance* suggests that as these new people come online and become part of the global economy, they will not just consume its products but will contribute ideas, products, and inventions that will benefit everybody.[6] As marketers, we'll need to market all those discoveries, products and inventions. I'm ready. How about you?

A Bias in the Nature of Technology—If you stop and think about it, there is a certain kind of *bias* in the nature of technology that shifts it in key directions over time. Think about the form of an Internet—a network of networks spanning the globe. This was going to happen, but the *specific kind* of Internet we chose to have was not. The Internet could have been commercial rather than nonprofit, or a national system instead of international, or it could have been secret instead of public. Telephony—long-distance electrically transmitted voice messages—was inevitable, but the iPhone was not. Instant messaging was inevitable, but tweeting every five minutes was not.

And it's important to keep this dynamic in mind as we progress into the future: We need to remain open to all possibilities and follow the trends and technology along its logical evolution. I think this will become easier over time as we all become more acclimated to rapid change in all areas of life.

> *Marketing used to be about creating a myth and selling it*
> *and is now about finding a truth and sharing it.*
> — Marc Mathieu, Unilever Senior VP of Marketing

Media Distribution Flipped on Its Head—Prior to the Internet, most media were defined by their respective distribution models. Newspapers were sold in newsstands and delivered to the home. Television came through television sets, and magazines arrived on newsstands and in the mail via subscription. High-speed Internet subsumed all of these physical distribution models. High-speed Internet connectivity has put the newspaper industry on life support, has negatively impacted all other print businesses, and is the fastest growing part of the television industry. The media business has always been a content-delivery business, which now happens on our individual devices. As 3G progresses to 6G and beyond in the coming years, we'll consume just about everything on our smartphone and then, eventually, in the air right in front of us through augmented reality (AR) and virtual reality (VR) technology. Some marketers out there are still caught up in the old distribution mindset. That will need to change.

The Technology Revolution—During the 2017–2030 period, the historic wave of innovation will crest. Will this be the emergence of the technological "Singularity"? Futurist Ray Kurzweil defines the Singularity as "a future period during which the pace of technological change will be so rapid, its impact so deep, that human life will be irreversibly transformed." You'll notice on the back cover of this book, I used the phrase "The Singularity is here." And that's because in many ways, especially for the marketing practice, it is: The foundation is in place. The inputs are there. Now, we

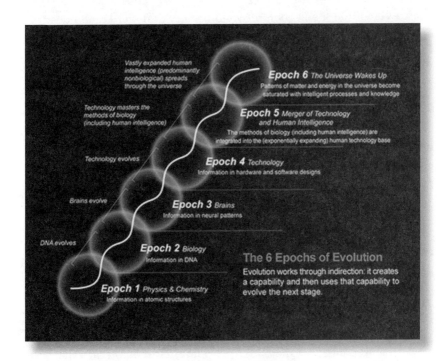

will watch it unfold before our very eyes. The technology revolution is on a high speed race to the future.

Things Are Changing Fast

All around us, in every part of our lives, we are witnessing the birth of new technologies, new types of companies, new forms of services, new ways of interacting with each other, a new globalized, interconnected world of promise and possibility. And through it all we see the breakdown of walls, the building of bridges, and the understanding and appreciation of people and cultures that are different than our own. All of these elements have a significant impact on the marketing that we do as organizations. From *how* we'll market, to what we'll market, to whom we'll market to, it's all going to change, as we have seen so clearly over the past several years. But now it will all accelerate and propagate. Think exponentially. Think opportunistically. Think of a "change the world" type of impact. Of course, that's a cliché, but it will soon prove to be very real—very real indeed. If you're the type of person who's always had one foot in the future, always thinking about tomorrow, this is your time, my friend.

"Legacy thinking" will hold some back. Futurist David Houle warns that humans tend to use past experiences and solutions to address present problems, and that such habits will be hard to avoid—particularly for those people who are part of older generations.[7] But it is the younger generations who are clearly leading the way here, showing us all how to embrace the thinking of *now*, the potential of now and...the promise and possibility of an exciting future. Considering the past and how things were done will still be important, as we don't want to repeat previous mistakes or missteps, but we cannot live in that space—not in our thinking nor in our doing. The future is the zeitgeist of today.

Megatrends—Ever since the book of the same name by John Naisbitt came out in 1982, the idea of transformative, global forces has been in the global consciousness. What are they? Here are just a few mega-trends that we'll

discuss in *Future Marketing*:

- Connectivity and Convergence
- Innovating to Zero
- Smart is the New Green
- Health, Wellness and Well Being

Mega-trends define the future world with their far-reaching impacts on businesses, societies, economies, cultures, and our own personal lives. In 2016, we now see these global mega-trends taking shape right before our very eyes. They aren't just ideas or talking points anymore, they are actually happening. And they will continue to roll out over the next fifteen years and beyond. As they do, our marketing methodologies and strategies will need to evolve right along with them.

Future Marketing Categories—And what are the big picture categories that are actively being discussed among futurists, innovators, and world changers at the top of the business agenda? Here are a few, as it relates to the marketing practice, some of which I'll discuss in *Future Marketing*:

- Business Strategy
- Workforce Issues
- Human Enhancement
- Natural Resources
- Artificial Intelligence
- Automation
- Money and Financial Systems

The other two, under the umbrella of consciousness and awareness, are the following:

- Mindset
- Purpose

With *mindset*, we need to ask this: can we transfer exponential thinking, via marketing, from the technology world to other domains to address society's grand challenges in areas such as diversity, healthcare and education, and overcome the scarcity of key resources such as food, water and rare earth metals? Yes, the marketing practice will take on a new importance in coming years. With *purpose*, the question is, "what would be a sustainable driving purpose and societal role for marketing in a world being transformed by all these forces of change?"

We all know that tomorrow's business landscape will be shaped and influenced by the world around us. But now the speed at which our world is being transformed will increase and so will the convergence of innovations and the ideas they give birth to. As we usher in the next fifteen years, it will be an awesome and historic time, where science and the technologies it spawns, are now at the heart of the agenda. And the marketing practice is right in the middle of that.

The Age of Abundance, Circular Economies

The subtitle of *Future Marketing* includes the phrase "The Prosumer Age," but the future will also be known as the Age of Abundance. Rohit

Talwar, in the symposium *The Future of Business*, predicts that between 2020 and 2050 the world will actually enter a "post-scarcity" phase, brought on by "the Singularity Movement." As manufacturing shifts to the biological and molecular level by way of genetic manipulation, nanotechnology, robotics, and artificial intelligence, resources will be used and managed more efficiently. What will marketing look like in an environment of abundance? It will be good, very good. But stay tuned and read on.

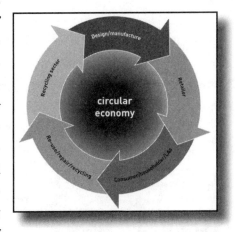

Part of this post-scarcity culture will develop out of increasing adoption of a "circular economy"—an economic process by which resources are reused and waste minimized before being returned to the world from which they were extracted. A 2012 report by the Ellen Macarthur Foundation estimated that certain manufacturing sectors in Europe could save $630 billion annually by 2025 if they adopted circular practices. The advantages of the circular economy are becoming clearer for both governments and businesses.[8] Personally, I think using the term "circular economy" is much better than "investing in sustainable business practices" or "sustainability," as these phrases have been politicized and misinterpreted. It's not about being a Democrat, Republican, Libertarian or anything else—it's about being *human* and doing right by our fellow human beings. And, of course, showing how we can practice circular economics through our marketing campaigns and initiatives.

Required Reading: *The Inevitable* by Kevin Kelly

In his epic 2016 book, *The Inevitable: Understanding the 12 Technological Forces That Will Shape the Future*, Kevin Kelly explains that "the wide, fast-moving system of technology bends the culture subtly, but steadily, so it amplifies the following forces: Becoming, Cognifying, Flowing, Screening, Accessing, Sharing, Filtering, Remixing, Interacting, Tracking, Questioning, and then Beginning.[9] Kelly uses these powerful (and spot-on) terms to define the way the future will play out. Each of them have far-reaching implications for how we will work, live and play, individually and collectively. And each will help us redefine and re-interpret what marketing is and could be in ten or fifteen years. In 2016, we've already seen the power of *flowing, sharing,* and *filtering* on the Web. But what about *cognifying, remixing,* and *beginning*? Exciting times truly beckon.

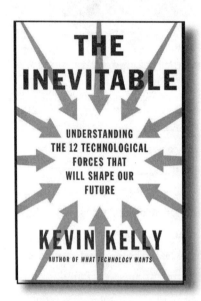

Kelly goes on to say that "in the coming 30 years the tendency toward the dematerialized, the decentralized, the simultaneous, the platform enabled, and the cloud will continue unabated."[10] Again, a masterful and succinct way of categorizing what will be our new reality. We know about the platform and the cloud, but what about the rest? I'll get into it all in coming chapters.

AOL cofounder Steve Case predicts that the "future Internet will be defined not by the Internet of Things; it will be defined by the *Internet of Everything*." He sees the Internet becoming part of our life, our education, our health, our finances, our ways transporting ourselves, and even our daily meals. Like Toffler, he uses the metaphor of a "third wave," one that threatens to disrupt the entire economy and the companies that presently lead it.[11] Many of us will naturally rise to this challenge and adjust accordingly. And beyond the disruption lies a collective actualization and that rising consciousness I referred to earlier. The potential for all of us is simply breathtaking.

The Future Marketing Department

In chapter fifteen, I discuss in detail what the future marketing department could look like. Obviously, there will be differences in its makeup and size depending on industry, company, target audience and more. But today and in the future, *all* marketing leaders will need to consider the big questions, including:

- Why do we do what we do and does it mean anything to our customers?
- What values and goals best align us to our customers?
- What capabilities do we have that can help us transition part of the brand experience to a platform experience?

Over the next few years, there will never be a greater time of change in the corporate structure. We'll all need to be more efficient, more customer focused and more attuned to the changes happening all around us. It will, no doubt, be an exciting, but challenging time for everyone.

Who is the audience for *Future Marketing?*

I wrote this book for forward-thinking, progressive marketers here in the United States and around the world. I wrote it for corporate marketers, small business marketers, entrepreneurs and for the thousands of marketing agencies out there, two hundred of which have been loyal clients of my firm, Content Launch, over the past several years. As I've mentioned, I did my very best to make this book grand in scope and sweeping in its vision, so I hope it appeals to business leaders everywhere, not only the marketing folks. In fact, I'd love to see executives in Operations, Finance, IT and Human Resources pick it up. I think there is something substantial and relevant for each of these groups in the pages that follow. After all, everyone in our organizations are involved in marketing now.

In addition, it is my hope that futurists around the globe find meaningful sections in *Future Marketing*. From the late, great Alvin Toffler to the brilliant Ray Kurzweil and everyone else in between, futurists everywhere have served as one of my primary inspirations in writing this book. I look forward to feedback from everyone who reads it. Finally, to prosumers and everyday influencers around the world: Each of you has contributed a small part in what has become *a revolution*. Your passion, enthusiasm, energy and devotion to the companies and causes you believe in has also been a driving force for me in putting this collection of thoughts and ideas together. The future is bright, in large part, because of you. Thank you.

What You'll Learn in *Future Marketing*

Future Marketing includes seventeen chapters, covering six major areas:

1. Making the Case
2. The Changing Customer
3. The Changing Economic System
4. Marketing in the Year 2021
5. Marketing in the Year 2030
6. Evolution of Marketing Fundamentals

In "Making the Case," I'll cover where we've been in marketing over the last year, where things stand today and how that's set up what's coming next. In "The Changing Customer," I'll cover the rise of the prosumer, the influencer, the evolving power structure between company and customer as well as how to engage through experiences. In "The Changing Economic System," I'll discuss post-capitalism and the impact it will have on the marketing practice. In "Marketing in the Year 2021," I'll cover how you'll need to connect with your audience and the marketing strategies that will pay off. In "Marketing in the Year 2030," I'll take it one step further and explore all the game-changing tools, technologies, approaches, and more that are a bit farther out. Finally, in "Evolution of Marketing Fundamentals," I'll propose a new marketing mix construct as well as ideas for the future marketing department. We'll wrap up with a showcase of companies showing the way now.

Why I'm Qualified to Write About the Future of Marketing

Marketing is my chosen profession, it's something I have done for over eighteen years. But it's much more than that for me. Not only is it my profession, it is my *passion*. As a big-picture, "idea" guy, it's something I think about all the time. As the founder and CEO of Content Launch, I've been hard at work helping hundreds of companies in a wide range of industries, B2B and B2C for a long time. What's my current big idea? My company offers the very first complete content marketing software built for small and medium sized businesses (SMB's) and digital agencies. Content Launch also provides content writing and content strategy services. As I mentioned earlier, my 2012 book, *Content is Currency: Developing Powerful Content for Web & Mobile,* helped thousands of businesses worldwide learn how to plan, create, distribute and manage content. It helped a lot of folks do marketing better. That book naturally led to this one.

I've also been a real presence at a wide range of marketing industry events over the last eight years, having spoken at Content Marketing World, Online Marketing Summit, South by Southwest, Marketing Profs B2B Forum, Search Marketing Expo, Social Media Marketing World, New Media Expo, Intelligent Content Conference, Content Marketing Retreat, Lavacon, ADMA in Australia, the BIA Kelsey Small Business Forum, the Media Relations Summit and for many companies and industry organizations, including Hubspot, Intuit, Konica Minolta, Raytheon, the American Marketing Association and Shop.org as well as industry groups in the areas of content marketing, mobile marketing and entrepreneurship.

Finally, I've been listed as a marketing industry thought leader by countless print publications and blogs since 2008. And I'm willing to bet that nobody has researched the future of the marketing practice more than I have! This book is the proof. Over many years, I've helped to carry the mantel for the content marketing cause, now I'd like to do the same within the wider marketing community and serve as a spokesperson for the future of marketing. After you finish *Future Marketing*, I'd love to have your endorsement in that regard. I look forward to hearing your feedback.

A Few Extra Bonuses for Your Investment

Future Marketing has been a labor of love for me, a true extension of my passion for writing, connecting and teaching. So, as I've done with my two previous books, I'd like to give you some free stuff! Since you have taken your precious time and energy to read this book, it's the least I can do in a spirit of pure gratitude. Of course, I am a content marketer, so you expect it, right? Gotta give up some high quality content here! So, as a loyal reader, here is what else you get:

- An **audio program** that discusses key topics from the book
- An **online video** of the live version of Future Marketing
- A **15 percent discount** on all content marketing consulting, strategy and/or writing projects (through November, 2017)
- A **complimentary membership** in my Future Marketing Power Group ($50 value)
- A **10 percent discount** on a subscription to Content Launch, my companies new content marketing platform (contentlaunch.com)

To redeem this offer, simply go to *www.futuremarketingbook.com* and subscribe to my blog. That's it!

After you finish the book (or any time as you're going through it), feel free to reach out via email or Twitter. I'd love to get your thoughts, feedback and ideas. And of course, if you'd like to have me come and speak at your event, I welcome that as well. You can reach me at *jon@contentlaunch.com* or *@jonwuebben* on Twitter. Of course, I'd love a review of the book on Amazon. If that's something you like to do with books you enjoy, feel free to review away! I appreciate your time.

In Closing...

As you make your way through *Future Marketing*, I encourage you to really dig in—go ahead and highlight, dog-ear, make notes, and just sit and think once in a while about what you've read. As this is a book of big ideas and grand concepts, it's important to unleash your creativity and imagination as you take in the information. Unlike many business books, this is not a book of tactical, "how-to" information. It's a thought starter, the impetus for a new conversation with your team, a light to shine into the darkness of that thing we can sometimes be fearful of: uncharted territory. After all, in the future, we are going to a place none of us have ever been.

So, see *Future Marketing* as a guidebook for helping your organization grow, prosper and change and for using the finer points of the new marketing I discuss in these pages to get you there safely and soundly.

With that, let us begin.

SECTION 1
MAKING THE CASE

CHAPTER ONE

The State of Marketing Nation

So, when you look around, talk to your customers and review your current marketing initiatives, where do you think we are today in the practice of marketing? The vast majority of marketing professionals out there, especially those who are reading this book, have a good read on the current state of digital marketing, so I'll just provide a cursory overview here. But I do think it's important to set up the wider discussion and lay out the current state of things so we can have some context and a starting point for everything else that follows in the upcoming chapters of *Future Marketing*. As the saying goes, how can we know where we're going if we don't know where we've been?

Keeping in mind the historical context will be important as we move forward in the coming years with such massive change to the status quo. And that is what's so important to understand: *that things will change faster now* and we need to think of the *larger picture and overall strategy* in addition to the tactical stuff. It won't be, "hey, Snapchat looks really cool, let's see how we can integrate it into our marketing mix!" It will be: "We have twenty customers who want to create virtual reality content for us in the next week. How do we manage that?" and other, even larger marketing-related concerns, driven by prosumers, peer-to-peer networks and more. This tide has been coming in for the past fifteen years, Kevin Kelly says, and its momentum is such that it will only deepen during the next fifteen.[1]

The Foundational Principles of Modern Marketing

Before I discuss the current state, let's go back fifty-three years to the release of Philip Kotler's *Principles of Marketing*, the landmark book that for all intents and purposes was the foundation of all "marketing" to come. Many of Kotler's concepts have become such an integral part of modern marketing that we have forgotten that they were ever revolutionary.

And here's the other thing: I'm guessing that half of the folks out there aren't even aware of Philip Kotler and his remarkable contribution to the study and practice of marketing. Here are a few of the marketing concepts that we now take for granted, but were first introduced by "Mr. Marketing" in 1963:

- The idea that you need to attract customers with powerful promotional messages
- The idea that you should show your customers that the use of your product or service is a rational choice for them
- The idea that marketing research and statistics should drive all business decisions
- The idea that marketing is all about "the big idea"
- The idea that brands are king

In 2003, the *Financial Times* cited Kotler's three major contributions to marketing and to management:

> First, he has done more than any other writer or scholar to promote the importance of marketing, transforming it from a peripheral activity, bolted on to the more "important" work

of production. Second, he continued a trend started by Peter Drucker, shifting emphasis away from price and distribution to a greater focus on meeting customers' needs and on the benefits received from a product or service. Third, he has broadened the concept of marketing from mere selling to a more general process of communication and exchange, and has shown how marketing can be extended and applied to charities, political parties and many other non-commercial situations.[2]

As you make your way through the chapters of *Future Marketing*, keep this all in mind. Besides the fact that Kotler's teachings are important to know just for general marketing knowledge and to understand the context, I'll show how the coming years of change will upend some of what he taught in *Principles of Marketing*.

The fact is, things will be changing so fast and there will be so many decisions to consider, that the idea of "principles" really goes away. Instead, it will be "options" or "choices." In fact, his next edition of the book should maybe be titled, *Exploration of Marketing Decisions for a Changing World*. Of course, there will be some key tenets or principles in the future marketing practice, but the jury is out on what those will be exactly. My personal feeling is there will be lots of dependencies on the principles. Are you business-to-business (B2B) or business-to-consumer (B2C) or peer-to-peer (P2P)? Are you a startup, small- or medium-sized business (SMB), or a large enterprise? Are you for-profit or not-for-profit? Are you targeting the virtual space? An augmented reality content play perhaps? AI enabled? You get the idea.

2016 Benchmarks, Budgets & Trends—B2B Content Marketing

Every year, Content Marketing Institute (CMI) and Marketing Profs combine forces for their "Benchmarks, Budgets & Trends—B2B Content Marketing" Report.[3] It always provides a wealth of great information

and insight and this year's report is no exception. A total of 3,714 re-
cipients from around the globe—representing a full range of industries,
functional areas, and company sizes—completed the survey during July
and August 2015.

As I believe that content marketing *is* digital marketing, it's important to include the latest information here in *Future Marketing*. As well,
according to a recent Gartner survey,[4] 98 percent of marketers no longer
see digital as a distinct approach from other marketing practices. Digital
marketing is now the context for *all* marketing.

In addition, the majority of my readers are in the B2B area, so I
wanted to provide relevant data that's pertinent to their day-to-day operations. As B2C folks will see, there is quite a bit of overlap and applicable points in this report. I encourage you to read the full study on the
CMI website.

As with the inclusion of Philip Kotler's major messages in *Principles
of Marketing*, the CMI-Marketing Profs study is foundational information
and will positively inform the rest of the discussion in this book.

Here are the key takeaways for 2016:

- Only 30 percent of B2B marketers say their organizations are effective at content marketing, down from 38 percent in 2015. Effectiveness levels are greater among respondents with documentation, clarity around success, good communication, and experience.
- 44 percent of B2B marketers say their organization is clear on what content marketing success or effectiveness looks like; 55 percent are unclear or unsure.
- 44 percent of B2B marketers meet daily or weekly—either in person or virtually—to discuss the progress of their content marketing program; however, the more effective the organization is at content marketing, the more often its marketers meet.
- Fewer B2B marketers have a documented content marketing strategy compared with last year (32 percent vs. 35 percent), even though the research consistently shows that those who document their strategy are more effective in nearly all areas of content marketing.
- Respondents' content marketing maturity levels were roughly equally apportioned: approximately one-third were in the early stages, one-third in the adolescent stage, and one-third, in the sophisticated/mature stage. In general, marketers become more effective as they gain experience, the findings show.
- B2B marketers allocate 28 percent of their total marketing budget, on average, to content marketing—the same percentage as last year. The most effective allocate 42 percent, and the most sophisticated/mature allocate 46 percent.
- Lead generation (85 percent and sales (84 percent) will be the most important goals for B2B content marketers over the next twelve months.
- Over the last six years, B2B marketers have consistently cited website traffic as their most often used metric. This year, however, we also asked them to rate metrics by importance. The most im-

portant metrics are sales lead quality (87 percent), sales (84 percent), and higher conversion rates (82 percent).

- B2B marketers, as in years past, continue to be heavily focused on creating engaging content (72 percent), citing it as the top priority for their internal content creators over the next year.

The Current State of Digital Marketing

The other critical marketing report in the industry, I think, is the Salesforce "State of Marketing" report.[16] This is a more all-encompassing review that also includes B2C companies. For the third annual version, Salesforce Research surveyed nearly 4,000 marketing leaders worldwide to discover:

- Overall trends changing the role of marketing
- How high-performing marketing teams approach marketing intelligence and customer experience
- Key insights on primary digital marketing channels

As with *Principles of Marketing* and the CMI-MarketingProfs report, this is the final piece of the puzzle that will provide you with the current landscape overview you'll need to get the most out of *Future Marketing*. It's my hope that by providing the current situation, the future possibilities and a potential action plan for how you can start thinking about how your organization can begin to find a place in the future view, you'll have all the tools you need to achieve your future objectives.

So, here are the nine key takeaways from the Salesforce *State of Marketing* report. I encourage you to read the entire study on the Salesforce website.

1. Top marketing teams win with a "customer journey" strategy—High-performing marketing teams are 8.8 times more likely than underperformers to strongly agree that they've adopted a customer journey strat-

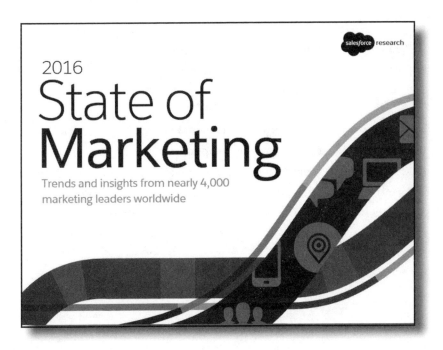

egy as part of their overall business strategy. Successful marketers are connecting with customers in new ways across mobile, email, social, and the Web. Seventy-three percent say that a customer journey strategy has positively impacted overall customer engagement—the second biggest priority for marketers this year.

2. Top marketing teams are integrating the customer experience—Successful marketing leaders are crossing the boundaries of business units to create a single view of the customer. High-performing marketing teams are 7.7 times more likely than underperformers to strongly agree they're leading customer experience initiatives across the business—bridging the gap between marketing, sales, and service. Sixty-four percent of top teams also say they are excellent at creating a single view of the customer, versus only 4 percent of underperformers.

3. Top marketing teams get smart with tech adoption—To keep pace with a dynamic industry and continually make marketing communications smarter, 72 percent of top teams will increase spending on marketing tools and tech in the next two years. Fifty-three percent of high performers qualify as heavy tech adopters, compared to only 7 percent of underperformers. Top teams are more likely to extensively use marketing analytics and predictive intelligence, among other tools.

4. Top marketing teams align with business leadership—The world's best marketing teams have buy-in from company leaders. As such, marketing budgets are more likely to be prioritized. Eighty-three percent of high performers say their executive team is completely committed to supporting the overall marketing strategy, compared to only 31 percent of underperformers.

5. Real-time channel orchestration strikes a chord—Leading marketers understand the value of a cross-channel approach. In fact, top teams are 3.2 times more likely than underperformers to strongly agree they've integrated their social media activity into their overall marketing strategy (3.4 times more likely for integrating email marketing and five times more likely for mobile marketing). Among high performers who have integrated their digital marketing channels with their overall marketing, at least 95 percent rate the integrations as very effective or effective.

6. Mobile momentum hits a tipping point—From 2015 to 2016, every aspect of mobile covered in the research has risen significantly in usage. This growth encompasses both mobile as a marketing platform (such as mobile apps) and mobile as a marketing channel (such as texting using SMS). With 98 percent growth in mobile app usage and 111 percent growth in SMS usage, a majority of marketers are now using these mainstream mobile tactics to engage customers.

7. Intelligent email is driving higher revenue—As email personalization capabilities grow more sophisticated, the channel becomes even more integral for marketers to deliver a holistic customer journey. Top teams are 4.2 times more likely than underperformers to leverage predictive intelligence or data science to create personalized emails. Forty-nine percent of marketers say email is directly linked to their business' primary revenue source—a notable jump from the 20 percent of marketers who said the same in 2015.

8. Social sees massive return on investment (ROI) growth—Last year, three of the top five areas where marketers planned to increase their spending involved social outlets. Now, those investments appear to be paying off; 75 percent of marketing leaders report that social is generating ROI. Top teams are also 1.7 times more likely than underperformers to align their social media marketing strategy with other social activities such as customer service, pursuing a more unified customer view.

9. Advertising accelerates on social platforms—Nearly two-thirds of marketers boosted budgets for advertising on social platforms in 2016, making it the third largest area for increased investment. Among high performers, 80 percent will increase spending on advertising on social platforms. In order to create a unique experience based on real customer identity, 83 percent of top teams use customer data (e.g., email or phone data) to segment or target ads.

So there you go—an overview of the current digital marketing landscape at the end of 2016. From real data coming from actual organizations around the world to the trends that are positively impacting the marketing practice and creating new audiences for these organizations, you now know what's going on out there in the "real world." What's interesting for me as I've researched and written *Future Marketing* has been the stark difference between what's been discussed in this chapter and what the future holds for marketers. It's a massive—and very encouraging and exciting—difference. The opportunities for all of us are simply stunning.

But before we get into what marketing will be like five years and fifteen years from now, let's continue setting the stage by looking at what the current cultural, economic, and societal mega-trends are telling us as well as how the most popular predictions from a group of widely respected futurists are informing the coming years of marketing.

CHAPTER TWO

Mega-Trends: Cultural and Technological Shifts

"*Mega-trends.*" Just the phrase itself conjures up the thought of exciting possibilities, the potential advancement of civilization, the calling on our collective human talents to make great things happen and, of course, the question, "what if?" What if a particular global trend becomes a reality that then becomes the "new normal?" What if we can see it coming but don't know how it will impact other things? What are the positive and negative ramifications? Again, a "mega-trend" is a really *big* trend, like the "sharing economy," for example, that defines the future (and current) world with its far reaching impact on businesses, societies, economies, cultures, and our own personal lives.

The term "mega-trends" and the book *Megatrends* really both began in 1982. The scholar and author John Naisbitt led the charge. Futurists like Alvin Toffler were fully aligned with Naisbitt and praised him for taking the ideas mainstream, which is exactly what happened. As the result of ten years of research, it hit the public consciousness like a thunderbolt. On the *New York Times* bestseller list for two years, *Megatrends: Ten New Directions Transforming Our Lives* was eventually published in fifty-seven countries and sold more than 14 million copies.

For my younger readers, allow me to offer a brief history lesson. In 1982, the U.S was buried deep in a serious recession that saw unemployment hit a postwar record of more than 10 percent. There was no Internet or iPhone or sharing economy. For the jobless, you couldn't simply freelance online or drive for Uber to make up for the lost paycheck; the options were much fewer. Billy Joel wrote the popular song "Allentown" in response to the malaise. Welfare lines went around the block at local government offices. Ronald Reagan was in deep trouble, just one year into his presidency. *Megatrends* predicted a coming recovery and much better days ahead. As a result, it gave hope. It told an optimistic story. And the crazy thing was, Naisbitt was right on a lot of what he said then.

To craft his epic book, he used the research technique known as "content analysis" employed by the American intelligence services during World War II. Naisbitt and his team read thousands of newspaper articles (which were effectively the Internet of that time) in the late 1970s and early 1980s to see what ideas and issues were being discussed. By 1982, he came up with the final list of ten massively influential ideas that he called "megatrends." So, what did he say and what was he right about when we consider current business and marketing related issues?

1. Shift to an information society—He said: *"We have shifted from an industrial society to one based on the creation and distribution of information."* Naisbitt hit the nail on the head here. As his most important and most accurate prediction, some say now that it was a forgone conclusion. But it wasn't. Again, the public Internet was nowhere close to being made a reality in 1982. We were using Apple II and Commodore 64 computers at the time! The fact that Apple is now worth more than Ford, US Steel and General Electric clearly illustrates high tech's achievement.

2. Shift to a global economy—He said: *"We are moving from being a self-sufficient national economy to being part of a global economy."* Absolutely dead-on correct. We now buy American-designed cars with electronics from Asia and steel and plastic parts made in Latin America, with the final assembly plants in Canada. Money and jobs flow freely across national borders.

3. Participatory democracy revolutionized—He said: *"The new information technology will revitalize participatory democracy."* This is definitely true because the last three national U.S. elections have seen record numbers of votes cast, many by people who got much of their information online. The Internet has greatly enhanced democracy and will continue to do so around the globe. Let's just hope we can come up with ideas and solutions that will bring resolution and compromise to the extreme political polarization we see currently.

4. Rise of informal networks—He said: *"Society will shift from hierarchical structures to informal networks."* Bingo! The decline of the old massproduction industries like auto and steel, followed by the rise of small high-tech companies (Apple, Microsoft, Dell and more) that ballooned into nimble, highly adaptable enterprises shows us how this mega-trend has played out and become real. Another proof point: The classified sections of major newspapers have been replaced by something way better, easier and cheaper: Craigslist. Big marketing impact, right?

5. A society of multiple options—He said: *"Society is changing from a narrow 'either/or' perspective with a limited range of personal choices to one of 'free-wheeling' multiple options."* Correct again. See the shift from three television networks in the 1970s to 300-plus channels today on a typical cable television package. The development of specialty foods and restaurants, cars, clothes, music and family structures all prove that this prediction was right on the money. Huge ramifications for marketing, correct?

Naisbitt was clearly correct on the growth of high-tech industries, globalization, the information explosion enhancing democracy, the boom in social networking. and the massive increases in consumer choices. It's great learning for anyone involved in marketing, as it begins to open one's eyes to the possibilities and potential of current trends. As innovation is becoming central to both the organization as a whole as well as the marketing practice, it's critical to adopt the "visionary mindset."

The Mega-Trends of Today

In 2014, the analyst organization Frost & Sullivan published an incredibly valuable and interesting piece of research, *"The World's Top Global Mega Trends to 2025 and Implications to Business, Society and Cultures."*[1] Here are the highlights.

1. Urbanization: City as a Customer—Urban areas will grow to form megacities, mega-regions and even mega-corridors such as the Boston to Washington, DC (BosWash) corridor, which will have a population of 58 million and account for 20 percent of United States GDP in 2025. Businesses will regard these mega-population centers as key areas for investment and put "city as a customer" as a key tenet of their outreach and marketing strategy.

2. Smart is the New Green—"Going Green" has been a mega-trend for many years, even going back as far as the 1970s. What's different now is there will be a shift towards "smart" products, which are intelligent, connected, and have the ability to sense, process, report, and take corrective action. We'll see this in almost every product, which will have tiny sensors (otherwise known as the Internet of Things) embedded to connect to the Web. It will be a key component of the move towards mass efficiency in all processes, and in all industries, across the globe.

3. Connectivity and Convergence—By 2020, there will be over 5 billion Internet users, with over half of them accessing the Internet over handheld tablet devices and 80 billion connected devices worldwide. Our work, home and surrounding environment will come together into one seamless, "connected living" reality. This connectivity will enable "big data" to create market opportunities for new products and services—some that already are here today, like social sentiment analysis, open innovation, and micro-personalized marketing and medicines.

4. Bricks and Clicks—This will become the retailing norm by 2020, with every retailer expected to have an online identity as well as a brick-and-mortar presence. Nearly 19 percent of global B2C retail will happen online, with online retail sales expected to reach $4.3 trillion by 2025, resulting in the emergence of virtual stores, virtual hypermarkets, interactive stores, and "click and collect" retailing models. A key micro-impact of this will be the focus by businesses on creating a seamless online/offline customer journey and a unique and personalized customer experience throughout the life cycle of the product or service.[2]

5. Innovating to Zero—This means having cars with zero emissions, zero accidents, and zero fatalities. It means cities and buildings that are carbon neutral (Copenhagen may be the first in 2025). It means a zero-concept world with zero defects, and zero breaches of security. Companies will shift focus and develop products and technologies that innovate to zero, including zero-emission technologies such as wind power, traveling wave reactors, solar photovoltaic (PV), and 3rd-generation biofuels.

6. New Business Models: Value for Many—With the advent of online aggregation and cloud-based platforms, many businesses are finding new ways to monetize new markets and opportunities.[3] Different types of business models are applied in different stakeholder relationships—right from Business to Consumers (B2C) to Business to Business (B2B) to Government to Business (G2B).

Personalization and Customization: Brands will focus on designing products as per their customers' choice and requirements, providing value addition, and helping retain customers by developing a personal rapport.

Kevin Kelly predicts that the current trend by which we trade ownership of things for access through subscriptions will only increase. And that, of course, will have a dramatic impact on marketing. "Ownership can be casual, almost fickle," Kelly writes. "If something better comes along, you may grab it." Subscriptions, on the other hand, are like a firehose of new features, fixes, and updates that connect producer to consumer with a dependable, predictable stream that's hard to turn off.[4] Personalization and customization will be an expected component of this relationship.

Value for Many: Companies are seeing the benefit of pricing their products and services competitively to achieve a larger customer base. Lower costs for consumers and economies of scale for companies will lead to a win-win situation.

Sharing Economy: Facilitators and intermediaries have begun to adapt to the new form of peer-to-peer or people-to-people marketplace, as the concept of the shared economy has started to take effect. Key commodities shared are cars, clothes, money, goods, and space and the forms of sharing these commodities include renting, swapping, reusing, distributing, and lending. The sharing economy was something of a natural development of market forces being applied to social problems, Kevin Kelly suggests. Collaboration has helped poor people get health care, students get free college textbooks, and helped develop drugs for obscure diseases. He points out in many cases such sharing has proven quite practical, and that it continues to surprise us with its power.[5]

Another early influencer in the sharing dynamic was Twitter. It tapped into the power of simple sharing through 140-character updates. By enabling people to share quick quips and, in the process, gather a following, Twitter proved how valuable sharing could be. It showed how short updates could be turned into shared gold when collected and processed in the aggregate, and then organized and disseminated back to the individual and sold in analytic clumps to corporations.

7. Future Infrastructure Development—The global investment in infrastructure development is expected to cross the $27 trillion mark by 2025, with Asia-Pacific (APAC) accounting for 37 percent share and with expected investments of $10.50 trillion from 2010 to 2025. In terms of transportation, new corridors will form connecting economic clusters to enable better trade and use of technology. Large investments are expected to be made in the Northern American and APAC region.

The water infrastructure ecosystem, including dams, reservoirs, and drinking water supply systems, will be a key focus area of governments worldwide to ensure water security and economic development. Ageing infrastructure will be replaced, capacity will be increased, and operational efficiency will be improved. Finally, energy hungry developing nations will need to up their game in power generation by investing substantial amounts in their existing infrastructure.

8. Health, Wellness and Well Being—We're clearly seeing this with the debate and discussions around the Affordable Care Act (Obamacare), the popularity of health monitoring products like the "FitBit," the introduction of "cold-pressed" juices to the marketplace, and more. The definition of healthcare will change as economies struggle to afford healthcare costs, which will affect 20 percent of a nation's GDP in a developed world. Focus will shift to mass prevention and diagnoses and to wellness aspects of the mind, body and soul.

9. Future of Energy—The energy industry will focus on three major areas: alternative sources, storage, and efficiency in distribution. Smart grid infrastructure will use digital technology through advanced metering, distribution grid management, and high-voltage transmission systems for the distribution of power. Solar photovoltaics (PV) power-generation capacity is set to increase five-fold by 2020. The contribution of shale gas to the total gas production supply in the United States is likely to increase to almost half in 2035, backed by government support and parallel investment in fracking and drilling technologies. The future of energy management is expected to drive a multiple convergence of technologies, markets, competition, and business models, resulting in greater operating efficiency in storage and distribution.

10. Future of Mobility—In the future, we'll have personal mobility solutions (not always an automobile) to get us to where we need to go. The traveling experience will become integrated with smart technologies, enabled by a single ticket or membership to provide seamless travel on multi-modal transport systems. Car sharing will become a commonplace model and shared cars will become autonomous.

The Adjacent Possible

All of these mega-trends are pointing us to another benefit and fundamental property of technology: the fact that it expands into what theoretical biologist Stuart Kauffman calls "the adjacent possible." Before the invention of the wheel, for example, the automobile, the wheelbarrow, the roller skate, and a million other offshoots of circularity were not imaginable. They existed in a realm that was off-limits until the wheel was discovered, but once discovered, these pathways became clear. This is the adjacent possible. It's the long list of first-order possibilities that open up whenever a new discovery is made.

"The strange and beautiful truth about the adjacent possible is that its boundaries grow as you explore them," wrote author Steven Johnson in the *Wall Street Journal*.

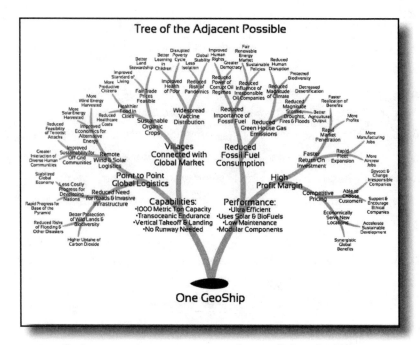

Tree of the Adjacent Possible

One GeoShip

Each new combination opens up the possibility of other new combinations. Think of it as a house that magically expands with each door you open. You begin in a room with four doors, each leading to a new room that you haven't visited yet. Once you open one of those doors and stroll into that room, three new doors appear, each leading to a brand-new room that you couldn't have reached from your original starting point. Keep opening new doors, and eventually you'll have built a palace.

In *What Technology Wants*, Kevin Kelly says,

For most of history, the unique mix of talents, skills, insights, and experiences of each person had no outlet. If your dad was a baker, you were a baker. As technology expands the possibility space, it expands the chance that someone can find an outlet for their personal traits.... When we enlarge the variety and reach of technology, we increase options, not

*just for ourselves and not for others living, but for all genera-
tions to come.*

The dynamic of the adjacent possible will help lead us to a world of abundance and, in the process, produce some spectacular leverage.[6] As marketers, we need to understand how we can tap into this dynamic, utilize the technologies coming online and leverage our resources accordingly.

Identifying the Mega-Trend Is Just the Beginning

Ultimately, values, implications, systems, design and aspirations must combine to create *guiding narratives*. These are more than just stories, they help us to explain the world in which the trends exist, why different trends have not emerged, what new trends and patterns might arise, and how designing new outcomes can change our dominant culture and trajectory.

Stories have always been a powerful element in futures thinking due to a focus on scenario planning, but such plans have often been misused as a showcase for individual trends and their linear ramifications. Guiding narratives are much bigger, catapulting us far beyond trends by illustrating values, implications, systems, design, and every other component that details who we are, where we have come from, and where we are going.[7]

Now let's move on to a discussion on the interesting predictions of respected, well-known futurists and how their predictions will impact the marketing practice.

CHAPTER THREE

Futurists' Predictions

Futurist: *a person who studies the future and makes predictions about it based on current trends.*

A s discussed in the introduction, the futurist Alvin Toffler was one of my first influencers. His books and ideas had a huge impact on my thinking as a young person growing up in the uncertain late 1970s and early 1980s. As I mentioned earlier, for those to young to remember, times were different then. In many ways, it was

Alvin Toffler

a simpler time. But, in many ways, it was a scarier time as well. The Cold War with the Soviet Union and the threat of nuclear war, high inflation, gas lines, a sputtering American economy: my family felt the pain for sure.

Toffler's book, *The Third Wave*, gave me hope for the future. And now that so many of his predictions—or versions of his predictions—have come to pass or look like they will, my feeling remains the same: These futurists are smart people who need to have seat at the table for long-range planning. When it comes to business planning and marketing planning, I believe including their ideas is critical. We need to seriously consider what they are saying.

42

The whole "futurist" thing started with such books as Bertrand de Jouvenel's *The Art of Conjecture* and Dennis Gabor's *Inventing the Future* in the early 1960s, both considered key early works in the futurist movement. The first U.S. university course devoted entirely to the future was taught by Toffler at The New School in 1966. Futurists study the "possible, probable, and preferable" futures, plus the effects of "wildcards"–low-probability, high-impact events.

A survey of 108 futurists[1] found the following shared assumptions:

1. We are in the midst of a historical transformation. Current times are not just part of normal history.

2. Multiple perspectives are at the heart of futures studies, including unconventional thinking, internal critique, and cross-cultural comparison. This is key, I believe.

3. Futurists do not see themselves as value-free forecasters, but instead are aware of multiple possibilities and consider the alternatives.

4. Futurists generally see their role as liberating the future in each person, and creating enhanced public ownership of the future, or "participatory futures." This is true worldwide.

5. While some futurists are more policy-oriented than others, almost all believe that the work of futures studies is to shape public policy, so it consciously and explicitly takes into account long-term policy transformation.

6. Part of the process of creating alternative futures and of influencing public (corporate or international) policy is internal transformation. At international meetings, structural and individual factors are considered equally important.

7. Futurists believe in complexity: a simple one-dimensional or single-discipline orientation is not satisfactory. Trans-disciplinary approaches that take complexity seriously are necessary. Systems thinking, particularly in its evolutionary dimension, is also crucial.

8. Futurists are motivated by change. They are not content merely to describe or forecast. They desire an active role in world transformation.

9. They are hopeful for a better future as a "strange attractor."

10. Most believe they are pragmatists in this world, even as they imagine and work for another. Futurists have a long-term perspective.

11. Futurists work for sustainable futures, understood as making decisions that do not reduce future options that include policies on nature, gender, and other accepted paradigms. This applies to corporate futurists and those in nongovernmental organizations. Environmental sustainability is reconciled with the technological, spiritual and post-structural ideals. Sustainability is not a "back to nature" ideal, but rather inclusive of technology and culture.

So, who are the current top futurists and what are they saying that could impact the marketing practice?[2]

Dr. Michio Kaku—Kaku is a professor of theoretical physics at the City University of New York and author of *The Future of the Mind.* He writes,

Dr. Michio Kaku

In the next 10 years, we will see the gradual transition from an Internet to a brain-net, in which thoughts, emotions, feelings, and memories might be transmitted instantly across the planet. Scientists can now hook the brain to a computer and begin to decode some of our memories and thoughts. This might eventually revolutionize communication and even entertainment. The movies of the future will be able to convey emotions and feelings, not just images on a silver screen. Historians and writers will be able to record events not just digitally, but also emotionally as well. Perhaps even tensions between people will diminish, as people begin to feel and experience the pain of others.

Alphabet (formerly Google) Chairman Eric Schmidt predicts that new systems will help us move beyond the limits of our human biology. Just as electronic calendars and to-do lists have in effect already become "prosthetics," helping us overcome our fallible memories, so social networks can extend our reach to others with expertise and abilities beyond our own. Such systems will help us use our time better, allowing us to think more deeply—or simply to turn off the thinking cap for a while. At the same time, he says, devices and holograms will allow us to project virtual versions of ourselves into places where we aren't physically present, and give us access to more and more content.[3]

See some marketing opportunities here? Absolutely—dozens of them. With so many potentially massive changes, it will be a question of prioritizing based on your marketing goals, budget and audience. Of course, some of these predictions may not come to pass. But some of them most definitely will.

Dr. Ray Kurzweil—Kurzweil is an inventor, pioneering computer scientist, and director of engineering at Google. He writes,

Dr. Ray Kurzweil

By 2025, 3D printers will print clothing at very low cost. 3D printers will print human organs using modified stem cells with the patient's own DNA providing an inexhaustible supply of organs and no rejection issues. 3-D printers will print inexpensive modules to snap together a house or an office building, lego style. We will spend considerable time in virtual and augmented realities allowing us

to visit with each other even if hundreds of miles apart. We'll
even be able to touch each other.

Some of the 'people' we visit with in these new realities will be avatars. We will be able to create avatars of people who have passed away from all of the information they have left behind (their emails and other documents, images, videos, interviews with people who remember them)."

Dr. James Canton—Canton is CEO of the San Francisco-based Institute for Global Futures and author of *Future Smart: Managing the Game-Changing Trends that will Transform Your World.* He predicts,

Dr. James Canton

Wearable mobile devices will blanket the world. By 2025, there will be a massive Internet of everyone and everything linking every nation, community, company and person to all of the world's knowledge. This will accelerate real-time access to education, health care, jobs, entertainment and commerce. Humans and robots merge, digitally and physically, to treat patients who may be around the world. Robo-surgeons will operate remotely on patients. RoboDocs will deliver babies and treat you over the cellphone.

Artificial intelligence becomes both as smart as and smarter than humans. AI will be embedded in autos, robots, homes and hospitals will create the AI economy.

Kevin Kelly notes that Alphabet and companies like it "have had AI in their DNA from the very beginning." Google's Larry Page confounded critics who questioned the company's ability to continue expanding its search business. His answer, as the competition in search expanded, was prescient: "Oh, we're really making an AI."[4] And remember, that was fifteen years ago!

Such visionary thinking continues at Google and its parent company Alphabet, where Eric Schmidt is working to realize once far-fetched ideas like self-driving cars, robots that respond to our thoughts, and augmented reality that is a seamless part of our everyday lives, overlaying data about the world that we see when we use our six senses. In effect, he says, they will make our natural world better.[5]

So, Dr. Michio Kaku, Ray Kurzweil and Dr. James Canton are incredible thinkers with some mind-blowing predictions, but who do I consider the most interesting and inspiring of them all? This man:

Thomas Frey

Thomas Frey—Frey is Google's top-rated futurist. In 2015, Frey released an article, "Future of the Internet–8 Expanding Directions," which was a very compelling read. Of all the Futurists, Frey's commentary and predictions are perfectly aligned with the interests of business people, and specifically for our purposes, marketers. With the Internet being a "multidimensional communications network" as Frey calls it, the future of the Web is not any one thing; it's many. He believes there are *eight causal dimensions* that can help expand our understanding of this super-complex communication system:

THE EIGHT EXPANDING DIMENSIONS OF THE WEB:[6]

Speed

Pervasiveness

Capacity: Data Transmission, Processing, & Storage

Durability

Human Interfaces

Dimensionality

Privacy, Security, Trust, Ethics, & Standards

Intelligence

In terms of *pervasiveness*, Frey says both Larry Page and Mark Zuckerberg are driving the effort to create a more pervasive Internet filled with satellites, drones, and balloon systems that connect us to even the most remote regions of the earth. Eric Schmidt predicts virtually everyone will be connected in some manner by 2020, with each of these 7 billion-plus unique nodes becoming a critical source of data collection and transmission.

In terms of *capacity: data transmission, processing, and storage*, Frey points out that over 90 percent of Internet traffic is video, and the Internet wasn't designed for this level of video data. To handle all the video needs of the future, we'll need the "exascale" computer, which won't come online until 2025. Exascale computing refers to computing systems capable of at least one exaFLOPS, or a billion billion calculations per second. Such capacity represents a thousand fold increase over the first petascale computer that came into operation in 2008. Transmission, processing, and storage are all interrelated. The Internet cannot progress unless all three are somewhat in equilibrium.

In terms of *human interfaces*, Frey says that optical interface de-

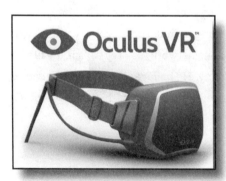

vices such as augmented reality and virtual reality are picking up steam—as we are seeing in the marketplace. Microsoft HoloLens, Facebook's Oculus VR, Google's Glass, and Samsung's Game VR are all part of a growing cadre of devices aimed at rewriting how we experience the world. As we add growing levels of intelligence to everything around us, our devices will begin making many of our decisions for us. For example, driverless cars will eliminate the need for us to make 10,000 micro decisions per hour while we drive.

In terms of *dimensionality*, the Internet of Things, which will provide connection to objects we never dreamed connectable, will add an entirely new dimension to the Web. Sensor technology is expected to break through the "trillion sensor" threshold around 2024, creating data streams from virtually every surrounding surface. We will soon see sensors embedded on the sides of house, bridges, cars, and even woven into the fabric of our clothing. In addition to sensors, microchips will add computational power to whatever is being detected. Skin sensors and body sensors combined with microchips will monitor a person's health in real time.

Future devices will tap into ambient power in a form of wireless energy, so we will no longer have a need for cords, or be limited by batteries, or have to remember to plug things in at night. Every new sensor, microchip, transmitter, and receiver will add tiny new dimensions on the microscales, while satellites, drones, and balloon systems will add macro-scale dimensions.

In terms of *intelligence*, Frey says that whether it's human intelligence or artificial intelligence (or both), the Internet is the tide that raises all boats.

The Internet gives us the ability to function together in a form of *swarm intelligence*. Think of a "swarm" as a cohesive grouping of individuals, all working together as a dynamic unified system. As humans, we don't possess the natural ability to form real-time swarms, but Internet technologies can help fill in the missing pieces, using artificial means to form the critical interstitial connections. In the coming years, human swarming will transition from an intellectual curiosity to a powerful tool that unleashes group intelligence in a wide variety of fields, applications, and settings.

Alphabet's Eric Schmidt says we may be surprised at how a once-vast world is made manageable by better tech, easier connection, and international cooperation. Imagine not just communications systems like Skype, but ones that enable instant translation, virtual reality, and editorial collaboration in real time. Such advances will change how companies and enterprises connect and interact with people and customers everywhere.[7] All of this will make our marketing work that much easier.

A future Internet will even help us expand our understanding of what intelligence is and how to apply it. Major businesses and even entire in-

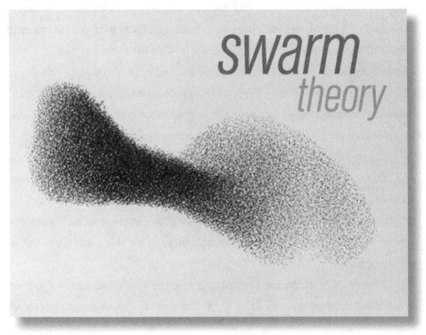

dustries will form, expand, and collapse far faster than ever before.

A New Source of Value—Experiences

As I'll discuss later in the book, customer *experiences* and the marketing that surrounds them will take on a whole new life in the future. But I wanted to bring it up here as well because I see "experiences" as a megatrend unto itself. Usually, there are key people that help lead the way in these movements and innovations. When it comes to experiences, we can trace the root of it all to one man: Walt Disney. As just about all of us are well aware, after making his name by continually introducing new levels of experiential effects on to cartoons, Disney opened Disneyland— a living, immersive cartoon world— in California. Before his death in 1966, Disney had also envisioned Walt Disney World, which opened in Florida in 1971. Rather than create another amusement park, Disney created the world's first theme parks, which immerse guests (not "customers") in interactive, entertaining, and groundbreaking rides and attractions. For every guest, cast members (not "employees") staged a complete production of sights, sounds and more to create unique experiences. Fifty years after his passing, Walt Disney remains a central figure in any marketing discussion. In the future, we'll see more marketers and other

Walt Disney

business leaders like him. Innovation and innovators will be everywhere and touch everything.

Now let's move on to content marketing and its future state as well as a discussion on the importance of marketing technology and where it's taking us.

CHAPTER FOUR

Power of Content Marketing: Ushering in the New Age

First, a declaration: Content marketing *is* marketing. It's the standard now and it will still be the standard for connecting with your audience in 2030. And that's why I'm covering it, once again, in *Future Marketing*, as I've covered it in my last two books. Now, understand that creating content for experiences—customer and user experiences—will also be a part of that connection in fifteen years, but that's still content marketing. It's just the "experience" version of it. In addition, creating content for "the platform" (and not only for the brand) will also be critical in the future. More on that in coming chapters.

The other thing to understand is this: the practice of using valuable, relevant content instead of ads has been one of the key changes in marketing over the last ten years. And it has helped usher in the new age of marketing. Why? Because content *connects you with your customers in better ways*. It builds the relationship. Ads don't do that. I don't know about you, but an ad has *never* helped me feel closer to the companies I do business with. The only thing I feel and think when I see an advertisement is, "oh, this company wants me to buy something from them. And they're interrupting what I'm doing right now. Not interested." Need further convincing? Ask a Millennial or Generation Z'er. The key here for my advertising friends is that we need to make ads better. And with the coming new technologies, we'll be able to do that. So all is not lost!

Again, it's *all about* content and it always will be.

So, for those who are new to content marketing or simply want to brush up on the topic, here is your chance. What follows is a introductory mini-course on the finer points of using content to connect with your audience. I'll follow with a discussion on the future of content marketing.

What Exactly Is "Content Marketing?"

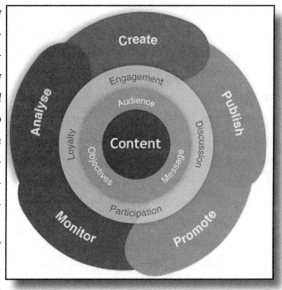

Content marketing is the strategic marketing approach of creating and distributing valuable, relevant and consistent content to attract and acquire a clearly defined audience—with the objective of driving profitable customer action.

In short, instead of pitching your products or services, you are delivering information that makes your buyer more intelligent. The essence of this content strategy is the belief that if we, as businesses, deliver consistent, ongoing valuable information to buyers, they ultimately reward us with their business and loyalty.

Content marketing is the act of sharing tips, advice, and other value-added information as a means of converting prospects into customers and customers into loyal, lifelong, repeat buyers. Utilizing the power of opt-in permission to deliver content via email, RSS feeds, social media channels, and other methods, your goal is to become a valued resource for hundreds and thousands of people who, in time, will want to buy what you sell. Over a period of weeks, months, and years, you'll build a solid relationship with them and earn their trust. You don't want to sell to them once and never see them again. You want to make a friend—a friend who enjoys buying from you—for life.

So, there you go, plain and simple. That is content marketing in a nutshell. But, how do you make it work for you?

Content marketing is about doing lots of things right: having a blog and establishing a platform? Check. Having a social media presence on Twitter, Facebook, YouTube, and other networks? Check. Providing free content in exchange for contact information? Check. Getting people on your autoresponder list and regularly sending them informative tips and advice about things that are important to them? Check that, too. In essence, you want to leave no stone unturned, showing up everywhere and anywhere your prospects may be hanging out online. Wherever they go, there you will be as well—with their permission, of course. They won't be able to miss you. And you won't miss them. Casting a big net that covers every area of your target sea will help you find all types of fish you've never seen or even thought you'd see. And that's the key.

If you start to feel like a publisher with all this content marketing stuff, well, then you'll know that you're doing things right. Like it or not, everyone is a publisher in today's business world. You business veterans out there should just take a look at all the marketing activities you've done up to this point—it feels a lot like publishing, doesn't it? Like a magazine or television station, you need to produce content—all types of content—for your consuming prospects. Before, you were just a provider of products and services. Now, you are a trusted expert resource for your customers!

How do you create compelling content? By focusing on delivering relevant, valued information that people will notice. When you do this, you'll generate trust, credibility, and expert status in your particular industry, and people will come to you when they are ready to buy. That's it. Some people will be attracted to your content immediately. Some will only want the free stuff. Others will be "just looking." And some will have the big bucks and want to spend it with you.

Why Do You Need Great Content?

Well, besides what we've already mentioned, great content ensures your long-term success and helps build your brand. In the future, it will be a question of survival. What is brand building? It's the notion of establishing a familiar presence, having a standard way of doing things, and establishing a certain level of confidence in the minds of your customers. They'll always know what they're going to get with you, and in return for that peace of mind they'll spend their money with you. You need great content because great brands always communicate very well. They don't just keep pace, they *set* the pace. And really well-produced Web and mobile content can do that for your business. Think Starbucks. Think Apple. These companies are leaders for a reason. Through their powerful brands, they are champions of content and content marketing.

Effective Web and mobile content also capitalizes on "pull" marketing techniques and the power of being where people are searching, which can clearly revolutionize your business, especially for those who are still operating from a "push," or pre-Web, strategy. Effective content is powerful because it's one of the most important elements of Google's search algorithm; if you produce content that the search engines deem important, they will reward you for it. And let's not forget the social media networks and mobile devices. The same goes for them.

Content also makes you *really interesting*. It puts you in the driver's seat. You set the pace for your industry. People come to you for editorials and feedback, and your content establishes you as an authority. The media will want you. Your clients will want you. People will retweet your tweets and "Like" you on Facebook. They will want to come to your party. Doing content right is a one-way ticket to industry dominance. Of course, having great products and services is important too.

Maximizing Its Effectiveness—The Content Marketing Machine

In my seminars and talks, I frequently mention the "three pillars" of content marketing success: (1) the content itself, (2) design, and (3) us-

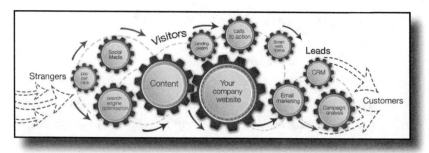

ability. Essentially, these pillars are what your content communicates, how it looks, and its ease of use. This is a good place to start with what I call your "content marketing machine," otherwise known as your total content marketing effort. It relies on certain inputs and steps that build upon each other and slowly but surely create a perpetual, automated lead-generation and business-growth machine.

Using the three pillars as your foundation, you need to consider three things:

- What types of content you produce
- How you put your content in front of your prospects and customers
- How you are supporting your content

In terms of the content you produce, think of it divided into three channels. The first is the content that makes up your site: your home page, your services pages, your case studies, your blog. Next, is the content you use for lead generation. This could be content that's on your site or off your site, but it includes materials like white papers, "webinars," and free e-books. Finally, there is your off-site content. This would be your tweets on Twitter, your PowerPoint presentations on SlideShare, your status updates on Facebook, your videos on YouTube, your mobile apps, and more.

It is really the careful practice of producing content in all three of these areas that will grow your influence and your brand. And, as we have mentioned, you need to produce all types of content: hard-hitting copy, powerful audio, and visually appealing video. You'll also want to automate the distribution process and leverage it with tools like HootSuite, Buffer and others.

Next is how you get your content in front of your target audience. One of the best ways is through a blog. Like a must-read newspaper—think of *The New York Times* or *The Wall Street Journal*—your blog is a perfect way to build a strong base of support for your mission, capturing those all-important eyeballs and building a solid relationship with your target market. The search engines love blogs because of the fresh content. Your audience will love you because you are making their lives more interesting, their brains smarter, and their pocketbooks a little heavier with your great ideas. And here's where it gets really good: They sign up for your RSS feed, your newsletter, and/or your autoresponder series. That's when you have them!

It's also where you use content marketing fundamentals to start creating a relationship. Obviously, you still deliver terrific quality. You teach and entertain more than you sell. You use metaphors and stories to make your writing conversational and easy to read. But you also use subtle techniques to create an audience of buyers, not just loyal readers. You begin to call on your content bag of tricks, adding more persuasive elements to your writing, your videos, and your other content. All the while, you're getting more and more information about your audience, their likes, their dislikes, where they live, how they buy, and more.

Essentially, you're building your case, establishing trust, and making your target market fall in love with you. On that magical day when they're ready to buy (and it will come), send your loyal reader to a well-crafted landing page on your website. Of all the Web pages you have, your landing page does the most explicit selling, with a great offer and a clear, direct call to action. Once customers buy the first time, chances are very good that they'll buy again and again and again, especially if they are happy with your product or service. They'll tell people about you. They'll follow you wherever you go. And *voila!* The content marketing machine has done its job.

The Biggest Content Marketing Trends in 2017

What follows here are selected areas of another report from Content Marketing Institute (CMI) on the most important content marketing trends for 2017.[1] I thought it was good to include this right alongside the "content marketing 101" review in *Future Marketing*.

Popular content marketing trends include:

1. Creation of a real content marketing strategy—Most companies aren't doing this and are still too focused on campaigns and talking about their products, instead of truly driving value outside of the products and services they offer. If your company is confused about content strategy, Kristina Halvorson's book, *Content Strategy for the Web*, is a great place to start.

2. Native advertising—This is a form of paid media where the ad experience follows the natural form and function of the user experience in which it is placed. It's relatively new in the past few years. You see native ads on Facebook, *Huffington Post* and many other online portals. Joe Pulizzi,

Founder of CMI, calls native advertising the "gateway drug" to content marketing (in a good way). CMI is starting to see a number of enterprises experiment, and succeed, with paid, native promotion of their content. Why is this so important? Five years ago, enterprises were spending 80 percent on content creation and 20 percent on content promotion. CMI believes this ratio has switched, with successful enterprises creating differentiated content and putting advertising and promotion dollars behind it now.

3. Influencer marketing—CMI says this topic and practice has vaulted into the top five most popular topics since the start of 2016. They say that just about every enterprise has some kind of content and influencer strategy, but few organizations execute a real strategy that makes sense. This one plays big in the future of marketing.

4. Purpose-driven marketing—CMI asked: What's your *why*? Why do you create your content? Does it have a real impact on your customers and prospects? Is there a deeper purpose behind what you do, instead of just creating content as part of your sales and marketing machine? The "Why" will become ever important in the future of the marketing practice. This one is with us forever from this point forward. And that's a very good thing.

5. Video and visual—Using video and having a visual storytelling strategy are never more important than they are right now. But CMI says most brands are still hanging their video strategy on the viral video instead of building a process and organization around the ongoing delivery of valuable information through video. There is huge future marketing impact with this one by 2021 and 2030.

6. Content technology—Be sure to review Scott Brinker's mammoth marketing technology infographic on Chiefmartec.com to understand the importance and growth of content technology. CMI says it's not just a futuristic look at content anymore, artificial intelligence and machine learning are here right now, and we need to start paying attention. I agree!

By the way, if you're in the market for content marketing software, check out my company at contentlaunch.com.

7. Email and marketing automation—CMI says email is far from dead, and may be more important than ever for content marketing programs. Most enterprises (99 percent of them) send spam disguised as content every day to key stakeholders. They say as many B2B enterprises move from just email right into marketing automation but only use 10 percent of the functionality behind marketing automation. Simply put, most of us are using marketing automation the wrong way.

8. Construction of a media organization—CMI is fascinated by the movement of enterprises to becoming media companies. Red Bull Media House was, of course, one of the first to formally create a media company inside its organizations. PepsiCo and Mondelez recently announced their efforts to structure part of their content organizations as profit centers. This is a huge movement that has some momentum behind it.

How Content Marketing Will Change in the Future

The pace of technology change is synced with the pace of change in the content marketing industry. It's a constant. Fortunately, thanks to several years of experience with all types of new technologies, platforms and user behavior data, we can make intelligent predictions about where those technologies are heading.

The emergence of virtual reality content is probably the most exciting thing ever to happen in the industry. It is clearly on its way to not only change how companies do content marketing and advertising, but also to dramatically shift how consumers engage with the companies they love to do business with. Virtual reality has the very real potential to improve the content marketing efforts of companies everywhere and engage consumers like never before. Experiential marketing, with a twist of storytelling, is about to be unleashed into the world!

Used effectively, virtual reality will positively impact the future of how we market and engage with consumers. With it, brands have the exciting opportunity to leave stronger and more lasting impressions on audiences, tell more engaging stories, and introduce more unforgettable experiences.

The future of content marketing is all about virtual and augmented reality experiences. Virtual reality is on its way, and over the next few years, it will go mainstream. Facebook acquired Oculus VR, the forerunner in virtual reality technology, so you know they have big plans for it. Of course, visual content is on the rise—videos are more easily produced and in higher demand. That won't change. Consumers are only going to demand more visual engagement over the next few years.

How Brands Are Using Virtual Reality Today

A few forward-thinking brands have already benefited from the virtual reality trend by providing unique content marketing experiences to achieve high levels of consumer engagement in ways that standard digital marketing could never accomplish. Here are a few examples:

- **Marriott**: Using virtual reality, Marriott created a "tangible experience" of traveling to one of its hotels, allowing viewers to experience the hotel in a way that seemed like the viewer was there, on the property.
- **Lexus**: The company provided an opportunity to experience the Lexus NX by virtually driving the car using a VR headset.
- **IKEA**: Rather than just looking at sets in stores, IKEA introduced a way for shoppers to virtually explore a living room.
- **Hacienda Patrón Tequila Distillery**: The company provided consumers with a 360-degree educational seminar offering a behind-the-scenes look at the product.
- **United States Air Force**: The USAF gave candidates the ability to fly a fighter jet through the use of virtual reality.

VR Content is Picking Up Steam with the Media Companies

The Cannes Lions Advertising Festival in France a few months ago saw VR content as a hot topic.[2] It was a popular talking point among ad agency executives, tech companies such as Samsung were demonstrating their latest hardware, and online services such as YouTube were showcasing the content now available on their platforms.

Publishers and media companies also were joining in, pitching marketers on the idea of branded virtual reality content, which they hope to produce and distribute on behalf of paying brands in the latest frontier for marketing. Salespeople and VR experts from Gannett's USA Today Network, spent time demonstrating a sizzle reel for its weekly VR show called "VRtually There," as well as branded VR content it's already produced for companies such as Honda.

Gannett also demonstrated a new VR ad unit it created, which it's calling a "cubemercial," that effectively places the viewer inside a virtual-reality room. Brands will be given the opportunity to showcase videos or products on each of the cube's six sides, said Gannett's chief revenue offi-

cer, Kevin Gentzel. "We've been showing this to industry leaders throughout the week and we've been seeing a great reception," Gentzel said, although no brands have yet committed to a trial with the unit.

The company said it recently signed a deal with a new client to create three
new pieces of branded VR content, due to be published across its network of sites
and properties. Meanwhile, AOL's recently acquired VR production company
RYOT was also in Cannes touting its own content creation capabilities. AOL
CEO Tim Armstrong said RYOT had taken meetings with multiple marketers
and agencies over the course of the festival and expects to sign deals as a result.

Elsewhere, publishers were picking up accolades for their VR efforts
at the Cannes Lions awards ceremonies. T Brand Studio, the brand marketing unit of the *New York Times*, won a Mobile Grand Prix prize for the
newspaper's virtual reality app, NYT VR. Since launching in November,
2015, NYT VR has been downloaded 600,000 times, the company said, and
has featured branded films for both GE and Mini.

Factors to Consider Before You Invest in VR Content Marketing

The first factor is the cost of production, which can be fairly high right
now for early adopters. The cost varies across platform and device: Using

Oculus Rift, for example, is pretty pricey. It produces a better, higher-tech experience, but devices such as Google Cardboard and Samsung Gear are less expensive and can be used with a smartphone to produce virtual reality content experiences as well. By 2021, VR will be mainstream and the costs to run a VR content marketing campaign will be much lower.

The other issue your team will need to determine is whether the content produced through virtual reality would be relevant to your target market. If your content wouldn't be better delivered through VR, then perhaps you'll want to wait another few years until costs come down. Just because VR is new and exciting doesn't mean it's the best way for you to connect with your audience.

Finally, understand how your target audience interacts with you and what they expect from you as a brand. Is virtual reality content something that will meet their needs? Does your audience have access to VR devices of their own, or would you need to provide the devices? This is a key question. And, another reason why VR content marketing is discussed in *Future Marketing*. It really is a type of content that is on the horizon, something you should start planning for now. Just try googling "VR content marketing agency." There is are only a few listed now, but in five years, look out!

So, there you go: your introductory education on content marketing is complete (for now). Keep all of this in mind as you make your way through the rest of *Future Marketing*. As a longtime practitioner of content marketing and someone who has studied a great deal of research on the future of business and the marketing practice over the past few months, I'm bullish on the power of content to connect with audiences, now and far into the future.

As organizations and professional marketers, we must never lose sight of customers, of their needs, and of connecting with them in meaningful ways. As I'll show in coming chapters, in some cases the customer is really a "part" of your organization in many ways and certainly will be in the future.

CHAPTER FIVE

Rise of Marketing Technology

C ontent. We know we need it. Our customers and prospects demand it. But how in the world do we write it, produce it, distribute it and get it all done? Utilizing technology solutions and platforms will be critically important in your future marketing endeavors. In this chapter, I primarily discuss content marketing software, but I'll also briefly discuss general marketing automation platforms like Hubspot, Marketo and Act-on as well as CRM platforms like Salesforce and Nimble, SEO solutions and other types of marketing technology later in the chapter.

Most companies claim that they're seeing success with content marketing,

but not as many have an actual documented strategy to reach their goals. Content Marketing Institute reports that only 44 percent of B2B marketers have a dedicated plan for content marketing; on the B2C side that number is at 39 percent.

But as companies expand their content operations, workflows, and publications, many are finding that they need solutions to centralize the process and improve efficiencies. Enter content marketing software. This technology can help organize your strategy, automate some of the process, assist with content curation and drive creation of original content.

Still, marketers continue to fumble with spreadsheets, informal techniques, email campaigns and other jumbled tactics to execute their content approach. Instead of investing in a long-term solution like a content marketing platform, they deal with inefficiencies. When 69 percent of marketers consider creating unique, engaging content to be an obstacle, perhaps they fail to see the reason why.

Obviously, marketing departments should be concentrating on content that appeals to prospects, not obtaining proper approvals and reinventing the workflow wheel. Content marketing software puts the focus on the right tasks: streamlining the content creation process, handling distribution and delivering key performance indicators so you can measure and improve your content techniques.

What is Content Marketing Software? Content marketing software helps to define and manage a company's end-to-end content process—or some part of it. It is used to plan, create, manage and distribute content, and/or measure content effectiveness. Some core functionality of content marketing software systems includes[1]

- **Collaboration and content creation**. Your content marketing solution should provide a platform on which content can be created. Content teams should be able to solicit ideas and collaboratively create pieces of content.
- **Calendaring**. Content marketing solutions should provide users with a calendar that allows them to plan the creation of content and launch dates.

- **Workflows and resource assignment**. The content marketing solution should support a content workflow that ensures that proper resources are assigned and proper approvals are gained.
- **User permissions**. The solution should differentiate between user types. Admins should be able to allow or deny access to functionality and decide which users can create, approve, publish or view content.

Who Should Implement Content Marketing Software?

The short answer is that companies of all sizes can benefit from implementing a content marketing platform to optimize their strategy. In fact, the Content Marketing Institute (CMI) reported that 59 percent of B2C content marketers plan to increase their content marketing platform budgets within the next twelve months.

It's clear that as organizations increase content production and the staff involved with process and distribution channels, the greater the need becomes for technology to streamline workflows, publication and analysis.

Content marketing solutions are most advantageous for companies that meet certain criteria:

- They dedicate resources to content creation on an ongoing basis
- They have a documented content strategy
- They've successfully established management buy-in for content marketing
- They have attainable objectives for the organization and its content that are ambitious, yet flexible
- They're committed to serving buyers' interests and needs with educational content rather than sales copy

Why Should Your Organization Implement Content Marketing Software?

Content marketing technology can benefit any company when properly executed to align with goals, budget, and current workflows. It doesn't need to mean upheaval for your existing processes, but can actually improve workflow with automatic task assignment, notifications, centralized distribution and delivery of performance metrics. As you explore your options for the right fit with content marketing software, bear in mind specific benefits. As you investigate options that best meet the needs of your business, consider the following benefits.

Benefits of Content Marketing Software

1. The quality of your content improves–Technology enables you to produce quality content consistently and frequently because your team has access to all material from one platform. This is an advantage for companies that want to prevent conflicting messages within the process, especially when content creation and distribution duties are spread across

various departments. Each item of content should stand apart, but also relate back to previously published materials in order to establish one cohesive experience.

Content marketing platforms make it possible for teams to review, edit and collaborate on nearly any type of content, in real-time. All members can confirm that the material stays true to brand expectations, guidelines and voice. The result is a dramatic reduction in the time spent editing, as you streamline the quality control process.

2. You'll get guidance from production and performance analytics—Are you measuring marketing success with estimates? Accurate analysis of content performance is essential. Analytics enable marketers to evaluate various components of the content management process, both in its creation and during the post-publication phase.

Insight on these metrics is critical, as they track productivity and identify the content that tends to resonate with your target audience.

Production metrics track how much content you create in a designated period, separated by asset type, category, topic, target prospect and creator or owner. Assessing these figures can assist you with identifying obstacles in the creation process and weaknesses in your content inventory.

Performance analytics give you an in-depth look at how well your material performs post-production. They include such metrics as traffic, shares on social media, subscriptions, downloads, conversions, leads generated and other types of opportunities.

Both provide fundamental data for your content approach, presenting feedback on what material is working so you can optimize your future efforts. However, linking your content to return on investment isn't a simple calculation. Lead generation and nurturing toward sales conversion is complicated across various industries, and the investment of time and resources must figure in.

Content marketing technology makes evaluating the impact of your efforts not only possible, but truly valuable. A study by Forbes Media and IPG Media Lab[34] found that 41 percent of participants were more likely to express intent to buy from a brand when looking at pages with branded content than when looking at a regular webpage with no branded content. To determine which types of content drive this high level of interest, you must challenge yourself, your team and your organization to take a data-centric methodology.

3. Content marketing software streamlines workflows—It's clear that proper organization is essential to successful creation, management and distribution of your content marketing strategy. Still, though most marketers and companies realize this, many rely on a mishmash of tools and techniques for gathering together various collaborators, tasks, and project owners. Navigating among spreadsheets, documents, a content-management system (CMS), email, and other disjointed systems will slow your organization's progress.

A coherent, standardized approach to workflow will ensure your entire team functions smoothly. A seamless process saves not only money, but time and resources as well. A content marketing platform imposes standards at each phase of the process, collecting each team member's responsibilities, deadlines and duties in one central location. Collaborators have easy access to ensure they're accomplishing their tasks along the way.

According to a study conducted by Aberdeen Group,[2] companies with well-defined processes for managing content development perform significantly better in several key areas compared to organizations without defined processes. In fact, the average website conversion rate is twice as high for process-focused companies, and the average email click-through rate is 30 percent higher.

As proper time is allotted to identify and define procedural steps, and each component of your operation is running efficiently, your content approach won't be thrown off track by missed deadlines and workflow snarls.

4. You'll increase distribution efficiencies—Distributing your material across several content marketing channels is time-consuming, yet it's critical to deliver your videos, e-books, blogs, whitepapers, and other pieces through the right channels.

Content marketing technology facilitates the process by integrating with various channels and social sites, making publication and promotion easier. Instead of pushing to different channels manually, users can distribute to numerous end points at once. These might include such destinations as a blog, website, marketing automation software, and social media.

You can also enable guidelines within the solution so colleagues and other collaborators can easily implement best practices for content creation and sharing. Such standards typically identify the rules a user should follow or other requirements when distributing different types of content. They could include posting on social media, adding content to an email newsletter, or using a specific hashtag.

5. You'll get more use out of buyer personas—Marketers realize the effectiveness of buyer personas, which are essentially a documented description of each key customer type across all target markets. Success with personas means you need to align with the needs and concerns of the specific individual.

However, you can't always keep these personas in your head when creating a blog post, producing a video, or drafting a new e-book. Content marketing technology enables companies to invite their buyer personas into the platform so that every new concept, content piece, and campaign can be mapped to the right persona. Your material remains relevant no matter which user in the system is creating or assigning it.

Plus, by mapping your content by buyer persona, you can easily keep track of how much and what types of content you've dedicated to specific buyers. Keeping your content approach and buyer personas in alignment will make it easier to monitor content performance and assist when you need to adjust your strategy on the fly. You never know when you might need to boost production as a market sector or geographic region takes a new direction.

6. Content marketing software enables you to integrate all your solutions in one place—The number of marketing solutions used by marketers every day is staggering and will only increase as technology and demand require more precision. Content takes center stage among all these tools and techniques since buyers actively seek information and entertainment more often than product details.

Today's content marketing technology addresses this hurdle by integrating seamlessly with myriad solutions that marketers employ to create, distribute, optimize, and measure performance of their campaigns. The entire process can be managed and tracked via one platform, while still accommodating the needs of each individual contributor.

Content marketing software can integrate with the big-name players in publishing channels, video tools, marketing automation technology, social media outlets, and vital production tools. Most platforms also work smoothly with sales and collaboration tools. Proven integrations enable your organization to brainstorm, develop, publish, and assess content from multiple workstations—all housed in one centralized location.

As the creation of an individual asset or series progresses, any contributor's work syncs among the various channels and platforms; in many cases, the process takes place automatically and in real time. Each member of your team has access to the most current version of a piece at all times. Robust integrations are a primary advantage of content marketing software, merging the production process with distribution so your team spends less time on tasks that must be accomplished across a range of tools.

When is the Right Time to Invest in Content Marketing Software?

Long-term solutions may be a consideration when you want to get the most out of your content, from both a quantity and quality perspective. Tracking performance of your content should also drive your decision-making process.

1. Your workflow is becoming increasingly complex—According to a CMI report,[3] B2B marketing departments employ roughly sixteen different techniques; even their counterparts at smaller companies use twelve on average. In light of the sheer quantity and range of content being published, it only stands to reason that many organizations seek to fit their divergent workflows into one content marketing solution.

When you unsystematically manage various workflows, each one suffers. Issues within the process can easily escalate out of control as you scale your content efforts. If you analyze your team's content production quarterly to find that several assets are being published, the time may be right to implement a standardized—yet scalable—workflow.

2. Your branding guidelines delay distribution—As your company expands or more regulations apply to your industry, you must maneuver through more guidelines in order to secure the necessary approvals. Each content asset can journey through various departments, including legal, creative, editorial, and more. The painstaking approval process slows down content creation and distribution, but it's often a necessary evil for sticking to brand guidelines and industry best practices.

A content marketing platform consolidates all the various types of content pieces, as well as brand assets, guidelines, legal jargon, contributors and other factors to ensure that the approval process is efficient and effective. Your team can then scale your content operations without worrying about wandering outside existing approvals and procedures.

3. You deal with an extensive network of content contributors—A well-developed network of contributors is definitely a powerful asset when it comes to gathering diverse views, insights and a steady stream of compelling material. But if it isn't managed effectively, each participant can muddle the workflow and detract from your hard work.

A marketing team performs differently depending on the size of the organization and the type of content being produced. Internal contributors may be involved across several departments, from the marketing department and customer service to sales and lead development—to name a few. External team members might include freelancers, designers, principals, analysts and others.

There isn't a set number of contributors that should or shouldn't participate in the process. The bottom line is that you do, in fact, need the right team to strategize, create and distribute content. But the more members you have contributing efforts to your content approach, the more essential content marketing technology becomes as a means to properly manage strategy, content, collaboration, discussion and performance measurement.

4. You need your content to power business goals—Modern marketers are tasked with achieving measurable goals for their organizations, specifically by delivering qualified leads to the sales department and boosting revenue. Content marketing technology supports your content efforts to enable these objectives.

When your marketing department is held accountable for driving critical business objectives such as lead generation and increasing revenue, you need to establish proof that your efforts are getting the job done. Content marketing solutions can assist in identifying performance success and areas of improvement by tracking traffic, downloads, new leads in the database and first or last touches on converted sales.

In addition, knowing which content types and topics are the most valuable for meeting marketing goals will help you improve your content strategy and direct resources on assets that deliver results.

5. You can't keep up with content needs—A final indication that it's time to consider content marketing software is when the variety and quantity of your content outpaces your team's management processes. The amount of quality content your business should be producing depends on your industry, especially if it includes certain verticals that are far more competitive than others. But keep in mind that 30 million pieces of content are shared every day. Clearly, it's a challenge to stand out.

As your organization expands, it's essential that you boost production of quality content to reach your audience across various channels. This also means you'll likely need to increase the different types of content you're creating, whether they're videos, blog posts, presentations, e-books or other formats. Plus, the quality of your content becomes even more critical as the demand to produce greater quantities rises. Content marketing software can increase process efficiencies, enable your team to focus more on quality and less on procedure, and streamline the analysis of your efforts.

Content marketing strategies are central to the long-term success of any business that seeks to raise brand awareness, drive demand, and convert leads into profit. Content marketing software can improve upon the process by boosting content quality, providing actionable performance analytics, streamlining workflow, and improving distribution.

If you're committed to delivering content that your prospects find valuable, organization and collaboration are critical. A content marketing platform can help you surpass common logistics issues and obstacles that slow organizations down, thereby enabling you and your team to concentrate on creating unique, compelling content.

Other Types of Marketing Technology

Over the last few years, we've seen an explosion in the various types of technology and platforms available to marketers. Although I have a natural inclination toward content marketing technology, I wanted to briefly mention some of the other key types of mar-tech that are available. I briefly mentioned a few other types in the opening to this chapter. My good friend, Travis Wright, the author of *Digital Sense: The Common Sense Approach to Effectively Blending Social Business Strategy, Marketing Technology, and Customer Experience*, wrote a great piece for *Inc. Online* on choices in marketing technology and I wanted to share an excerpt with you here.[4]

Wright says, "Your marketing technology stack will likely depend on your business model, commerce versus media and whether you are B2B or B2C." He recommends looking at other sites' MarTech stacks in order to help you imagine what your own should be comprised of. He points to HomeDepot.com as a great example of a MarTech stack that is organized well, according to data pulled by Ghostery.

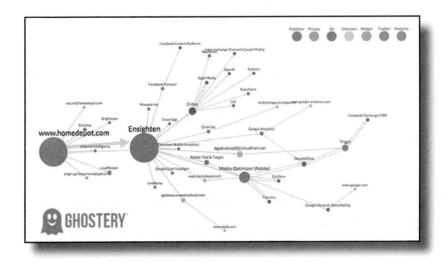

So what are the various types to consider? Wright discusses the following categories:

- **Customer Relationship Manager (CRM):** These tools manage the data of your current and future customers. It organizes, automates, and synchronizes prospecting, sales, marketing, customer service, and technical support. The world's most popular CRM is Salesforce. However, there are others like SugarCRM, Nimble, HubSpot Sidekick, and KarmaCRM. This type of mar-tech is required for any company, so that's why it's in the first position here. FYI: CRM is also considered a *sales* platform.

- **Marketing Automation:** This is the "swiss army knife" for marketing technology. In other words, these platforms do just about everything you need them to. It's a suite that usually includes analytics, tracking, online forms, and even email marketing. Popular platforms are HubSpot, SharpSpring, Infusionsoft, or Act-On for smaller businesses. Enterprises should check out Silverpop, Marketo, Eloqua, Pardot, and Adobe Campaign.

- **Analytics and Tracking**: We all have lots of areas we need to track—performance, ads, technology, and much more. Google Analytics is the most utilized tool here, with more than 80 percent of smaller businesses using it. Adobe Analytics is the go-to tool for larger enterprises.

- **Tag Management**: A tag is a chunk of code—often JavaScript—that performs a task on your site. Oftentimes, websites have several of these chunks that need deploying, including tags for analytics, affiliate marketing, advertising, and much more. If you're a small- or medium-sized business (SMB), look at Google Tag Manager. If you're an enterprise, check out Adobe DTM, Tealium, Signal, or Ensighten.

- **Data Management Platform (DMP)**: In lay terms, a data management platform is a data warehouse. It's software that grabs, sorts, and stores information—and then spits it out in a way that's useful for marketers, publishers, advertisers, and other businesses. Vendors that sell DMP technology to the digital media world currently include Adobe, Krux, Lotame, Aggregate Knowledge, BlueKai, and others.

- **Content Delivery Network (CDN):** A CDN works by providing alternate server nodes for users to download resources (usually content like images and JavaScript). These nodes are spread throughout the globe and are therefore physically closer to the end users, which ensures a faster response and content download time. While CDNs are a great solution for websites looking for speed improvements, not every site needs a CDN. Akamai is a popular CDN, but there are many CDN vendors to choose from.

- **Conversion Optimization**: You can lose your prospect with an unattractive site layout, long forms, or a slow site. Conversion optimization can easily double how many people fill out online forms, getting you that invaluable big data. Try out Optimizely for A/B testing of your pages, the complimentary Landing Page Grader from WordStream, or Ion Interactive to easily craft marketing apps with absolutely no tech background required. Enterprise businesses should consider Maxymiser, Monetate, or the original Adobe Target.

- **Email Marketing**: This is the tried and true and longest running mar-tech out there. Marketing using email has been with us since the late 1990s, but most companies still do it the wrong way. The key, of course, is to only send valuable, relevant content, not sales pitches. Content should be personalized and sent in just the right doses. Some great tools include Constant Contact, Exact Target, Emfluence, and MailChimp. Keep in mind that most marketing automation tools already have great email marketing tools within them.

- **Advertising Networks**: Even though I'm not a big fan of ads, there is no denying that ad networks are important. If you're an SMB, you probably use Google AdWords, or maybe Google Retargeting or DoubleClick for your ad network. Facebook is also a solid choice. Wright says that one of his favorite things to do is "to execute Facebook ad campaigns using a variety of these tools and retargeting platforms."

- **Remarketing**: You may not know it, but you already know firsthand what remarketing is. If you visit a website, then later see an ad for that website somewhere else, it's most likely no coincidence. Remarketing helps you reach people who have already searched for your offering--or something very similar. You can use Google AdWords, AdRoll, or Perfect Audience to get started.

- **Search Engine Marketing**: From search engine optimization (SEO) to paid search ads, search engine marketing has been massively important for many years. Search ads let you test and improve copy, forms, and keywords, then track potential customers via Google AdWords and Analytics. Of course, SEO demands regular, original, valuable content. Many companies depend on WordStream, gShiftLabs, or BrightEdge to complement Google's tools.

If you want to discover all of the marketing technologies in the industry, be sure to check out Scott Brinker's MarTech Landscape. Growthverse is also a great tool, it uses visualization mapping to show the entire marketing technology ecosystem.

The Power of Big Data

First, a definition:

Big Data: *extremely large data sets that may be analyzed computationally to reveal patterns, trends, and associations, especially relating to human behavior and interactions.*

There is no denying that we are entering a time where data—big data—is becoming highly insightful and actionable. We now have more information about more things than we've ever had before. And you can bet that in the future, big data will make an even larger impact on the marketing practice. In an article on Forbes.com[5] Louis Columbus discussed all of the myriad ways that big data is making a difference in the marketing—and sales—areas. He said, "the power of big data is providing insights into which content is the most effective at each stage of a sales cycle, how Investments in Customer Relationship Management (CRM) systems can be improved, in addition to strategies for increasing conversion rates, prospect engagement, conversion rates, revenue and customer lifetime value."

Here are a few selected areas that Columbus indicated are ways big data is revolutionizing the marketing practice:

- Supported by Big Data and its affiliated technologies, it's now possible to embed intelligence into contextual marketing. The marketing platform stack in many companies is growing fast based on evolving customer, sales, service and channel needs not met with existing systems today. As a result, many marketing stacks aren't completely integrated at the data and process levels. Big data analytics provides the foundation for creating scalable Systems of Insight to help alleviate this problem.

- Forrester found that big data analytics increases marketers' ability to get beyond campaign execution and focus on how to make customer relationships more successful. By using big data analytics to define and guide customer development, marketers increase the potential of creating greater customer loyalty and improving customer lifetime.

- 58 percent of Chief Marketing Officers (CMOs) say search engine

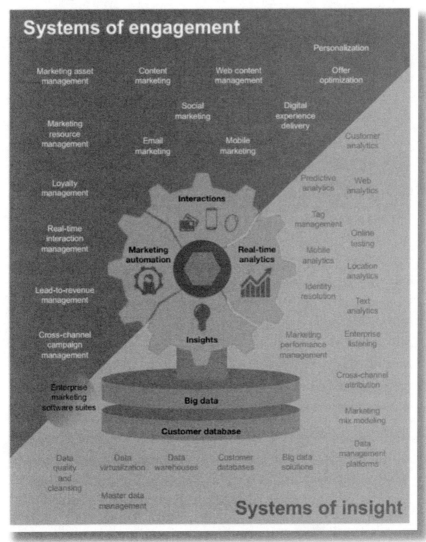

optimization (SEO) and marketing, email marketing, and mobile is where big data is having the largest impact on their marketing programs today. Fifty-four percent believe that big data and analytics will be essential to their marketing strategy over the long-term

And these represent just a few key insights. In fact, entire books have been written about big data. Many books. In *Future Marketing*, I simply wanted to touch on it and set the stage for a wider discussion. What will big data be like in the future? It will get faster and better and become a more ubiquitous part of our marketing decisions. In essence, there is nothing it will not touch. Just about every area I discuss in the rest of *Future Marketing* will be impacted by big data, in one way or another. The key will be in *how* we use it and—because there will be so much raw data at our disposal—how we *filter out the noise* from the stuff that really matters.

Factors Fueling the Rise of Marketing Technologists

DataXu performed a 2016 study, *Modernizing the Mix: Transforming Marketing Through Technology and Analytics.*[6] I thought their findings were pretty  interesting and should be shared here in *Future Marketing*. The increasing role of technology in the practice of marketing will only increase over the next few years. From their study:

- 100 percent of U.S. marketers surveyed say data and analytics will play a crucial role within their team as well as within other marketing teams in the future:
- 46 percent of U.S. marketers plan to increase investments in both

customer insight analytics and programmatic marketing in 2017

- 66 percent of marketing teams interviewed have a Chief Marketing Technologist (CMT) in place today, and 26 percent are looking to fill a CMT role in the next twelve months
- 23 percent of global marketers say "being stretched too thin due to working with and managing too many vendors" is their biggest threat.

So with that, we conclude Section 1 of *Future Marketing*. You now have a good "lay of the land" that shows where we are currently in marketing and a good understanding of some of the most important trends and predictions for the future. Let's go next to the subject of the changing customer and discuss how the customer will impact your organization in new and exciting ways over the next fifteen years.

SECTION 2
THE CHANGING CUSTOMER

CHAPTER SIX

Power to the People

As human beings, we are all consumers. We all buy things and use them to help us live our lives. We want the buying and consuming process, whether we're acquiring products or services, as consumers or businesses, to be easy and affordable and to add value. For many decades, we didn't have much decision-making ability in the whole process; our voice really didn't count for much. Before the Internet, where could we go to complain or build an audience? Of course, everything changed with the introduction of the Web. The question is: where do we go from here and what happens now?

As a modern day consumer, *you know* that you have changed the way you act when it comes to interacting with the companies you do business with. I know I have. So, some of what I discuss here in this chapter won't be a surprise. But some of it will, because this whole "changing customer" thing will take on new life over the next fifteen years. Some of it may seem like a fantasy or "pie in the sky" and some of it will be wrong. But some of it will be right on the money. And it will all sound pretty cool, I think. We, no doubt, live in interesting times.

As I mentioned in the introduction, the term "prosumer" was first introduced by Alvin Toffler in his 1980 book, *The Third Wave*, and explores the idea that as society shifts towards the post-industrial age, the producer and the consumer have amalgamated into the prosumer. Prosumers actively work to produce the services and goods they buy and consume. Examples of this that we see every day are the self check-outs at the supermarket, the DIY furniture of Ikea, automated ticket machines at train stations, or online order and delivery services such as eBay or Amazon. It's everywhere, and will continue to be.

Remember, just five years ago, there were no self-checkouts; employed cashiers and baggers did that for us. Thirty years ago, none of us built our own beds and dining room furniture; some guy in North Carolina at a furniture mill did that. A train station attendant gave us our train ticket and in the 1980s we shopped at Sears or Kmart to buy what we now get online from Amazon. As people *buying* the stuff, we are now actively engaged in the *production or delivery or marketing* of the stuff. This is a critical and key distinction now, and will be in the future.

The Producer Gets Loyalty—The Consumer Gets Attention

If you're a company that has prosumers as customers, you'll enjoy a level of loyalty that most companies can't even pay for. But your prosumer customers will enjoy many advantages as well: uninterrupted quality, continuous improvements, attentive personalization—assuming it's a great service.

Think about it: If you *access* software, instead of own it, then you can share in its improvement. As the prosumer, you'll be encouraged to identify bugs and report them (replacing QA), to seek technical help from other customers in forums (reducing the burden of the help desk), and to develop your own add-ons and improvements (replacing product development). And most importantly for the subject of this book, as a prosumer, you'll tell others about your experience, you'll create content on behalf of the software company, and in so doing you'll generate new users and new sales. You'll be the new marketing department! Access amplifies the interactions we have with all parts of a service.

Kevin Kelly observes that the shift away from ownership of products has come at the cost of the benefits companies get from having users modify and experiment on the products they own. Services presently offered by many popular platforms don't permit such tinkering.[1] In the future, we'll see this change. If the company wants to win in the Prosumer Age, they'll need to give up a little control. But it will be good for all parties involved.

The first stand-alone product to be "servicized" was software. Today, selling software as *service* instead of as *product* has become the default mode for almost all software. In the future, we'll see this "product to service" transition in just about every industry, all over the world. And the world's prosumers will lead us.

The Internet Made It Possible

The Internet, of course, invited us into the "means of production," which had previously been sealed off from us. As the Web became more widely available, we as prosumers became more important. As prosumers, we now have the ability to create what we want to fit our needs. As prosumers who have unprecedented influence and power, we are no longer bound by the same old products and services produced by faceless multinational production companies. Technology innovations have given us the ability to generate content that not only appeals to us, but appeals to the companies we buy from as well.

One article quoted the author Jeremy Rifkin's description of those who own IoT devices as "prosumers—adopters of systems to help steer their own course in the economy. Such users are making Toffler's forty-year-old prediction prove true.[2]

It should also be noted that "prosumer," in addition to being a mash-up between "producer and consumer" can also mean "professional consumer."

Leadership expert Daina Middleton cites the book *Convergence Culture*, by USC communications professor Henry Jenkins, as an insightful look at how the shift is actually one of culture rather than technology. It depends on people being willing to take an active part in a new kind of society. Jenkins asked, "Does it make sense any more to speak about media audiences or, for that matter, consumers in this brave new world of spreadable media? Probably not." Instead he suggested labeling the "audience" that marketers will have to reach through what he termed "spreadable media" as "loyals, inspirational consumers, connectors, influencers and… prosumers." [3]

Web 2.0—The Critical Mass Arrives

Just about everyone knows that "Web 2.0" was the second stage of development of the World Wide Web, characterized by the change from static Web pages to dynamic or user-generated content and the growth of social media.

In 2005, Tim O'Reilly, who coined the term "Web 2.0," in discussing "the Web as platform," said,

> Like many important concepts, Web 2.0 doesn't have a hard boundary, but rather, a gravitational core. You can visualize Web 2.0 as a set of principles and practices that tie together a veritable solar system of sites that demonstrate some or all of those principles, at a varying distance from that core.

The development of Web 2.0 technologies enabled the rise of the prosumer. We can upload our own content on YouTube. We can contribute to Wikipedia, becoming producers by writing an article for a Wikipedia page or uploading a video to YouTube. Before the Web, audio, video and text production was only available from professionals who had access to the means of production. New technology means that anyone with a smartphone now has the capability to make a popular video by using the built-in camera, uploading it to YouTube, and getting people to see it and share it.

We participate in the production of online content for a number of reasons. First, we enjoy creating our blog, song, video or post. We also like sharing it with our community. Sometimes, we find others in the community that leads to some form of collaboration to create something together. We upload it to the community to enjoy, which gives us, as prosumers, a sense of belonging and purpose. The employees of YouTube aren't creating the videos, we are. In the 1970s and 80s, the employees of YouTube would have done the work. This sounds very strange to us now, but back then, it would have sounded really odd to say that in thirty years, people would be creating and sharing videos on their computers and building community around them!

Facebook is a good example of an "informational commune," Kevin Kelly observed. More than a billion "citizens" contribute to it from their own lives and in return get valuable communication and relations with others. "They are paid by being allowed to stay on the commune."[4]

Our Contribution Reduces Costs for Companies

Look at Amazon.com. This is an interesting case. Have you ever had the conscious thought that we're all doing lots of the work for Amazon? We post reviews, we post what we bought on Amazon on our Facebook page, we let them know when there is a mistake on their website or a problem with the product. *We help them do the work,* yet we are not paid for it. We also provide Amazon (and many other companies) with our personal data, which allows them to sell the data and make money off us without them really doing anything except asking for our data.

But we are rewarded by the low cost of the products, the easy ordering process, and the fact that we don't have to leave the house to get the things we buy. So, the operation of Amazon.com as an entity is really a *partnership* between them as a company and us as their customers—or prosumers. We all win! And this is a critical distinction. As prosumers, we are enabling Amazon to gain a larger profit due to our participation in cutting their "research" and other costs.

The "Open-Source" Revolution

Prosumption and the prosumers that practice it have been further enabled within the context of "immaterial production." Case in point: The production of open-source computer software. Its whole concept relies on prosumers to both develop and test the software. No money changes hands, and the software is used by millions because it's really good—the best, in fact. The open-source movement is a key part of the prosumer revolution.

For example, Linux is open-source software that is free and can be used by anyone and contributed to by anyone for free. And what are the big, established, profit generating companies now doing? Microsoft is moving much of its software to the cloud and changing the way it does

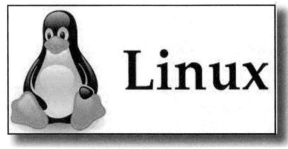

software licensing. In a huge departure for the company that analysts acknowledge will open it up to more markets, Microsoft says it plans to put its SQL Server onto the Linux platform for the first time in 2017. Merv Adrian, from Gartner Research, said recently that the company lost some key enterprise deals because it wasn't on Linux.[5] When big, traditional companies start making these moves, that's when you know we can start calling it "the Prosumer Age." And what about Tesla offering up its patents for the Model S for free to anyone in 2014, essentially making them open source? That's very "prosumer" of them.

Open source is thriving, in part because of the growth of big data. Big-data technology Apache Hadoop is celebrating its tenth birthday this year; since its introduction, a whole ecosystem of technologies has grown up around it. Technology vendors are recognizing that by putting some technology into open source, they gain collaboration from other great minds to help the project mature more quickly. Developers from different companies can collaborate on projects and develop solutions for the greater good of the entire community. That's not something that happens in a competitive commercial software market.

Plenty of room for growth remains for "decentralized collaboration," Kevin Kelly writes. For instance, one company that monitors open-source technology estimates that it presently touches some 650,000 people and nearly as many projects. "That total is three times the size of the General Motors workforce," he says. By way of comparison, he invites readers to imagine an auto company whose employees churned out cars even though the company wasn't paying them.[6]

What Motivates an Open-Source Developer?

Open-source developers are motivated in part by ego, and in part by curiosity and fun, says Stefano Mazzocchi, who invented the open source Apache Cocoon framework. Mazzocchi said he himself initially wanted to gain a reputation as a supreme programmer, but also did it because he was curious and enjoyed the work. His testimony dovetails nicely with one online survey of Linux developers whose motivations were shown to be slightly different. Peter Gloor, author of *Swarm Creativity*, says that the survey ranked learning and fun as the highest motivations, others were the following:

1. Community goals and other "collective motives."
2. The motivation of getting recognized by fellow coders, and interacting with people you respected.
3. Learning new techniques that led to more money and friends.[7]

What can your company open up to become "open source," or how can you partner with an open-source platform? And how can that impact the marketing you do? Could you garner more customers and more revenue or new markets in the process? I bet you can. At the same time, everyone will like your company a whole lot more, too.

The Impact of Technology

As with the rise of Uber and Airbnb, the advancements in smartphone technology have also made a huge impact on the prosumer movement. How about self-check-in terminals at airports or movie theaters? What was key to self-check-in technologies was the development of another technology in itself: the credit/debit card. No longer is it necessary to have a human cashier to make sure prosumers are paying the correct amount; technology does it all for them. Over the last twenty years, it's been a series of new technological moments that creates other new technology, technology that in turn creates the need for other new technology that then includes the prosumer as a part of it. It's a cascading and multiplying effect that then has an exponential benefit for all of us. And the world gets more efficient along with it.

And how about all the new *energy prosumers* being impacted by new renewable energy technology? These are the folks who are installing solar panels on their homes all over the country. These prosumers are energy consumers who move beyond passive energy consumption to become active energy producers. They are small-scale, DIY energy producers capitalizing on a number of different opportunities in an evolving market. It's the natural next step as the world transitions to a decentralized energy economy. The market is renewables. And it's not just about producing energy—being an "energy citizen" also covers measures like energy efficiency, storage, and participation in demand response.[8]

We even see the prosumer behavior with online music. Over thirty music streaming services now provide listeners with ways to "play" with the unconfined elements of popular recorded music. Spotify is a stand-out. As a cloud containing 30 million tracks of music, you can search to locate the most specific, random song imaginable. With the paid version of Spotify, you can download the digital files and remix tracks if you like. And, just like that, you are now the consumer *and the producer*. In our

"flowing" type of technology environment, you can consequently bring up your playlists and personal radio stations from any device, including your phone, or direct the stream into your home speakers.

We Consume Content, Then Instantly Add to the Conversation

With almost all Web 2.0 platforms, millions of prosumers simultaneously consume and produce user-generated content on a regular basis. Social network sites such as Twitter and Facebook, content-sharing sites such as YouTube, Instagram, and Flickr, blogging sites such as Wordpress, and the collaborative encyclopedia Wikipedia are only a few examples.

You see this prosumer behavior up close at industry conferences when an audience is watching a speaker in a conference session. Before Web 2.0, mobile phones, and apps were invented, you would find "speakers" at these events who "produced" speeches, and there was an audience "consuming" (i.e. listening to) them. Engagement would occur when the audience members would take notes and sometimes ask questions at the end of the speech. But that is so 1990s. The standard now is having audience members "tweeting" about what is being said in the speech or session they are consuming as it happens, and sometimes even being responded to by the speakers in real time.

In a way, the audience now has the most powerful role in the conference, as what is being shared on Twitter about the event is now on the Internet for a global audience to consume. The presentation may have been shared by the speaker as well, but the three hundred people that were in the audience create a critical mass of response, opinion, and feedback. And in the exchange, they have power and influence. All of this behavior happens on blogs as well, which is one big reason why they have become such a powerful force in our culture. This one dynamic can be applied to many marketing activities at your organization.

When we add to the conversation, we are providing lots of data about ourselves. More available data about everyone in the future will only intensify the trends we see today: Every opinion will find lots of listeners, real-time updating will encourage a hyperactive social network, and the ubiquity of social networking will allow everyone to play celebrity, paparazzo, and voyeur—simultaneously, if desired.

We will all produce and share a ton of data about ourselves—our past and present, our likes and choices, our aspirations and daily habits. This data will enable companies to do the same things they're doing now, but in much greater numbers and in a more refined manner: They'll be able to better respond to customer concerns, to precisely target specific people and, as we'll see unfolding with the emergent field of predictive analytics,* to predict what future patterns will emerge for their target audience and actually deliver what's needed before anyone even realizes they need it. That's powerful and that's...the future of marketing.

Influencers and Thought Leaders

The widespread use of social media has also given rise to the influencers and thought-leaders movement. This allows certain folks to create their own influence. Social media has enabled people to follow their passions to create, curate, connect with others, and attract a following. The roots of influencer marketing are in advocacy and public relations firms

---

*Predictive analytics is a young field of study at the intersection of statistics, data mining and computer modeling.

whose job it was to turn their business clients into industry thought leaders. Today, whether the influencer is a celebrity or not isn't really important; most influencers, especially in B2B, are not.

In fact, influencers can come in all shapes and sizes and your own company may have a few. Every day staff or employees like "Mary in the Human Resources Department" who speaks all over the country, or "Bob the UX Designer in the IT Department" who has a blog with 25,000 subscribers, could be key influencers. They don't have to be charismatic, camera-ready executives. Or, it could be that person out there with a million Twitter followers, celebrity or not. And, as I've discussed in *Future Marketing*, it very likely could be that prosumers are already advocating for your company or actively helping your company in some way. When you work with people who have subject matter expertise and an active network, you can gain some huge advantages. The main goal is to create an affinity for the brand through the influencer, and to reach the audience that influencer has been able to attract.

A thought leader is more someone who comes up with original thoughts and ideas. They're creating substantive, deep, research-based, game-changing content that makes a big impact. These are the people who write books, do webinars, and speak at industry events. Just as important as expressing interests and creating content is doing it in a way that inspires others to act.

Tomoson, an influencer platform, did a study that showed that businesses that implemented influencer programs get nearly a 7:1 return in advertising or content marketing value. Companies that engage influencers are seeking their reach, quality, and expertise; if they do it right, they can get just that.[9]

This type of activity will certainly accelerate and propagate over the next fifteen years.

Influencers in the Future

Kevin Kelly predicts that everybody will have the ability to be an influencer, if they want it. He cites the example of the Academy Awards in 2021: "Instead of retailers paying millions of dollars to have a place in the Oscar attendees' 'swag' bags, they could aim at a huge network of smaller influencers, saving money and being more effective in the process." Advertisers could even skip the Oscars program entirely and instead pay thousands of "small-time influencers" to generate attention.[10] It will be real people, with real influence motivating other real people to do something they are doing.

Self-Monitoring and the Prosumer Age

The Prosumer Age is also being influenced heavily by the self-tracking phenomenon we've seen over the last few years with products such as Nike+ and Fitbit. And it's not just about tracking our steps, our sleep, and our overall personal health. In the future, we'll be digitally tracking *our lives*. If we want them to, tiny wearable digital eyes and ears will record every second of our entire day—who we saw and what we said—to aid our memories. Our stream of email and text, when saved, will form an ongoing diary of our mind.

We'll be able to add a record of the music we listened to, the books and articles we read, and the places we visited. The important details of our routine movements and meetings, as well as important events and experiences, will also be trackable and will be merged into a chronological flow. This flow will be called a *lifestream*. First described by the computer scientist David Gelernter in 1999, a lifestream is more than just a data archive. Because it's tied to us, it will be like an Internet of Things (IoT) for people.

Exactly how will we benefit from our lifestreams? Kevin Kelly offers some predictions:

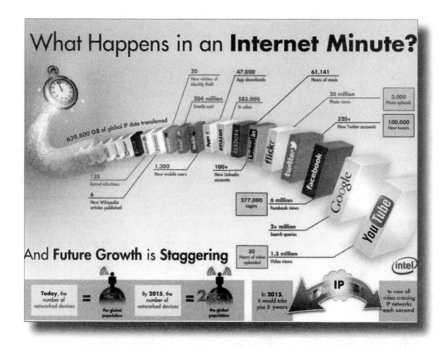

- **A personal warning system of bodily measurements**—From real-time blood sugar and blood pressure measurements to monitoring of environmental toxins, the data we get could warn us and serve as a personalized health resource. It could change public health dramatically.

- **An indelible aid to your memory of what you've said, where you've been, who you've met, and what you've done**—You'd be able to search and share this information as needed.

- **Complete archived details of what you've written, said, or made**—Detailed journaling to make you more productive and creative.

- **A method for giving form, structure, and legibility to life's events.**[11]

Self-Monitoring in Action

Kelly cites the example of a present-day lifestreamer, computer scientist Larry Smarr, who changed his life by self-diagnosing the onset of ulcerative colitis. Smarr had obsessively tracked data about his body, from skin temperature to microbes in his stool, and his findings about the microfauna in his body helped anticipate the onset of the disease before his doctors even suspected it. The diagnosis was later confirmed surgically.[12] Although some would find this behavior odd, or way too time-consuming, it won't be odd or time consuming in the future. It will be easy and ubiquitous. What Smarr discovered was powerful. And *that's* the future.

The marketing impacts of widespread lifestreaming are self-evident: With all this data about all the people, the idea of target marketing will take on a whole new life. Of course, some of us will sell or give access to our data and others will not. But the benefits for opting in will be very attractive. I've mentioned that marketing will get easier in many ways, right? This is one key way.

Convergence of Company and Customer

The gap between company and customer is shrinking all the time. The lines between lifestyle industries, between forms of art and entertainment, and between the senses are increasingly blurred. As collaboration, co-creation, and personalization increase, industries are beginning to adopt a bottom-up approach to community-led development and market impact. They have to do so to keep up with the Etsys, Nikes, Ubers, Airbnbs and other disruptors of the world. (By the way, Nike was founded in 1964, so you don't have to be a young company to capitalize on this.)

With prosumers helping to transition the power from large enterprises to smaller communities, well-executed customer-led marketing conversations now involve multiple facets such as design, prototype, testing, production, distribution, marketing, and community. Customers have taken brand conversations *away from the company* in the form of tweets, posts, blogs, comments, videos, and more.[13] In this hyper-converged reality, prosumers (who in turn are brand advocates) will be exactly what companies need to remain relevant and to be successful in the long run.

The Story of *Wired* Magazine

Consider *Wired* magazine, which Kevin Kelly examines in *The Inevitable*. They chronicled the rise of the tech world even before the Web, along the way experimenting with how news and information was shared and used. Since they were pioneering ways of telling stories about tech, they experimented with allowing their readers to become part of the magazine in unprecedented ways. They could contribute and edit online. "So the *Wired* team asked: What happens if we turn the old model inside out and have the audience/ customers in charge?" Kelly writes. These were producing consumers—Toffler's prosumers—and the question was how much to trust them. Should *Wired* crowdsource large parts of its content, or follow more traditional editorial paths? Should editors change from always assigning and instigating stories to approving the crowd's wisdom?

"Well, that's exactly what they did," Kelly says. "*Wired* thought they could get further faster by unleashing people with strong voices, lots of passion, and the willingness to write without any editors getting in the way." As with Facebook, and online blogs today, editors were not creators of the content. This model of creativity now results in billions of writers pouring vast amounts of content onto the Web each moment—far more than professionals could produce. No one edits most Web content today, and it is grassroots writing at its most basic. Does it work? Is it worth attention? Kelly notes that *Wired* was recently sold for $24 billion.[14] Yes, it works.

What Did Philip Kotler Say about Prosumers?

In 1986, Philip Kotler, the author or the landmark book *Principles of Marketing*, said in his paper, "The Prosumer Movement: A New Challenge for Marketers," that

> we can imagine further examples of consumer participation
> in designing manufactured goods and services. A person will
> enter a clothing store, stand before an electronic mirror and
> press appropriate buttons that will project various suits on
> him in different colors, style, and materials. After finding the
> most pleasing look, he will press another button and laser
> beams will cut and prepare the clothing.

He went on to say,

> In many ways, prosumers should be looked at as another
> market segment. We would want to identify those who have
> a strong need to produce their own goods and figure out
> ways in which marketers can help them meet this need. The
> aim of marketers should not be to protect the exchange
> system. The purpose of exchange networks is to facilitate
> the pursuit of human satisfaction. If the market system is
> overextended, and if people want to meet more of their
> own needs, on what grounds should marketers object? The
> market, after all, is a human invention and it will last as long
> as it serves human needs.
>
> Before markets, there were other ways for goods and
> services to be created and distributed, including reci-
> procity and redistribution arrangements. Societies that
> move in new directions to meet human needs should not
> surprise us. Whether Toffler's saying that prosumerism
> spells the end of marketing or only a contraction in its

scope, he has raised some worthwhile issues for market-
ers to consider.[15]

The big key is when Kotler says, "prosumers should be looked at as another market segment." This is the *Eureka!* moment. And this has been the missed opportunity in countless for-profit organizations. Of course, it's not too late. The Prosumer Age has really just begun. True prosumers can only be created when they are integrated across a company's product, process, environment and business model. This means there is a lot of work to do for most companies. True brand power is then about enabling customers to *share the journey* and have *their own unique prosumer voice.*

The Uber Model

In looking at Uber as a company, it's pretty clear what we see: they own some pretty cool software that does something very popular and adds value (providing people with easy, affordable transportation), but they do it without one key ingredient: they operate without any employees. Or, rather, the people that do the actual work—the drivers—aren't salaried employees, they are contractors. This is pretty  revolutionary. These drivers, who are essentially freelancers, would also be known as prosumers (although they are getting paid). We'll see many more companies appear on the scene in coming years using the same prosumer operator dynamic—yet another key pillar in the Prosumer Age.

The other future marketing lesson from Uber is the *zero marginal cost* dynamic. Businesses like Uber are able to set up a website with low fixed costs, connecting thousands of potential drivers to their service at very little cost. Uber trumps traditional taxi services by utilizing GPS guidance on a Logistics Internet to connect riders with drivers, at near-zero marginal cost to the company. How can we, as marketers, enable zero marginal cost to new campaigns and prosumer experiences in the future? This is something to seriously think about.

Impact of the Collaborative Commons

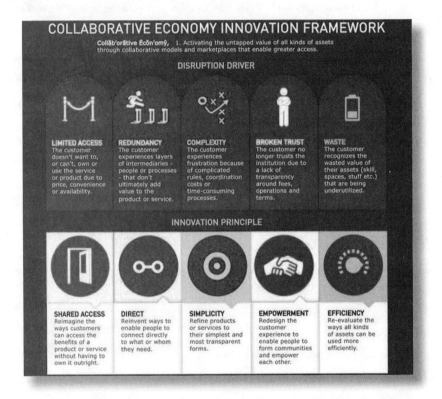

The collaborative commons is a digitalized space where providers and users share goods and services. It's prosumers working together. As a new economic system, it's flourishing alongside the conventional capitalist market, causing turmoil in traditional industries.

Over the last ten years, millions of consumers turned prosumers have produced and shared their own music, videos, news, and knowledge for free in a *collaborative commons* called Creative Commons (CC) on the Internet, disrupting copyright practices of the recording industry, film and television, newspapers and magazines, and book publishing.

Capitalism's logic dictates that the entrepreneurial spirit of a competitive market will continually drive productivity increases and marginal cost decreases. *Marginal cost*, the cost of producing additional units of product, is the focus, as this is where entrepreneurs and businesses make their profits in a market-exchange economy—at the margin; and when marginal cost approaches zero, so too does profit.

Education is becoming freely accessible through open online learning environments, such as "massive open online courses" (MOOCs). Digital cryptocurrencies, such as Bitcoin, are enabling peer-to-peer finance options for a decentralized age, where instant transactions of any denomination to anywhere on the planet can be made with next to no transaction fee and without the involvement of a third-party such as a bank.[16]

While the market is based on self interest and driven by material gain, the collaborative commons is motivated by *collaborative interests* and driven by a *deep desire to connect* with others and *share*. If the former promotes property rights and the search for autonomy, the latter advances open-source innovation, transparency, and the search for community, which, of course, are hallmarks of the younger generations.

As marketers, are we competing with the collaborative commons? We sure are. And that will only increase over time. The real opportunity here, however, is the potential of forming a partnership with those who participate in these communities in order to further build the platforms our companies manage and operate. Or you could create your own version of the CC for your organization. And of course, if you can show value and passion and authenticity, then collaborative commons prosumers may actually buy something from you.

The Prosumer and the Experience Economy

Another great book I recommend to everyone is *The Experience Economy* by Joseph Pine II and James Gilmore. It was published in 2011, and it was ahead of its time. I've touched on the growing importance of creating experiences for your customers in the future, but let's take a deeper look into how they suggest prosumers will play a role and why the push to experiences is happening now (and will escalate).

Tech makes much of this possible, as does creative competition, but Pine and Gilmore say that the biggest thing behind this development is

economic—the progression in value like "that of the coffee bean—from commodity to good to service and then to experience."

As people become more affluent, things like fancy dinners become commonplace, the authors write: "Economist Tibor Scitovsky notes that 'man's main response to increasing affluence seems to be an increase in the frequency of festive meals; he adds to the number of special occasions and holidays considered worthy of them and, ultimately, he makes them routine.'" And economic value increases.[17]

The prosumer, of course, will be the one enjoying the experience. And ironically, this is the one activity where many customers will want you, the company or the marketing department, to actually do all the work. They would only retain the title "prosumer" if they are actively a part of staging the experience—which is entirely possible, of course. For the most part, I think this is one area where your customers will truly stay in the customer "column." However, we do see a huge increase in customer or user "summits" over the past several years by many large companies in the marketing space, including DreamForce (SalesForce), Inbound (Hubspot), and dozens of others. And some of these customers participate as producers at these events. But most simply attend.

The Value of the Experience Lasts—When it comes to producing experiences, the work of the experience stager perishes with its performance, but the *value* of the experience lingers in the memory for those engaged by the event. Much as prosumers get added personal value by being a part of the operation, so to do attendees of experiences. Sometimes, the impact of an experience can last many years or even a lifetime. If you can do that, you can bet your customers will keep coming back for more. In the future, they absolutely will.

When we look at retailers like Bass Pro Shops Outdoor World, Recreational Equipment, Inc. (REI), and Cabela's, they sell goods as equipment for use in all types of outdoor experiences. But what's so cool is that their retail space *is an experience itself.* At REI, you can climb a rock, pedal a bike, or get a running analysis right there at the store—for free. How can you "REI" your company?

What Motivates People to Become Prosumers?

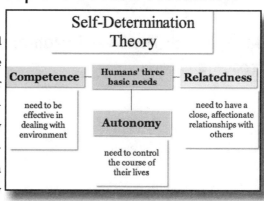

Edward Deci and Richard Ryan from the University of Rochester think they know what motivates prosumers. They developed the self-determination theory in an effort to explain why humans are motivated to become involved in activities in a manner that results in enhanced performance, persistence, and creativity (i.e., to become prosumers). The idea behind this theory is that individuals are intrinsically motivated to seek challenges and discover new perspectives—and in doing so, the activity itself stimulates their desire to actualize their individual human potential. If someone is intrinsically motivated, they will choose to actively engage and participate, and the experience will feel rewarding. Daina Middleton writes that the studies looked at what made people want to take part—basic psychological needs to feel competent, independent, and related to others.[18]

Self-determination theory hasn't been applied to the marketing practice in the past because it wasn't relevant to do so, since marketing as a discipline has traditionally been considered a *passive activity*. As we all know, up until just a few years ago, the marketing practice consisted of a one-way persuasive message broadcast to an audience with the intent of changing perception and ultimately causing a behavior change that resulted in product demand.

But now, and in the future, every part of the product or service decision-making process involves individuals taking some form of action. If we want to find out more information about a product or service, we simply go to the Web on our laptop, tablet, or phone or crowd source an opinion from a social network of choice. Technology has enabled participation. And self-determination theory helps explains the rise of the Prosumer Age.

3-D Printing: The Manifestation of Alvin Toffler's Prosumer Ideas

The arrival of 3-D printing really is the ultimate manifestation of Alvin Toffler's prosumer ideas in *The Third Wave*. In the book, he discussed a concept known as "the electronic cottage," where we produce all types of products at home in the future. Well, thirty-six years later, that future has arrived. 3-D printing is the technology behind the manufacturing model that will accompany an IoT infrastructure.

Already, 3-D printers are producing a wide range of products, from jewelry and artwork, to car and airplane parts, human prostheses and bionic implants, bioprinted cells and tissue, furniture, to full-scale buildings and parts of infrastructure; even food is now being 3-D printed. If people are "printing" products at home, then they won't be buying as much from traditional companies perhaps. But that's not the important message.

The good news for marketers is that 3-D printing provides many opportunities to deliver unique marketing campaigns and connections. 3-D printing also allows innovative ways to develop and strengthen relation-

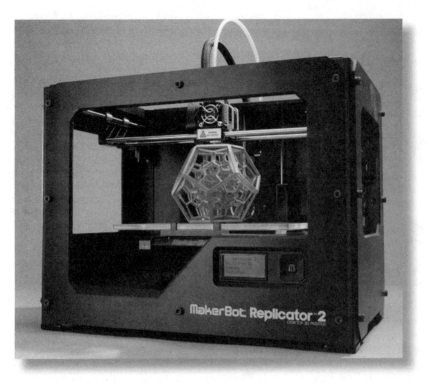

ships with existing and potential customers. Some well known companies are already expanding marketing possibilities by using 3-D printers.

Coca-Cola created miniature statues of consumers to promote smaller Coke bottles. Some of the other companies experimenting with the technology are Nokia, Volkswagen, and eBay.[19] Marketing is a competitive business where individuality becomes the secret to success. A major factor in a successful marketing campaign is in its distinctiveness. Originality by utilizing 3-D printing could be the secret ingredient in the recipe for success of tomorrow's marketing campaign. When considering what use 3-D printing can be for marketing, it is important to see the technology as *part of a mix* rather than as a solution in its own right. By 2030, 3-D Printing will be a part of almost every marketing experience.

Prosumers and Future Control of the Internet

Although none of us really think about it much, today's Internet, though "free," is still effectively controlled by the companies who control the data. But a backlash against the controlling power of the Internet elite is taking shape, and prosumers will take a very active role. Several of the most exciting emerging and anticipated technology breakthroughs will challenge the currently centralized nature of the Internet.

A venture called Ethereum builds upon the blockchain concept with

a goal of decentralizing the communications, contracts, and transactions that occur in both the physical world and cyberspace. It provides tools that enable users to program self-activating, self-managing smart contracts. In the future, this could lead to a more secure, transparent, and democratic Internet that could replace the current one in scale and usage. So, just as we've seen with corporations needing to give up some control of their brands and communications to customers, some of whom become prosumers, we'll also see this with the Internet itself in the near future. And we'll all benefit from that. Centralized control of anything in the future will be seen as archaic or a construct of the twentieth century. High-profile prosumers, prosumer groups, and innovative organizations like Ethereum will lead the way to our future decentralized Internet.

An Abundant Future and the Pursuit of Happiness

The Prosumer Age and the marketing work prosumers will contribute will help enable an *abundant* future, where our incomes go much further than they do today. Not only will prosumers impact this new abundance but the sharing economy, the mass efficiencies we'll gain and more will help to usher it in as well. And this future abundance will make our marketing work easier.

How far will our money go? Peter H. Diamandis and Steven Kotler note that one writer has estimated that worldwide, by 2030 or 2040, the average person will need about $10,000 annually for basic well being and a chance at doing better in the future.[20] Wow. Of all the research I reviewed for *Future Marketing*, this is one piece of data that blew my mind.

So why else will we have an abundant future? Here are a few other reasons:

- Dematerialization and demonetization
- Exponential price-performance curves
- Bootstrapping potential
- The domino effect

In addition, each step up prosperity's ladder saves time; because those extra hours add up to additional gains.

So now that we understand the power of prosumers and the key elements of the Prosumer Age and how this will lead to easier, more effective marketing as well as abundancy in all its forms, let's explore prosumer and peer-to-peer groups.

CHAPTER SEVEN

Prosumer and Peer-to-Peer Groups

Throughout *Future Marketing*, I discuss the rise of the prosumer, how these former "customers" now take on new meaning when they help you, the company, produce some of the work.

But what about when prosumers help other prosumers in a peer-to-peer construct? How does that impact your marketing and your connection to customers? Where do you fit in? How could this dynamic be rolled into your marketing efforts in the future? Perhaps you'd have ten prosumer customers working on a collaborative video for a new product your company is launching. Maybe you'd have five prosumer customers writing code for a community portal for your company, at no cost to you. Well, these types of things are happening now for sure, but the point I want to make is that by 2021 and certainly by 2030, these types of arrangements will be very commonplace. The other thing you need to be concerned with on the "challenging" side of the equation is what happens when these peer-to-peer groups decide they no longer need you, the company, anymore. What happens then? You need to be aware of this possibility and how to prevent it from happening.

> *Never doubt that a small group of thoughtful, committed*
> *citizens can change the world. Indeed, it is the only thing*
> *that ever has.*
> —Margaret Mead, American Anthropologist

As most of us know, large groups of people like those in big corporations aren't inherently nimble, and they don't like taking large risks. Their mission is to make steady progress. They stand to lose a lot if they place the big bets that certain breakthroughs require. Fortunately, this is not the case with small groups. With no bureaucracy, little to lose, and a passion to prove themselves, small teams like prosumer or peer-to-peer groups consistently outperform larger organizations when it comes to innovation.

Oracle, PeopleSoft and JD Edwards Peer-to-Peer Super Group

James Whalen, a member of the Board of Directors for Quest International Users Group, a community for Oracle, People-Soft and JD Edwards applica-tion customers, shared some very interesting insights into  how their peer-to-peer group works.[1] One of the key lessons here is the idea that in the marketing practice, these types of user or peer-to-peer groups rarely happen. Whalen's group is an *IT* user group. In this category, we've seen dozens of user groups at the corporate level. He says,

> I've relied on the opportunities—both virtual and in-
> person—that our user group provides for benchmarking,
> discovering solutions to problems, finding out about new
> tools, collaborating with vendors, sharing ideas with col-
> leagues, and cultivating new, and sometimes life-long,
> friendships. There are countless reasons to get involved with
> peer networks, regardless of your industry—including user
> groups for those of us in the IT sector.

Whalen shared four applicable ways his company benefits from its peer-to-peer group:

1. Reinvent the Wheel? No Time, No Need, No Way! The pace of business today, demands unprecedented speed and agility. Peer networks present a ready-made community for absorbing best practices and learning from the collective experience of members. In addition, peer networks can help reduce the risk of new initiatives.

2. Many Minds are Better than One. Tapping into the collective knowledge and enthusiasm of a peer group can be extremely powerful, especially when the forum offers a safe place to float new ideas and collaborate with colleagues who have similar goals.

3. There's Power in Numbers. User groups provide mutual benefits to customers and their vendor partners. Recommendations from and concerns voiced by user groups command attention as they represent the collective voice of a vendor's most knowledgeable and engaged customers. Progressive vendors understand the importance of engaging with peer networking groups in their industry.

4. Gain a Fresh Perspective and Greater Awareness. Professionals who work in isolation are at higher risk for burnout and professional stagnation. User groups are a vital conduit to new ideas and fresh perspectives, offering numerous opportunities for in-person and virtual interaction.

The Power of Decentralized Systems

There are very good reasons to have a decentralized communication (or marketing) group in place. In a large-scale emergency, for example, when electrical power is out, a peer-to-peer phone mesh might be the only system working. A network of rooftop repeaters and millions of phones would create an ownerless network. More than one startup has been founded to offer this type of mesh service. However, an ownerless network upsets many of the regulatory and legal frameworks now in place for our communication infrastructure. But will there be ownerless organizations in the future? There are now! That's what Linux and Wikipedia are.

Can Peer-to-Peer Groups Replace Your Digital Marketing Agency?

So, what if advertising follows the same trend of decentralization that other commercial sectors have? What if your prosumer customers created, placed, and paid for ads and content?[2]

Here is one way to think of this novel arrangement. Each enterprise that is supported by advertising—which is currently the majority of Internet companies—would need to convince advertisers to place their ads with them in particular. The argument a publisher, conference, blog, or platform would make to companies is that no one

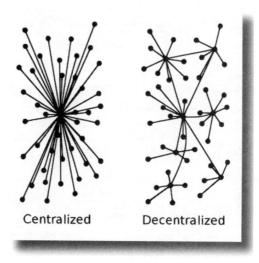

Centralized   Decentralized

else can reach the particular audience they reach, or reach them with as effective a relationship. The advertisers have the money, so they would be picky about who gets to run their ads. While a publication would try to persuade the most desirable advertisers, the publications wouldn't get to select which ads ran. The advertisers, or their agents would. A magazine or TV show with lots of ads or commercials would consider itself lucky to have been picked as the vehicle for the ads.

But what if anyone with an audience could choose the particular ads they wanted to display, without having to ask permission? The result would create a platform that curated ads as well as content.

This arrangement completely reverses the power of the established ad industry. Like Uber and other decentralized systems, it takes what was once a highly refined job performed by a few professionals and spreads it across a peer-to-peer network of amateurs. No advertising professional in 2016 believes it could work, and even reasonable people think it sounds crazy, but one thing we know about the last thirty years is that seemingly impossible things can be accomplished by amateurs when connected smartly.

The missing piece between this idea and reality is the *technology* to track the visits, to weed out fraud, to quantify the attention that a replicating ad gets, and then to exchange this data securely in order to make a correct payment. This is a computational job for a large multisided platform such as Google or Facebook. The success of this system would only prosper in addition to, and layered on top of, the traditional advertising modes. The tide of decentralization floods every corner. If amateurs can place ads, why can't the customers and fans create the ads themselves? Technology may be able to support a peer-to-peer ad creation network.

No Longer Zero Sum with the Peer-to-Peer Dynamic

Big corporations are no longer the only ones getting big things done. Again, look at Linux. Look at Wikipedia. In the future, we'll have five hundred examples we can point to. If there is a societal problem or a marketing problem, we don't have to wait for corporations or governments or non-profits to solve it. We can take matters into our own hands. From

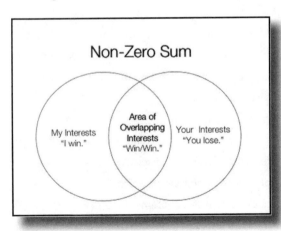

the social media influencer to the DIY innovator to the classic prosumer, we can and will get the job done. And as with Linux, sometimes the big corporations have to cede the win to the peer-to-peer group. Linux became the standard and IBM had to capitulate.

As Peter Diamandis describes in *Abundance*,

> most importantly, the game itself is no longer zero-sum. For the first time in human history, we don't need to figure out how to divide our pie into more slices, because we now know how to bake more pies. Everyone can win. Perspective shapes our reality. The best way to predict the future is to create it yourself. Where there is vision, the people flourish. The impossible becomes the possible. And abundance for all becomes imagine what's next.[3]

Swarm Intelligence for Social Insects

There is real power in decentralized self-organized groups of people. In the context of *Future Marketing*, we're calling them prosumers. I mean think about it: an efficient, productive organization without bosses!

Entrepreneurs like me dreamt of that scenario in our twenties when we were faced with the prospect that we may have had to work for "the man." No one is in charge because everyone is in charge. It's revolutionary in today's multi-national, global corporate-plex.

As Peter Gloor, author of Swarm Creativity said, "Flash mobs are striking examples of how the Internet can be tapped to coordinate "swarming" behavior, a concept popularized by computer scientist Eric Bonabeau.[4] Having studied the amazing world of swarm intelligence, the collective intelligence of social insect colonies, Bonabeau is now applying his insights to human interactions and computer technology.

He says, "Individually, one insect may not be capable of much; but collectively, social insects are capable of achieving great things. They build and defend nests, forage for food, take care of the brood, divide labor, form bridges, and much more. Look at a single ant, and you might not think it is behaving in synchrony with the rest of the colony. But we sometimes observe "ant highways"—impressive columns of ants that can run from tens to hundreds of feet. They are highly coordinated forms of collective behavior. Swarm intelligence in social insects is based on self-organization; no one is in charge, but social insects successfully solve complex tasks."

According to Bonabeau, self-organization has four properties:

1. Positive feedback reinforces desired behavior, such as when a bee recruits other bees to help exploit a food source.

2. Negative feedback counterbalances positive feedback, such as when bees overcrowd a food source, which stops them from exploring it.

3. Amplification of randomness leads to positive reinforcement, such as when bees that get lost trying to locate a known food source discover new food sources.

4. Amplification of interactivity has a positive outcome, that is, when insects make positive use of the results of their own activities as well as those from the activities of other insects

Social insects combine these four properties into predefined patterns, which have evolved over time, to efficiently accomplish a given task. Bonabeau reasons that our world is becoming so complex that it cannot be comprehended by any single human being. Swarm intelligence offers an alternative way of designing "intelligent" systems in which autonomy, emergence, and the ability to distribute tasks to replace control, preprogramming, and centralization. During most of our history, we human beings have suffered from a "centralized mindset": we like to assign the coordination of activities to a central command.

The self-organization of social insects, through direct and indirect interactions, is a very different way of performing complex tasks—and it closely resembles the behavior of open source developers, for instance,

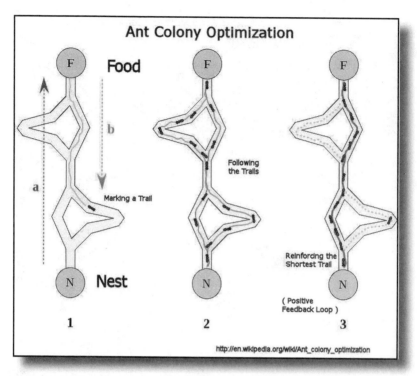

Ant Colony Optimization

http://en.wikipedia.org/wiki/Ant_colony_optimization

who exhibit behavioral patterns similar to those in an ant colony. While the behavior of the individual programmer might appear random, open source developers are, like ants, self-organized to build impressive software systems, directed by lead developers such as Linus Torvalds (the open source "ant queen"), who impress their distinctive brand and flavor on their "colony" of software developers. Wikipedia, the online encyclopedia, thrives on swarm creativity.

The lesson of bees and their swarm intelligence has massively positive implications for the marketing practice over the next fifteen years. Imagine if you had such a group as a part of your marketing efforts. In this book, I have explained how large group of your customers can serve in this role, if only you will see the benefit of it and let it happen. Many of them are already influencing your brand in big ways, but what's stopping them from doing more is *us*, the company, the CMO, the VP of Marketing. In the future, we can no longer allow ego and control and greed and pride to influence our marketing decisions. Many of your customers *desperately* want to be a part of the marketing work you are leading. Let them. The decentralization train is leaving the station and you need to get on board! Your competitors may beat you to the destination if you don't look out.

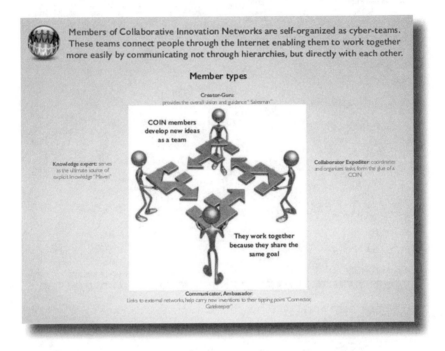

COINs—Collaborative Innovation Networks

Peter Gloor, also in his book, Swarm Creativity, discussed the idea of COINs—collaborative innovation networks.[5] Most of us have probably never heard of them, even though COINs have been around for hundreds of years. Many of us have already collaborated in COINs without even knowing it. What makes them so relevant today is they have reached their tipping point.

What is it exactly? A COIN is a cyber team of self-motivated people with a collective vision, enabled by the Web to collaborate in achieving a common goal by sharing ideas, information, and work.

Famous COINs include the groups that created the Web and Linux, as I've discussed already in *Future Marketing*. And there are hundreds of others. So the question becomes, how can a marketing department in the future create or partner with a COIN? This will be an important endeavor. And as I've discussed many times, it's all about the prosumers out there leading us in new and exciting directions. The prosumers make up these COINs. The decentralization of society will bring these collaborative innovation networks to the forefront.

COIN Creation—As Peter Gloor describes, COIN creation[6] is a fluid process—a COIN cannot be mandated into action. The progression of COIN growth is similar to chemical crystallization, where a nurturing liquid and a crystallization germ are enough to start the process. Just as a crystal grows from the germ on its own by adding more molecules through chemical attraction forces, the trigger for COIN members to join the community stems from their own motivation. Growing the largest crystals with the most desirable properties requires a thorough understanding of the procedure and ingredients of the crystallization process. The same principle applies to the COIN growth process. Nine success factors are involved in bringing a COIN to fruition. It is not necessary to accomplish them in sequence, but each one is critical.

1. Establish swarm creativity and give up central control.
2. Nurture the critical roles of creator, communicator, and collaborator.
3. Establish distributed trust.
4. Establish a common code of ethics.
5. Establish a small-world structure of high connectivity, interactivity, and knowledge-sharing.
6. Set up a collaborative Web workplace.
7. Know when to change the organizational structure.

Gloor explains that senior executives in organizations that host COINs must create an environment in which their COINs have the opportunity to achieve all nine of these critical success factors, and in which all COIN members can become the best at playing whichever COIN role they fill. The potential benefit is huge. So how could you get a group of fired-up marketers to be fascinated with a particular problem and then come up with a shared vision for an innovative solution (and not for the money or glory)? Think about that one.

Yes, the peer-to-peer group is here and it's not going away. By 2021, these groups will be growing significantly. By 2030, it will be strange if your company doesn't work with one. So, the question now becomes, how do we engage them with our organizations, with our marketing work?

CHAPTER EIGHT

The New Way to Engage: Experiences

I f you think about the most memorable times you've had with something you've spent money on, they most likely had an experience attached to them. Whether it was the first time you went to Disneyland or Disneyworld as a kid, a corporate team trip to China to visit suppliers, a night out with the family to Dave & Busters for arcade games and pizza, the Cirque du Soleil Beatles *Love* show in Las Vegas, your honeymoon to the Bahamas or an industry conference you attended, experiences mean so much more than just buying something on Amazon. Experiences are also tightly wound to our loved ones and friends, as we are typically with these special people while we are enjoying the experience, which makes them even more significant.

But individual experiences can be just as impactful. Think about a professional massage you enjoyed, or the first time you spoke in front of a large group, or a half marathon you may have run by yourself (these are three from my own life). Speaking of individual experiences, probably one of the most meaningful in my life over the last couple years was when I visited the Deer Park Buddhist Monastery here in San Diego County near where I live. And that one didn't cost me a dime!

I discuss experiences in detail in Chapter 15, "The Future Marketing Mix Construct," but I wanted to discuss them here as well because experiences are a big part of the changing customer dynamic. We're expecting experiences now. And whatever we expect, we better receive, right? Or we'll go to the nearest competitor.

So the big idea is this: *in the future, products will turn into services which will turn into experiences.* By 2021, you'll need to be "experienciz-ing" everything your company sells. Creating an experience for your customers will be everything.

A Betterness Consumption Paradigm

In *The Future of Business,* Anne Lise Kjaer talked about the Better-ness Consumption Paradigm[1] in a section titled, "Understanding Tomor-row's Consumer Landscape." In the future, she said, "people will be asking, "How does this product make me feel," "How is it made," and "How will it impact the environment?" Business must start exploring the impact of the products and services they offer beyond face value, and this means more equal partnerships with your stakeholders to be a force for good. Aiming for betterness participation and experiences will be key in the future.

A recent study by psychologists Leaf Van Boven and Thomas Gilovich verifies this, indicating two key principles of consumption:

1. Doing things makes people happier than having things.
2. Anticipation of an experience is more exciting than anticipation of a material purchase—regardless of the price of the acquisition.

Making experiences a guiding principle in our customer engagement models fosters a brand loyalty that becomes critical in any future-proof strategy.

Exploring the Many Experiential Angles

In *The Experience Economy,* B. Joseph Pine II and James H. Gilmore argue that "-inging" experiences will result from manufacturers and retail-ers adding value to our goods by adding services to the things we buy: the *wearing* experience, the *cleaning* experience, the *hanging* or *drawering* experience, the *briefcasing* experience, the *wastebasketing* experience, the *computer screening* experience, and so on. Such experiences make using the products memorable for consumers, and make more money for the companies.

Key to this will be giving customers the kind of sensory interaction with the products that makes them memorable. Not only those goods that are inherently sensory—such as toys, treats, video and music, cigars, and wine—but also accentuating the memorable qualities of any good that can convey sensory experience to the person using it. Making products memorable this way will be part of the future.[2]

Creating Holographic Experiences

When we think of experiences in 2016, we consider trade shows, special customer events, perhaps a customer appreciation day, and things like that. But in the future, due to all the technological advances in AI, VR, AR and more, experiences will be so much more. So why not a holographic, augmented reality experience?

Consider this: Eric Schmidt suggests that soon we'll be able to create holographs from still or moving images. This will allow us to make a "memory room," where images, videos, and geographic information are combined through a single device that will bring them alive. He writes, "A couple will be able to re-create their wedding ceremony for grandparents who were too ill to attend."[3] Just think about the holographic experiences you could create! Creative directors at marketing agencies around the world could stay busy dreaming up amazing things for weeks and months with this one.

Experiences as Entertainment

Not only memories would be found in such a memory room. Schmidt envisions the device as a source of entertainment, too: "If you're feeling bored and want to take an hour-long holiday, why not turn on your 'holograph box' and visit Carnival in Rio?" Or maybe you would want to buy a "holographic pass" to the Olympics, and watch the women's gymnastic team's floor exercises in your own home, live.

Holographs could even make work more fun, he writes. Emails could be projected in front of you in three dimensions, you could get to know clients face-to-face without ever having met in person, and interact with 3-D avatars of contacts that move around as the client moves, and talk like he or she talks.[4] Maybe not all of us would agree, but personally, I would find that pretty entertaining. The big idea is there will be an experiential or entertaining edge to *everything* by 2030.

Consider what services like Spotify provide us right now: a large catalog of live, streaming music for free. This gives us a sense of what the future will be like: an endless amount of content, available anytime, on almost any device and at little or no cost to users, with copyrights and revenue streams preserved. The one thing that will be different in the future is that all of this great music and the accompanying video will be happening as a true experience; we'll be *in* the video for the song while it's playing!

Pike Place Fish Market Experience

Have you ever been to the Pike Place Fish Market[5] in Seattle? It's definitely a sight to see. There's nowhere in the world where more big fish are thrown and caught and where people are entertained by the spectacle of it all, than this place. Their entire operation is based on providing an experience—for everyone and anybody. You don't have to buy a fish, you can simply sit there and watch the show. But truth be told, the Pike Place Fish Market makes a ton of revenue from its little show. The cost to put the show on? Just about zero. Many years ago, ChartHouse Learning produced a video called *Fish!* which shared the magic of the Pike Place experience—including the legendary tossing of fish from worker to worker. In the video, they came up with four key principles to explain their success. And when you think about experience, the word "entertainment" comes up too, right? The reason this is important is because each of the four principles is really an *acting* technique:

Play: Although it's a serious business, it's also about having fun, with workers as well as customers put on stage for the enjoyment of everyone.

Make their day: The focus is on customers—the audience of the show—and doing everything possible to create wonderful memories within them.

Be there: A variation on famed director and acting teacher Konstantin Stanislavski's dictum to "be present," this means forgetting about everything else that is going on to be there in the moment.

Choose your attitude: As Aristotle first pointed out, acting is fundamentally about making choices. We all act differently in front of colleagues than with customers, when with our children than with our parents, before friends than with strangers. It is not that we are fake or phony in any of these circumstances; we are simply choosing that part of ourselves to reveal to those we are with.

In the future of marketing, creating customer experiences will be a very important endeavor. Think about it: A really great experience with your brand or platform is something that no cultural or technological change can ever diminish or impact in a negative way. There is no commoditization risk. You'll instantly differentiate your offering. You don't even need to be that concerned with cost or price; people will always pay for a great experience. Isn't that why Starbucks came out of nowhere in the early 1990s to become the largest coffee retailer the world had ever seen in ten short years? They carefully, consistently crafted a retail *experience* that could not be duplicated by everyone else. Think about this one example as you consider how you could turn your suite of products and services into a wide range of engaging customer experiences by 2021.

SECTION 3
THE CHANGING ECONOMIC SYSTEM

CHAPTER NINE

Post-Capitalism

Nothing is ever expected to last forever; no job, no relationship, no home, no life, and as we are seeing now, no economic system. Everything is always in a state of *becoming*. Like probably most of you out there, I have always thought that capitalism was the "last stop on the train"—the ultimate market construct, as perfect an economic system as human beings could ever devise. What we know now is that there is *a next phase*. Call it *post-capitalism*. In this system, economic welfare is measured less by the accumulation of market capital and more by the aggregation of social capital.

And it really has *nothing* to do with socialism, even though there are collective social elements to it. But I want to be perfectly clear about this: all of the tenets of socialism—like the welfare state, no ownership, and making sure we are all equal in every way—are notions simply not reflective of human nature and have been effectively dead on arrival ever since wacky Karl Marx gave the idea a voice. Human beings are competitive by nature and, as a result, there are winners and losers. It's not the job of the winners to support the losers. The winners may help teach others, so that others may be empowered, but as the saying goes, "there ain't no free lunch." In addition, *nothing* is changing about democracy in the context of post-capitalism. What it is really, is bringing greater efficiency and decentralization and democratization to capitalism, where instead of having thousands of owners (of businesses, organizations, etc.), we are *all* now owners.

Post-capitalism still retains the profit motive and private ownership, but introduces a new idea: in some cases, the financial means of production is not privately owned, it has been *socialized*. The socialization of the supply of productive wealth is one of the prominent features of the post-capitalist economy.

In the coming era, both capitalism *and* socialism will lose significance, as participants in the Prosumer Age increasingly identify with a type of "collaboratism." Jeremy Rifkin envisions collaboratists who take something from both capitalism and socialism, but without the centralization presently built into markets and bureaucracies. People using the Internet of Things could be entrepreneurs in a social economy, empowered through democratized communication, logistics, and energy to make the system more diverse and stronger. Rifkin writes, "the very notion that an economic system that is organized around scarcity and profit could lead to an economy of nearly free goods and services and abundance is so counterintuitive that it is difficult to accept." Hard to envision, perhaps, but already happening.[1]

In the context of post-capitalism, with all the change it will bring, determining the future of marketing takes on far greater importance than simply defining what new strategies and tactics will be in play. Fundamental questions need to be discussed about the purpose and nature of business, its relationship with society, and the meaning and importance (or not) of profit in tomorrow's world.

The Prosumer Age—Consciousness and Connection

David Houle proposes that unlike the Agricultural Age (defined by tools), the Industrial Age (defined by machines), the Information Age (defined by technology), the Prosumer Age will be defined by how we connect with one another and our shared consciousness.[2] Kevin Kelly likewise cites the theories of Yochai Benkler, author of *The Wealth of Networks*, who says, "I see the emergence of social production and peer production as an alternative to both state-based and market-based closed, proprietary systems." Benkler envisions this as producing a more creative, productive, and free society.[3]

Impact of the Crowd—As we've seen over the past several years, crowd-sourcing has had massive impact in business and society. Crowdfunding in particular has emerged as a practical, alternative financing method for companies and individuals to help finance a product or project. A reward or donation in exchange for a financial contribution is the standard way that deals get done on the crowdfunding platforms.

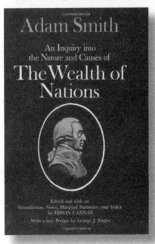

There is no offer of equity or financial return on contribution, so those who contribute are not capitalists. The productive wealth or contributed capital is not supplied by a capitalist elite but by the contributor. So, crowdfunding has created a micro-economy where prosumers contribute the productive wealth (vs. private investors or shareholders) that enables the company, product or project to be successful. This dynamic is one very obvious and popular way that the post-capitalistic era is being ushered in.

Paul Bailey, in his excellent dissertation, *Branding Post-Capitalism*, offered up this simple and brilliant comparison:[4]

> **Capitalism:** *where things happen to you (consumption)*
>
> **Post-capitalism:** *where you make things happen*
> *(contribution)*

Capitalism Has Evolved—The system that we call capitalism has been so successful that it's actually changing itself, says Jeremy Rifkin. "At the center of capitalism there lies a contradiction in the driving mechanism that has propelled it ever upward to the heavens, but now is making it morph into something new," he writes.[5] That "something new" transforms the old system's process of turning most aspects of our lives into commodities that can be exchanged into one in which the marginal costs of the transformation begin to disappear.

"Capitalism's operating logic is designed to fail by succeeding," Rifkin says. Supply and demand balance one another in classic capitalism, of the sort proposed by Adam Smith's *The Wealth of Nations*. Like Newton's law that for every action there is an equal and opposite reaction, the system self-regulates. But Rifkin imagines what would happen if capitalism's very competitiveness produces a sort of "extreme productivity" that produces more and more efficient technology until the marginal cost of that technology becomes negligible. "In other words, the cost of actually producing each additional unit—if fixed costs are not counted—becomes essentially zero, making the product nearly free," he writes. That could mean the end of profit. Not for everything, of course, but many things. And Rifkin sees us heading there.

E-books and Craigslist: FREE!—As we have seen, the marginal cost of producing and distributing some products is

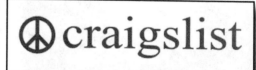

already plummeting to near zero. Look at books. The cost of marketing and distributing each copy of an e-book is nearly zero. The only cost is the amount of time consumed by creating the product and the cost of computing and connecting online. And this phenomenon has also impacted the communications and entertainment industries as well. So now the question is, what's next? What industries will be affected by 2021? By 2030? The answer is: just about all of them.

Craigslist has embodied this process. It is far more than just classified ads, Kevin Kelly tells us. It scaled up a "community swap board," pictures and all, presented it to a regional audience, and made the customers do the work. Craigslist's users type in the descriptions of the goods and services they're offering, update them in real time, and do all of this for a service that doesn't even charge for it. How could newspaper classified ads compete? It may have been bad news for newspapers, but Kelly sees it as "a viable alternative to both profit-seeking corporations and tax-supported civic institutions." If Craigslist isn't a forerunner of post-capitalism, what is it?[6]

John Maynard Keynes Saw the Coming Age in the 1930s—John Maynard Keynes, the legendary economist, saw all of this coming and he was optimistic about it, unlike many other economists. In 1930 he wrote a paper, "Economic Possibilities for Our Grandchildren." Keynes observed that new technologies

John Maynard Keynes

were advancing productivity and reducing the cost of goods and services at an impressive rate. Technology was also reducing the amount of human labor needed to produce things. Keynes talked of *technological unemployment*, which is unemployment due to our discovery of means of economizing the use of labor outrunning the pace at which we can find new uses for labor. Keynes said this means "that mankind is solving its economic problem."

Keynes believed that "a point may soon be reached, much sooner perhaps than we are all of us aware of, when these economic needs are satisfied in the sense that we prefer to devote our further energies to noneconomic purposes." When Keynes looked to the future, he envisioned an eightfold increase in standard of living in progressive countries by 2030. That world, he predicted, was one in which people could live the good life while working only fifteen hours a week.[7] And this is right in line with that $10,000 annual salary I discussed earlier. Remember, with mass efficiency and revolutionary technology, everything changes.

Keynes was optimistic about a future where machines (what we'd now call AI) would produce an abundance of nearly free goods and services, allowing human beings to do what they really wanted to do: enjoy their time, pursue hobbies that interested them, and transcend towards self-actualization.

Impact of The Internet of Things

As mentioned in Chapter 2, the Internet of Things (IoT) is also having a big impact on marketing. But did you consider its role in the changing economic system? As the coming together of the Communications Internet with the fledgling Energy Internet and Logistics Internet, it will truly be our new intelligent infrastructure. In fact, it's already boosting productivity to the point where the marginal cost of producing some goods and services is nearly zero, making them practically free.

Jeremy Rifkin envisions a world in which sensors from a vast Internet of Things tie us together with devices, the natural world, factories, networks of logistics, appetites and habits, the circular economy described in my Introduction, and all providing Big Data continually. It will flow "to every node—businesses, homes, vehicles—moment to moment, in real time," he writes.[8]

The Collaborative Commons—As you're well aware, the subtitle of *Future Marketing* is *Winning in the Prosumer Age*. And I discuss the prosumer throughout the book, especially in the preceding chapters. There are many names given for this dynamic; participants, contributors, influencers, and more. Another term that I came across last year was "Collaborative Commons" (mentioned on page 102), which Jeremy Rifkin described in great detail in his epic book, *The Zero Marginal Cost Society*. He said, "the rise of a Collaborative Commons will be the dominant model for organizing economic life." I think this term extends the "prosumer idea" a bit and is more descriptive.

Clearly, how Rifkin explained it really struck a chord with me. In fact, his book was one of my early inspirations for writing *Future Marketing*. When I read it, I started thinking, *now wait a second, this is something very different, something very significant that is coming our way*. I was right.

He went on to say that the capitalist market and government-based socialism are two means of organizing economic life, but they aren't *the only* ways—not any more. In fact, the

> Commons predates both the capitalist market and represen-
> tative government and is the oldest form of institutionalized,
> self-managed activity in the world. The contemporary Com-
> mons is where people engage in the deeply social aspects
> of life. It is made up of millions of self-managed, mostly
> democratically run organizations, including charities, reli-
> gious bodies, arts and cultural groups, educational founda-
> tions, producer and consumer cooperatives, credit unions,
> health-care organizations, advocacy groups that generate
> the social capital of society.[9]

QOL: Quality of Life

Capitalism is based on self-interest and driven by financial gain. It's all about property rights and the search for autonomy. The social commons is motivated by collaborative interests and driven by a deep desire to connect with others and share. It advances open-source innovation, transparency, and the search for community. The IoT is the technological side of an emerging collaborative commons.

GDP vs. Quality of Life Indicators—So, considering the whole idea of post-capitalism, how should we evaluate economic performance in the future? This is an important topic when we consider the marketing practice because it will help us plan programs and set success metrics accordingly. Interestingly enough, the European Union, the United Nations, the Organization for Economic Co-operation and Development, and a number of industrialized and developing countries have introduced new metrics for determining economic progress. The big idea is that emphasizing "quality of life" indicators rather than merely the quantity of economic output will be the new zeitgeist. Social priorities will be critical. Here are the important ones:

- Educational attainment of the population
- Availability of health-care services
- Infant mortality and life expectancy
- Extent of environmental stewardship/sustainable development
- Protection of human rights
- Degree of democratic participation in society
- Levels of volunteerism
- Amount of leisure time available
- Percentage of the population below the poverty level

The gross domestic product (GDP) metric will likely decline in importance as an indicator of economic performance in the next three decades. By 2040, all indicators point to quality of life indices being the de-facto test for measuring the economic well being of all countries of the world and the global family as a whole.

Any marketing activity that supports the items in the above list will go a long way to being a part of the solution. In my opinion, educational attainment of the population, protection of human rights and percentage of the population below the poverty level are the three most important ones. Amount of leisure time available is the most interesting. We all want more of that!

Is 2017 the Year of Takeoff?—Green technologies, information systems, and e-commerce, are among the technologies converging in the short-term future, and suggest that resurgent growth may be just around the corner. If so, Bill Halal in *The Future of Business* symposium thinks it will be in keeping with a pattern of thirty-five-year cycles that have marked U.S. stock markets. According to his calculations, one cycle of the Dow Jones Industrial Average peaked in the 1920s and crashed in 1929; a second cycle that began under Eisenhower was succeeded by one begun under Reagan. That thirty-five-year cycle ended with the crisis of 2008, and the author predicts that a new boom will start about 2017—one based on the technologies discussed in *Future Marketing*.[10]

Post-Capitalism and the "Awakening"—Daniel Pink's *A Whole New Mind* quotes the famous psychologist Viktor Frankl's observation that "people have enough to live, but nothing to live for; they have the means but no

meaning," and compares it to Nobel Prize-winning economist Robert William Fogel's discussion of a "Fourth Great Awakening" in which "spiritual (or immaterial) inequity is now as great a problem as material inequity, perhaps even greater."

Robert William Fogel

Other scholars and thinkers have diagnosed a similar problem, Pink writes. One survey of values found that people were more worried about "spiritual and immaterial matters." Another survey said that more than half of all Americans question life's purpose and meaning. This reflects, according to Ronald Inglehart, "a gradual shift from 'Materialist' values (emphasizing economic and physical security above all) toward 'Postmaterialist' priorities (emphasizing self-expression and the quality of life).''

Pink cites journalist Gregg Easterbrook's description of the problem as "a transition from *material want* to *meaning want* ... on an historically unprecedented scale—involving hundreds of millions of people—[that] may eventually be recognized as the principal cultural development of our age."[11]

The "Noosphere" and Unified Consciousness—Futurist David Houle looks back to the philosopher Pierre Teilhard de Chardin, who proposed the idea that our evolution is becoming more and more complex, and moving toward something like a single consciousness. "He used the word 'noosphere' to describe the ever-increasing accumulation and expansion of the knowledge and interactions of humans,"

Houle writes—"an ever-expanding sphere of human thought." Teilhard suggested that the culmination of this would be something he called the "Omega Point," where consciousness was unified.[12]

Capitalism Will Not Go Away Forever

Capitalism, as we know it now, will never totally go away. It won't be replaced by the post-capitalism construct, it simply will be supplemented by it. In essence, the capitalist market will no longer exclusively define the economic agenda. There will still be goods and services where marginal costs are high enough to warrant their exchange in markets where they will see a profit and ROI. But if so many products and services are nearly free, social capital will be a bigger player than financial capital, and economic life will be way more collaborative that we could ever dream today.

From Coordination to Cooperation to Collaboration to Collectivism—One media theorist, says Kevin Kelly, has ranked the coming era's social arrangements according to how well they coordinate with one another. These include both tools and attitudes "that promote collaboration, sharing, aggregation, coordination, ad hocracy, and a host of other newly enabled types of social cooperation." According to this theory, we start with simple sharing, then begin to cooperate, then collaborate, and finally form a collective. "At each step of this process, the amount of additional coordination required enlarges." Kelly sees much online evidence that this is already happening.[13]

The Measure of Brand Success—Paul Mason is the Author of *Postcapitalism: A Guide to Our Future*. In an interview from 2015 he said,

I think the realization that we are in this long transition to a world of sharing, collaborative production, and free stuff might prompt a brand to react like this: "Buy our stuff because, though the brand commands a higher selling price, there is a measurable social good." I am not talking here just about the usual CSR metrics: one of the key metrics might be "we automated our Asian production line and our workers enjoy dotcom-start-up-style conditions"; or "a third of our factories are co-ops."

Campaign magazine quotes Mason as further saying that

> organizations (and marketers) will measure their success in a
> post-capitalist world by the extent to which they are utilizing
> free stuff to create more useful free or cheap stuff. There'll
> be a market sector as long as there is scarcity; and reward
> for entrepreneurship will be short and sharp, but real.[14]

How Post-Capitalism Affects the Marketing Practice

So, why are we discussing this—our economic system—in the context
of the marketing practice? Well, let's look at it from the prosumer perspective. Let's says it's 2030. Let's assume you have a wide group of active
and loyal prosumer customers. They are engaged in what you are doing
and they have skin in the game. They are contributing *something* to your
brand, platform, product, or service. How and why are they contributing?
And what is their relationship with your company and brand?

Ownership by Contributor Prosumers—There is a perceived 'ownership'
by contributor prosumers created by the enabling quality of contributed labor or brainpower. Contributors are very aware that without their
contribution prior to production, the brand, platform, product, or service
would not be nearly as successful. The post-capitalist "value-chain" of
Market > Contribution > Production shows how the contributor prosumer
"adds value" to the company. They are aware of this and expect it to be valued by the company, because after all, they really are *a part* of the company.

Contributor Prosumers Share in Your Purpose—Contributor prosumers
see a value in developing an ongoing involvement with your company
through a shared purpose. The purpose of the project is what contributor prosumers align themselves with and then share their support for
with their personal network. It can also create the basis for a relationship,

encourage contribution, and help to create a community post-contribution. In the capitalist economy, people partly define themselves, or are defined, by *what they consume*. In the post-capitalist economy, people will define themselves by *what they contribute to*, and therefore what they enable to be produced. As Paul Bailey writes, "In the 20th century we were identified by what we owned; in the 21st century we will also be defined by how we share and what we give away."[15]

In conclusion, post-capitalism will impact the marketing practice in just about every way imaginable. By 2030, in many ways, marketing as an activity will be unrecognizable from what it looks like today in 2016. Even though it's just fourteen years away, the rate of change and new technologies, the rise of a large population of prosumers and, yes, a new type of economic system will re-make the marketing practice from the ground up. Will there still be products and services to market? Of course. Will the end goal only be market share and big revenue numbers? No. But in the end, we'll have more meaningful things to measure which will, in turn, positively impact our companies, ourselves and our worldwide global community like nothing we've ever seen in human history.

So now let's discuss what marketing could be like in 2021, shall we?

MARKETING IN THE YEAR 2021

CHAPTER TEN

Overview: Five Years from Now

As I've mentioned, in the 1960s, Philip Kotler, with his definitive *Principles of Marketing*, gathered insights from economics, social science, and analytics and applied them to the marketing practice. At the time, the ideas he espoused seemed really odd and new and not everyone agreed with his concepts. In time, every single one of his ideas became standard operating procedure for the marketing profession. And his concepts stood the test of time for forty or so years because life didn't change much when we were still using typewriters, personal assistants were called "secretaries," and the Internet was just pie in the sky.

In *Future Marketing*, I'm attempting to do the same thing as Kotler, but actually looking at it from far more many angles. As you read in the first section of the book, I discussed cultural and technological trends. I brought in ideas from world-renowned futurists. I looked at the history of "mega-trends" and what those massive trends are today. I took a deeper dive into cutting edge content marketing practices and how those practices will become *experiential and multi-sensory*, whether live, at in-person events and experiences, or through virtual/augmented reality, or through online events and experiences. I discussed marketing technology and its exponential growth in the coming years, which will be needed to support the new marketing function. Finally, I analyzed the changing customer, the evolving organization, and the changing economic system to show how these key pieces of the puzzle are factoring into the changes.

What are the symptoms and what are the causes? That's an open debate. But it doesn't matter, really. What is important is *embracing* the change and always being open to "the new." As I've mentioned through-out the book, we are always "becoming," never truly arriving at any spe-cific destination. The marketing practice will forever be a fluid dynamic from this point forward, much as the Web is becoming flowing streams of information.

Clearly, technology is at the root of this transformation. Over the last few years, with the entrance of Snapchat, WhatsApp, and more, we've seen how tactical the technology has been. By 2021, we'll see it as a strategic transformation. As marketers, we'll need to change what we do, how we think, the technologies we use, how we work, how we interact with custom-ers and much more.

The Future of Business addresses Microsoft's June 2014 report *Cy-berspace 2025: Today's Decisions, Tomorrow's Terrain*, which saw today's Internet technology possibly evolving into one of three scenarios—Pla-teau, Peak and Canyon.[1] I encourage you to read the report. But here is the spoiler: "Peak" is what we want and what I believe the future state will be. Essentially, the Peak state enables international cyber security coop-eration, innovation will thrive, and technology will peak, becoming more powerful as a force for societal well-being and economic growth.

Kevin Kelly argues that it is inevitable for *ownership* to decline as vir-tual reality, AI, and robots improve to make for new ways of working and doing business. We may resist this, but he argues that such technological "remixing" is something we should embrace. "Only by working with these technologies, rather than trying to thwart them, can we gain the best of what they have to offer," he writes. Just as Uber has begun to change the way we look at owning cars, many other services will tend to decentral-ize and do away with ownership. The technologies that make this possible can't be stopped.[2]

So, in the big picture, what will we see by 2021 in the marketing prac-tice? Here is the overall list. A discussion of each follows.

1. Brands Will Become Platforms
2. Focus on Mass Media Will Change to Memes & Movements
3. Brand Messages Will Become Multi-Sensory Experiences
4. Storytelling Will Connect to Audiences through Virtual Reality
5. Marketing's Focus Will Change from Pricing/Benefits Concern to "Show Me the Genuine Passion for What You're Pitching"
6. Strategic Planning Based Around Products/Services Will Be-come Adaptive Strategy Based around Customers
7. Uninformed Guessing Will Become Real World, Data-Driven Simulations
8. Web 2.0 Will Move to the Fully Realized Semantic Web
9. Human Thinking Will Gain Cognitive Enhancement
10. The Mass Market Will Be Eclipsed by a Niche Explosion

1. From Brands to Platforms

The scale economy will become the semantic economy, where value chains will be subsumed by value networks. Translation? *Competitive advantage will be conferred not on those who best reduce informational costs, but on those who create new informational value for the entire net-work.* Much like the interstate highway system, it's changing business for-ever. But let's break that down a bit.

In 1985, Harvard professor Michael Porter published *Competitive Ad-vantage*, which became the bible of business strategy.[3] The "value chain" was at the center of his ideas. To achieve competitive advantage, Porter said, you need to look at the entire value chain of a business, from raw materials to the point of sale. To be successful and grow the brand, Porter said companies must build competencies throughout the value chain, as Home Depot or McDonalds did so well for so many years with logistics and their supply chain.

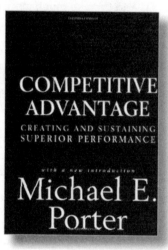

However, organizations today are centered around *the consumer* (prosumer). This is due, in large part, to the rise of the Internet and social networking. Because of this focus on the consumer, the advantage goes to the lean and nimble companies, like Facebook or Google (platforms), not General Motors (a big company with lots of brands). Even companies that were heavily product focused, like Apple, got the message and created platforms like iTunes and iCloud. Salesforce.com (a platform) became a billion-dollar company in record time.

And let's look at Facebook in a bit more detail. At the F8 developer conference in April, 2016, Mark Zuckerberg showed off the company's ten-year roadmap. Zuckerberg's intention was to show Facebook's three-stage game plan in action: First, you take a neat cutting-edge technology. Then

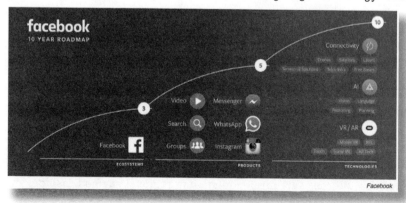

Facebook

you build a product based on it. Then you turn it into an ecosystem where developers and outside companies can use that technology to build their own businesses.[4] This is a great example of how to turn a brand into a platform. And then, so much more in the future.

One thing shared by today's giant, disruptive tech firms—Apple, Microsoft, Google, Facebook—is that they provide multisided platforms, Kevin Kelly observes. They also add value through third-party vendors and feature APIs that encourage creative experimentation by prosumers. Within this universe of apps, companies such as Uber, Alibaba, Airbnb, PayPal, Square, and WeChat contribute their own thriving multi-side markets. Such technical ecosystems derive from the basic platform, yet offer interdependent products and services independent of it.[5]

The ability and right to improve, personalize, or appropriate what is shared will be an important issue in the next iteration of platforms. Dematerialization and decentralization and massive communication all lead to more platforms. And what are platforms when it comes right down to it? Platforms are *factories* for services; and as we've seen, services favor access over ownership.

The bottom line: Digital technology is forcing marketers to change. By 2021, connectivity will drive total value and brands will increasingly become open platforms and ecosystems rather than assets to be closed off and protected. If you've connected to or created an API for your company, website, or app, then you know exactly what I'm referencing here. The fact is almost *all* companies fall into this category. We all need to connect with each other: internal departments, partners, users, customers, advertisers, freelancers... everyone. Connection in the semantic economy will be the standard.

2. A Move from Mass Media to Memes and Movements

Memes—Coined in 1976 by Richard Dawkins, a meme is a "package of culture." Pre-Internet, this meant things like regional sayings, fashion, and architecture. These are styles, concepts, and behaviors that are infinitely replicable and spread out to other cultures from the point where they started. Dawkins' complete definition of memes is:

An idea or element of social behavior passed on through generations in a culture, especially by imitation.

AND

A cultural item that is transmitted by repetition in a manner analogous to the biological transmission of genes.

So, what are some popular current memes?

1. Photo and video memes
2. Image (macro) memes
3. Word memes (like a Twitter hashtag)
4. Marketing-specific memes

Photo memes ask loyal fans and prospects to engage in an activity or take a picture of themselves doing something. The original behavior or posture is the same from person to person, but you add your own personal touch to it. Other marketing memes capitalize on existing memes and add their own caption.

Memes are shared on all social networks, with Tumblr and Reddit being most popular. Facebook and Pinterest are also meme-friendly platforms, but links to images and videos aren't quite as popular on text-based Twitter. Why are memes a big deal and why will they continue into 2021? They are easy to make, easy to consume, sharable, familiar, funny, and create a community where people understand a particular reference or identify with a message and can share it with the like-minded. They are also a great example of quality content marketing. Memejacking, where you take advantage of the momentum of existing memes, will also still be hot in 2021.

The meme dynamic will apply very strongly to the marketing of brands and platforms in 2021. A meme, once created and released, may not last long, but it can be very impactful in the short term. Sometimes, memes can permanently alter the image of a brand or platform. David Houle, author of the great book, *Entering the Shift Age*, said, "When the next evolutionary shift in human consciousness begins, memes will be what marketing becomes."

Movements—In terms of movements, we have seen these mobilizations of people behind a shared purpose many times over the past several years. Movements are all about people working together to generate ideas that create more involved, more meaningful cultural connections, which in turn drive business and societal decisions that create more involved and meaningful relationships. These then feed back into communities and companies as a virtual cycle of interactivity that can leverage a company's position to identify and effect relevant social, environmental, and world change. The Internet, smartphone, and social media have been the biggest technology drivers of the surge in movements. And members of the Millennial Generation have been the active doers behind it.

Scott Goodson wrote a very good book about movements called *Uprising*. He discussed the Arab Spring movement in Egypt, protests targeting government corruption in India, and the Occupy Wall Street (OWS) movement among many others. *Time* magazine named "The Protester" person of the year in 2011 because of OWS.

By 2021, we'll see even more movements around the globe, for a wide variety of causes. If you can spark one of these events by the marketing you do, that would be amazingly impressive. The more likely play will be to participate or help lead a movement, which your company and your prosumers can be a big part of.

3. A Move from Brand Messages to Multi-Sensory Experiences

This is where we see the diminishing power of ads, front and center. For decades, promotion and "push" dominated the field of marketing. It was all about TV, radio, and print advertising, and this is what drove marketing budgets and strategic thinking. And, of course, there were far fewer places to get your message out. Up until twenty years ago, there was no Internet, after all. The *message* was everything. Getting that message out to the right people at the right time was critical.

Of course, now we have the Web, and social media, and a whole new type of consumer known as the prosumer, and big data, and advances in digital technology. Consumers are less brand loyal, so we need to do everything we can to keep them engaged. We have more competition. Many of us compete globally, in fact. TV ads are way too expensive and 80 percent of them don't work. Plus, we have something really cool that we didn't have just a few years ago: the ability to "retarget" consumers when they respond to a message. And that is revolutionary in the field of marketing.

So what really happens when you create awareness for your products? If you're B2C, for example, do people go out and instantly rush to Target or Walmart and buy them? No. They start *searching online and researching you and your products* and weighing them against the competitive offerings. They see what their friends and family are saying about them. They go to Yelp and read reviews. And, of course, their online behavior will then be tracked by your competitors, who will then retarget those same prospects or customers with new offers. So, retargeting isn't always in your favor.

This move from messages to experiences is also why content and the practice of content marketing is so important. Brands have to learn to be more like publishers and develop content skills. By 2021, your customers will expect multi-sensory experiences or experiential marketing as it relates to your products and services.

If companies are doing ads, the ones that work are actually experiential campaigns on camera. Think of the Push For Drama video for TNT, or those Febreze commercials where people are blindfolded in the midst of garbage, or any one of those car spots where real people take real test drives. And then there are the experiential approaches that top agencies like Droga5 are taking—their work for Prudential, featuring giant dominos, was great and wholly experiential. These are all examples of experiential ideas becoming TV-centric work—more of this kind of hybridization is on the horizon.[6]

So the ads that will work are the ones that will use real people to tell brand stories for us. The ability to be authentic and credible through real-world experiences is critical for brand trust. Companies will need to create unfiltered engagements with their audiences, and experiential marketing approaches foot the bill. And this is at the heart of what's to come. We will increasingly rely on real-world campaigns that require authentic engagements and live experiences. In other words, experiential focus will make marketing more personal, more responsive, and more human. Once again, the influence and importance of your customers is absolutely central to success. Those who don't really care about the customer—and there are companies out there like that—will be gone, never to return.

When you think about trying to connect with your audience, we need fewer companies acting like the guy at the county fair trying to get people to gather around his booth to buy his magic mop. Instead, we need companies that serve as their customer's *personal concierge*, in their own version of the Four Seasons hotel lobby, and cater to their customers every wish and desire. If you have customers like this, they will reward you with a purchase and...their loyalty.

4. Storytelling and Audience Connection through Virtual Reality

In 2016, we now see that the era of consumer-ready virtual reality (VR) is here. By 2021, it will be the standard. Some augmented reality will arrive soon as well, but look for a full roll-out and mass use of this technology closer to 2030.

For the rookies out there, virtual reality uses computer-generated simulations to create 3-D environments that your target audience can interact with in seemingly real, physical ways.

What does the arrival of VR mean for consumers? It takes them completely out of their real-world context and puts them in another world entirely—which is exciting to consumers, with 70 percent indicating that they are "interested" or "very interested" in virtual reality.

The company Oculus VR was acquired by Facebook in 2014, and the first Oculus VR headsets started shipping in March, 2016. Companies will use VR technology to showcase products, simulate environments, or provide access to otherwise inaccessible perspectives (such as behind the scenes or far away). For example, outdoor gear company Merrell leveraged Oculus for its Trailscape campaign, in which consumers put on the VR headset along with a pair of newly-released Merrell boots, to hike in a simulated world full of rocky terrain. Nike recently leveraged VR to show fans what it's like to play on the field as the Brazilian soccer star Neymar Jr.[7]

The downside will be the cost of producing quality VR content. In addition, it will take some time before a critical mass of consumers (and businesses) owns a VR headset. It's not portable or affordable enough yet. Remember, this will be a B2C and B2B play. The B2B element seems to always be left out of the discussion. The other thing to remember, of course, is that there will be a marketing use case for VR; not all stories are meant to be told through enhanced reality.

Several other companies and industries are already starting to take advantage. These include the following:[8]

- The travel industry is using VR to sell the concept of "being there" to consumers. Marriott, for example, used Oculus to transport users from London to Maui in 90 seconds.
- The auto industry, with brands such as Audi and Volvo leading the charge, is using VR to allow customers to test drive cars or build their own auto.
- Zumba, the dance fitness craze, is using VR to show potential consumers what it's like to take a Zumba class.

● The North Face gave customers a chance to test out potential winter gear with Oculus Rift experiences in their stores.

So in 2021, when social engagements and commerce interactions come together, you can bet that VR will be the ticket.

According to Don Norman's *Things That Make Us Smart*, VR's ability to tell compelling stories in three immersive dimensions will be something new and exciting:

> *Stories have the felicitous capacity of capturing exactly those elements that formal decision methods leave out. Logic tries to generalize, to strip the decision making from the specific context, to remove it from subjective emotions. Stories capture the context and capture the emotions. Stories are important cognitive events, for they encapsulate, into one compact package, information, knowledge, context, and emotion.*

Daniel Pink cites this idea, and goes on to explain how recent technology has given us new and important ways to boil things down, add context, and bring in emotions into play. Good storytelling is something that even fast computers and affordable foreign freelancers have trouble producing effectively, and it becomes a more valuable commodity because of it. As our more abundant lives leave us more time to pursue deeper meaning and thought, the stories we use to define ourselves will be more valuable as ways to find such meaning.[9]

Virtual Reality & Hologram Technology—A big part of virtual reality will be the holograms we'll interact with in our physical space. In 2016, we're already seeing the early introduction of some cool technology. Microsoft has introduced its HoloLens, which is the first fully self-contained holographic computer. It is completely untethered—no wires, phones, or connection to a PC needed. Microsoft HoloLens allows you to place holograms in your physical environment and provides a new way to interact, learn, communicate and create. Very early holographic technology has also shown up in select concert performances with expensive reflection

devices, like Michael Jackson's posthumous "performance" of his song "Slave to the Rhythm" in 2014.

By 2021, even our handheld devices will come hologram-technology enabled. These holographic projection and communication devices will bring our interactions into 3D and into our physical space. Instead of video images on screens, there will be holographic interactions with team members, clients, partners, even holographic marketing industry events. There is a possibility that the *two-way communication capability* of holograms will be in place by 2021 as well. It will be expensive and limited, but most likely available. Holographic communication capability will be commonplace in the late 2020s. And it will change everything. Not just the marketing profession.

5. From a Pricing/Benefits Concern to "Show Me the Genuine Passion for What You're Pitching"

For decades in the business world it was all about communicating the "benefits story" to entice people to buy our stuff and support our brands. It was you against the competition. Whether you really genuinely cared about your products and services and whether or not they were produced or delivered in honest, ethical ways really didn't matter to your customers.

Then along came the Millennials and their igniting of what we call "the passion economy." With this new generation came new values. Career is a less important source of identity. Passion is the preferred currency. Millennials participate, trade, barter, create, and consume in a passion economy of products, services, ideas and memes. Kickstarter, Quirky, Lululemon, reddit, Twitter, and Etsy, are examples of brands, platforms, and channels that "get" the passion economy and are attracting Millennials.

Being "passionate" is another word for being a geek about something, and geeking out for fun and profit is one of Millennials' favorite sports.[10] And because it is theirs, it has become all of ours. Welcome to the new world order. The *psychology* of marketing has become as important as the technology of marketing. A sense of purpose will determine how people will act.

6. From Strategic Planning Based Around Products/Services to Adaptive Strategy Based around Customers

Marketing strategy has always been about your organization's products and services. The numbers were followed closely: We would survey a small selection of the population and then scale up those samples to make decisions, which could many times end up in being wrong, or worse, a total disaster. (Think "New Coke" in the 1980s or Kmart in the 1990s)

The evolution of big data, along with the increased influence of the customer, is now turning this whole idea on its head. With big data, we can collect massive amounts of data in real time, and over time we prove to be less wrong in our plans and estimates. To close this loop, we need a more Bayesian** approach to strategy that takes uncertainty into account, allows us to manage complex interactions that we have so far ignored but always knew existed and enable us to prepare multiple approaches rather than building a consensus around the lowest common denominator.

You'll also need to know your customers better than any competitor does. Understanding your customers is a continuous process and should be part of your organization's internal culture. Make use of the latest on-line tools to create an integral customer profile, which is continually updated. In addition, talk to and involve your customers in what you're doing. Get closer to them. Break down the wall that separates your company from them. You'll be able to anticipate your customers' needs and their emotional triggers.

The result? Marketing strategically rather than reactively. Plus, you'll get your customers help with some of the marketing! Which customer information metrics should you review?[11] Try these:

- Daily online and even offline habits
- Information about your buyers' professional, personal, and family lives
- Their interests, personal passions, hobbies, and assorted worries
- Their communications, social media, and online browsing preferences
- Awareness of advertising and different marketing platforms you might use or want to use
- The dynamics of your customers' buying, shopping, and desire-related habits.

**A method of statistical inference in which Thomas Bayes' theorem is used to update the probability for a hypothesis as more evidence or information becomes available.

7. From Uninformed Guessing to Real-World, Data-Driven Simulations

Wouldn't it be great if you really knew what was going to work in your marketing plan before you launched it? That is the goal. By 2021, you'll have a much better chance of getting there. So, big ideas have always been seen as the Holy Grail by marketers. But big ideas are risky. Many times, over the last few decades, marketers just threw stuff at the wall to see if it would stick, or based a new product launch or campaign on shaky data. If they were wrong, many times they would pay dearly by being shown the exit door.

Now machine-learning technology is enabling a new approach in the form of marketing simulations. Rather than argue the merits of a new approach, we can test them in simulated environments built from real-world data.[12] As the Internet of Things becomes more pervasive, this will allow us to truly co-create with our prosumers. In effect, by increasing our failures in the virtual world, we can improve our performance in the real one.

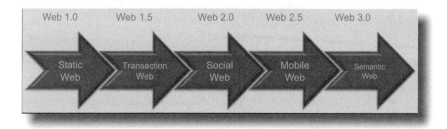

8. From Web 2.0 to the Fully Realized Semantic Web

Web 2.0 has taken us far over the past several years. On the horizon is the notion of the Semantic Web (some call it Web 3.0)—increasing the intelligence and intuition of the Web by annotating its content with self-descriptive information to enable more precise searching based on the context as well as the terms of the user inquiry.

According to the W3C, "The Semantic Web provides a common framework that allows data to be shared and reused across application, enterprise, and community boundaries." The term was coined by Tim Berners-Lee for a web of data that can be processed by machines. He foresees "a number of ways in which developers and authors, can use self-descriptions and other techniques so that context-understanding programs can selectively find what users want."

Most likely, the Semantic Web/Web 3.0 will not be random HTML pages called up by keyword searches on Google. It could be a simulated 3-D virtual reality filled with avatar replicas of our minds and bodies that greet our customers and friends when we are offline. These avatars will be automated and propagated with big data from our lives. Advanced AI algorithms will harvest information from our real world. Even without logging on to the digital simulation, it will gather big data from the real world.

Rohit Talwar in *The Future of Business* explained how a number of developments are underway in this domain and a range of platforms are beginning to incorporate basic semantic technologies. For example:

- **Google's Knowledge Graph**—It helps us see relationships between entities such as people and places.
- **Hummingbird**—It personalizes your search by considering where you are, what you've searched for before, who you know, and other data points.
- **Schema.org**—It describes, captures, and structures Internet data and provides useful cognitive schemas (ways of presenting and interpreting data) by way of a collaborative community.

The fully realized Semantic Web demands that participants form smart, emotion-aware, creative partnerships. Look for this to particularly affect areas such as travel and leisure with more immersive sensory applications that help virtually transport aspiring travelers. Artificial intelligence-based semantic search could be the standard within five years.[13]

9. From Human Thinking to Cognitive Enhancement

Cognition: the mental action or process of acquiring knowledge and understanding through thought, experience, and the senses.

Until just recently, we all needed to use our own minds to think and come up with ideas and solutions. By 2021, AI, powered through computers will provide cognitive enhancement to our own thinking, helping us get at the right answer quicker and more accurately.

IBM Watson has been the first major technology enabling this cognitive enhancement. Essentially, Watson is a question-answering (QA) computing system that IBM built to apply advanced natural-language processing, information retrieval, knowledge representation, automated reasoning, and machine learning technologies to the field of open-domain question answering. The key difference between QA technology and document search is that document search takes a keyword query and returns a list of documents, ranked in order of relevance to the query (often based on popularity and page ranking), while QA technology takes a question expressed in natural language, seeks to understand it in much greater detail, and returns a precise answer to the question.

According to IBM, "more than 100 different techniques are used to analyze natural language, identify sources, find and generate hypotheses, find and score evidence, and merge and rank hypotheses."[14] IBM has a whole host of services and solutions built for marketers that are powered by Watson. In researching *Future Marketing*, I was impressed with their website showcasing their ideas around how Watson can help marketers. Cognified content management is one of them. IBM can understand the content in your content library, can help you locate it, and even suggest gaps in your coverage. With cognitive content management, they can help deliver the right content at the right moment so you can create personalized experiences for your customers.

What will we see by 2021 in cognified marketing?

Take the amount of attention an individual reader or watcher spends on an advertisement. By 2021, we'll be able to use cognitive enhancement to easily multiply that attention by their social influence (how many people followed them and what their influence was) in order to optimize attention and influence per dollar. And there will be a hundred other use cases. This is just one.

According to an article by the advertising and PR firm Ogilvy & Mather, viewers respond involuntarily to effective marketing, whether by humans or machines. "AI/cognitive enhancement is already being used to edit videos which follow an emotional arc, encompassing a range of different feelings but always ending on a happy or satisfying note," they write. Such videos may even be more effective than work by real people at producing emotional responses. In one BBC test, measurement of involuntary facial muscle response suggested that people liked the AI-edited version of a David Attenborough video better than the traditionally edited version.[15]

AIs can also create. This year's Cannes Lions saw the screening of a music video which had been conceived by IBM Watson, based on a set of song lyrics. Google Magenta is exploring the possibilities of AI art and graphic design. VR landscapes offer up a whole new artistic canvas, and the potential for AIs to build entire worlds.

"So the next great visual artist, cinematic auteur or advertising genius might just be a robot," according to Ogilvy & Mather. But rather than worrying about it, they suggest brands and agencies incorporate the exciting new cognified platforms into their messaging strategies as ways of combining human originality with machine precision.[16]

We'll also see cognified music where it will be created in real time from algorithms and possibly employed as the soundtrack to a video game or a virtual world. Depending on your actions, the music would change. Hundreds of hours of new personal music could be written by the AI for every player.

By 2021, all of this will be very commonplace for the marketing practice.

10. From the Mass Market to the Niche Explosion

In a world of just TV, radio, and magazines, the mass market makes total sense. In the world of the Web and the world of the future, it makes no sense at all. If you market to the masses today, the masses won't respond the way you want them to. And it will be really expensive trying to reach them all. The fact is we have so many choices now; we don't all follow the same things. Whether it's music, movies, television programs, products we use, or services we enjoy, there is no one-size-fits-all. Even if you break it down to "women in their 30s in the state of California," you most likely still have a ways to go before you get to your target audience.

We've really seen the niche explosion in music. Pre-digital, music occupied a few niches: vinyl records and magnetic tapes, the radio, concerts, and in a couple hundred films made each year. Post-digital, music–all types, both signed by record labels and independent–can be found in the cloud, through our ear buds, on our smartphones, while playing video games; it's everywhere. The niches for music have simply exploded. Think about it: thousands of documentary movies require a soundtrack. Feature films need original scores. Even some YouTube creators need a soundtrack for their video work. Podcast creators need themes and jingles. Then there's the hundreds of hours of music required for each video game. Tens of thousands of commercials need memorable jingles. The music business is totally a niche-based industry now. By 2021, due to big-data growth and new marketing technology, we'll see this same dynamic happen to many other industries.

The Four Stages of Flowing

Kevin Kelly, author of *The Inevitable*, struck gold again when he discussed what he calls the "Four Stages of Flowing." I think it's very relevant to our discussion here on the niche explosion, because the idea of a technology flowing is what helps to enable the niche in the first place. You'll recall that I also touched on this concept in the introduction. I mentioned that "Flow" has become the basic organizing principle of the cybersphere and that the Web of the future will resemble an electric power network, with information coming through at volume and speed, based on what we want to see. Kevin Kelly added to the idea by saying this:

> What has happened to music, books, and movies is now happening to games, newspapers, and education. The pattern will spread to transportation, agriculture, health care. Fixities such as vehicles, land, and medicines will become "flows." Tractors will become fast computers outfitted with treads, land will become a substrate for a network of sensors, and medicines will become molecular information capsules flowing from patient to doctor and back.

These are the Four Stages of Flowing that Kelly describes:

1. Fixed. Rare. The starting norm is precious products that take much expertise to create. Each is an artisan work, complete and able to stand alone, sold in high-quality reproductions to compensate the creators.
2. Free. Ubiquitous. The first disruption is promiscuous copying of the product, duplicated so relentlessly that it becomes a commod-

ity. Cheap, perfect copies are spent freely, dispersed anywhere there is demand. This extravagant dissemination of copies shatters the established economics.

3. Flowing. Sharing. The second disruption is an unbundling of the product into parts, each element flowing to find its own new uses and to be remixed into new bundles. The product is now a stream of services issuing from the shared cloud. It becomes a platform for wealth and innovation.

4. Opening. Becoming. The third disruption is enabled by the previous two. Streams of powerful services and ready pieces, conveniently grabbed at little cost, enable amateurs with little expertise to create new products and brand-new categories of products. The status of creation is inverted, so that the audience is now the artist. Output, selection, and quality skyrocket.

These four stages of flowing apply to all media. All genres will exhibit some fluidity. Yet fixity is not over. Most of the good fixed things in our civilization (roads, skyscrapers) are not going anywhere. We will continue to manufacture analog objects (chairs, plates, shoes), but they will acquire a digital essence as well, with embedded chips.[17]

New Principles of Marketing Strategy by 2021

So now we know that identifying customer needs and communicating your benefits will just not be enough in 2021. You'll need to create immersive, multi-sensory, multi-modal experiences that engage people on an ongoing basis. That means having new skills and capabilities on your marketing team. Here are some guidelines to help you get there in the next four years:

1. Clarify Business Objectives & Simplify What You Evaluate—The proof of a solid marketing strategy is how effectively it achieves worthwhile goals. Therefore, how you define your intent will be a determining factor on whether you succeed or not. Instead of making it complicated, evaluate just three metrics: awareness, sales and advocacy (i.e. customer referral). While every business needs all three, it is important to focus on one primary objective or your strategy will devolve into a worthless pursuit.

2. Use Innovation Teams to Identify, Evaluate and Activate Emerging Opportunities—If you are a marketing professional, you are busy. It's difficult to keep up with the onslaught of emerging technology and tactics that seems to be arriving almost daily. Because of this and the overall importance of making innovation a key part of your company culture, it will be essential by 2021 to have a team dedicated to identifying emerging opportunities and running test-and-learn programs to evaluate their true potential.[18] Once an emerging opportunity has performed successfully in a pilot program, it can then be scaled up and become integrated into the normal strategic process as a viable tactic to achieve an awareness, sales or advocacy objective.

3. Separate Strategy and Innovation Practices and Re-define What "Failure" Means—Innovation is all about trying things out and seeing if they work. Strategy is not. With strategy, you need to stick to it to carry out the objectives. Sometimes it takes months or years. But in many organizations, it's seen as two sides of the same coin. The same people do both. That needs to change by 2021. Strategy is fundamentally different from innovation. A good strategy is one that achieves specific objectives. Innovation, however, focuses on creating something completely new and new things, unfortunately, tend to not work as well as standard solutions. Innovation is messy and unclear and needs to come from an open and optimistic mind. The innovation guy is the "creative, let's try anything, visionary" one. The strategy gal is the "conservative, good at implementation and measurement" one.

If we want an early lesson in taking risks and getting comfortable with failure, all we need to do is look at the Apollo Space Program under President Kennedy. Even though he made the promise in 1961 of "landing a man on the moon and returning him safely to the earth," you should know that very few of the necessary technologies existed at the time to actually deliver on that promise. *We had to invent almost everything*, in just a few years time.

And we did, but it was because the engineers involved didn't know they were trying to do the impossible, *because they were too young to know.* The engineers who got us to the moon were in their mid- to late-twenties. Many of the computer and Internet game changers over the past thirty-five years have also been young, whether it's Bill Gates, Steve Jobs, or Mark Zuckerberg. And this is clearly one of the great things about being young and confident. But we *all* need to be like this, it can't be a quality only possessed by younger folks. We're never going to get to where we need to go if that remains the case. As marketers, we all need to get way more comfortable with failure by 2021 and beyond. Personally, I believe this is one of the qualities/traits in human beings that will naturally evolve and change for the better over the next fifteen years.

Peter H. Diamandis and Steven Kotler cite an article for *Stanford Business School News* by Professor Baba Shiv who says "Failure is a dreaded concept for most business people. But failure can actually be a huge engine of innovation. The trick lies in approaching it with the right attitude and harnessing it as a blessing, not a curse."[19]

Companies That Are Getting Comfortable with Failure

Diamandis and Kotler praise failure further in their book, *Abundance: The Future is Better than You Think*. They say that some companies are focusing on how to make their working environment more tolerant of failure. At the financial software company Intuit, for example, the team responsible for a particularly disastrous marketing campaign received an award from Chairman Scott Cook, who said, "It's only a failure if we fail to get the learning." Similarly, Ratan Tata, CEO of the Indian conglomerate the Tata Group, told the Economist "failure is a goldmine" when explaining why his company instituted a prize for the best failed idea that taught the company an important lesson.

Another way that companies have begun strengthening their fearlessness muscles is rapid prototyping: the process of brainstorming wild new ideas, then quickly developing a physical model or mock-up of the solution. This process allows people to move quickly from the abstract to the concrete, and lets them visualize the outcome of their ideas. Because not all prototypes end up as the best or final solution, rapid prototyping also teaches that failure is actually a necessary part of the process.

Michael Schrage, a research fellow with MIT's Center for Digital Business and MIT's Entrepreneurship Center, has developed the 5x5x5 Rapid Innovation Method. "The idea is fairly simple and straightforward," he said.

A company looking to drive breakthroughs in a particular area sets up five teams of five people and gives each team five days to come up with a portfolio of five 'business experiments' that should take no longer than five weeks to run and cost no more than five thousand dollars each to conduct. These teams are fully aware that they are 'competing' with their colleagues to come up with the best possible portfolios to present to their bosses, perhaps winning the chance to implement the best performing concept.[20]

Innovation integrated with competition is a winning combination.

Open Apps/Assets that Create an Ecosystem/ Community

To get at the heart of this one, just look at what Salesforce.com or Google's Android apps community has done over the last ten years. They have built massive ecosystems around their brands and offerings with API's and huge partner networks. In fact, their brands *have become* platforms. And this has drawn millions of users and customers to their communities. People start using the apps in their ecosystem and they don't leave.

The primary focus of marketing promotion used to be to create cool ads that would drive awareness. Today, ads don't always lead to a sale and more likely result in an Internet search, where consumers' behavior can be tracked and then retargeted by competitors. It's not about getting a purchase anymore; it's about *getting them to participate*. And it's about having a purpose and passion that others can get behind and benefit from. That will be the new marketing superpower in 2021.

Attract, Assist, Affiliate Model

One of the best books I've read in the last year is *The Power of Pull* by John Hagel, John Seely Brown and Lang Davison. I really like a lot of what John Hagel says in the book. Much of what he espouses is in the same vein as the content marketing or inbound marketing crowd. He calls it "pull marketing," but it's all the same. I think his Attract, Assist, Affiliate model[21] is especially relevant to where we are going in marketing. By 2021, it will be commonplace.

How *Small* Moves, *Smartly* Made, Can Set *Big* Things in Motion

John Hagel III, John Seely Brown, and Lang Davison

"Attract" means motivating people to seek you out, to find you. "Assist" means finding ways to help people, both before and after a purchase, to get more value and use from the product or service. The third "A" is "affiliate." Instead of one-to-one marketing, the affiliate idea suggests bringing in any and all participants that could be helpful to the prospective buyer at relevant points in time. It's about creating a broader ecosystem of participants who can be more and more helpful to the customers you're trying to reach.

I love this idea, because it's in line with the social network construct that we've all created for ourselves on Facebook, Twitter, LinkedIn, Instagram, and all the rest. It's also customer focused. After all, these are companies and individuals that can help our customers, not the company selling to the customers. That's huge.

Hagel says that "Assistance" is not just waiting for the customer to ask you something; it's being proactive and becoming in effect a trusted advisor to the customer who says, "You know, I have some information about you and based on that information, I can give you some recommendations that are going to be really valuable to you and save you time and money." This is a really great way of seeing the customer relationship and it's clear that very few companies see it like this now, in 2016. Those companies that want to be successful and still around in 2021 need to adopt this type of approach in their marketing (and sales).

Along with that, Hagel talks about a new set of metrics: ROA and ROI. But instead of return on assets it's "return on attention." Instead of return on investment, it's "return on information." It's starting to track carefully how much it costs to accumulate information about a customer and divide that by what you can earn by using that information more effectively. This is a phenomenal example of evolving how we see the customer relationship in the future.

Return on Attention (ROA)—Return on Attention will be the new Return on Investment in 2021. It will be the metric to measure. With so many choices, our customers' attention is more important than ever before. People's time is valuable and we need to understand and appreciate that.

In fact, attention will be so important in the future, that we may want to pay people directly for their attention. Currently, we all spend our attention on content and ads for free. As consumers, why don't we charge companies to look at their content or watch their commercials? It may not be as authentic or meaningful, but with more competition than ever, it may be worth looking at. Plus, if we know who our prospects are, by using the power of big data, filtering and other new technologies coming online to laser-target them, it may be very well worth paying people for their attention, because the chances of getting the sale will increase significantly by 2021.

In 1995, the average hourly costs for various media platforms, including music, books, newspapers, and movies was calculated by Kevin Kelly. Twenty years ago, we spent $3.00 per hour on media. In 2010, and then again in 2015, he recalculated the values again. They stayed fairly stable: $3.08, $2.69, and $3.37 respectively. Kelly surmised that we have some intuitive sense of what a media experience "should" cost, and we don't stray much from it. The upshot is that an hour of our attention pays the companies seeking it an average of just $3 per hour— if the content is good enough. Can the filtering technologies return higher quality attention at scale in the coming decades?[22]

Those filtering technologies will be here by 2021. Look for it.

Power of Narrative vs. Story

The other key contribution to the future of marketing by John Hagel is his idea of the *power of narrative*, which I covered briefly in chapter two. To get true, authentic engagement from our customers, we need to move from stories to "narratives." Stories are a powerful way to attract attention and create emotional engagement, but "narratives" are even better. And here is the distinction: Hagel says stories are self-contained: they have a beginning, a middle, and some type of resolution. A story is about me, the storyteller, or some other people over there. It's not about you, the listener.

In contrast, a narrative is open-ended, about some opportunity, and whether the listener gets the benefit depends on the listener's choices. The resolution has not yet occurred. You're talking about some oppor-

tunity that hasn't yet materialized and the ability to embrace this opportunity hinges on the listener's actions. A narrative is a call to action. It says, "How it ends is up to you. What are you going to do?"

When you consider that millions of people have given their lives over the centuries for narratives—religious narratives, revolutionary narratives, social narratives of various types—you can see just how powerful they are. Very few companies have harnessed the power of narrative. Who has? Apple is one. The narrative of Apple's early days was captured in a tight slogan: "Think different." The narrative *wasn't about Apple.* It was about the people that Apple was trying to speak to. It was a call to action: "Think different."

One of the things that made "Think different" so powerful was the examples of Steve Wozniak and Steve Jobs. They were the perfect examples of people thinking differently and expressing their unique individuality. They *lived* the narrative. Companies in the future need to live a narrative that will engage and motivate the audience they're trying to reach. This is very similar to what I discussed earlier regarding the "passion economy" and the Millennial Generation.

Five Dimensions of Future Marketing Capability

Gavin Heaton is the founder of the Disruptor's Handbook—an un-Agency that brings startup culture to the challenge of digital transformation. In doing my research for *Future Marketing* I was intrigued by his 'Five Dimensions of Future Marketing Capability."[23]

Heaton says that when we look at the future of our marketing, we need to consider the challenges of our team's skill gaps, technology encroachment, and a shifting customer expectation. In short, we need to disrupt the way we do marketing and the teams that we create to deliver it. A skills audit is a great way to determine this. Your audit will classify low-, medium-, and high-level skills across five dimensions (rated according to your future needs):

1. Marketing foundations—You've got to have these. No matter whether you are a "seasoned professional" or a "digital native"—and no matter whether you have studied marketing or just picked it up—you need to know how to do everything from a SWOT analysis to copywriting, event planning, and management, to agency review and management.

2. Technology foundations—Didn't get the Slack announcement? Didn't read your own emails? Digital is now and it is the future, and that means getting a handle on technology. If you can't build a URL for tracking, tweak some HTML at a pinch, or create a landing page, then you've got some serious work to do.

3. Content production and publishing—Marketing has always had a close link to content and publishing. In a digital and mobile world, knowing how content works in different channels, and why is an essential skill.

4. Data analytics—You don't need to be a data scientist—but you need to be able to get your head around numbers. You need to be able to under-stand reports and reporting, the difference between metrics and mea-surement, and how to ask for the right kind of information to make your marketing better.

5. Social mindset—Have you ever done customer service? What about on-line community management? What used to be called "emotional intelli-gence" can be readily applied to the role of marketing. Do you understand your customer? Do you know your community? And, vitally, can you take that into a business context?

Personalized Pricing Options for Customers

Charging customers different prices for the same product isn't done much;[24] it's seen as unfair and discriminatory. We do see variable pricing when it reflects supply and demand (as in airline reservations and tickets to sporting events), but a company found engaging in this activity gener-ally incurs intense disapproval from consumers.

By 2021, however, we will reach a stage where individual consumer behavior is fully quantified and the incremental value of each transaction can be assessed in the context of that customer's total value to the busi-ness. Many customers will be enrolled in loyalty programs, have some kind of earned status based on their history, and collect tokens from various other forms of brand engagement (winning contests, participating in games, performing incentivized activities like social networking, or watching ads). When these are brought to bear in a purchase, along with any time/location-based contextual promotional offers, the result will almost always be a unique price for each customer, reflecting that customer's specific profile and level of engagement. Price is one of the original "4 P's" of marketing, so I wanted to be sure and mention this.

So now you know what to keep your eye on for 2021 as an organization/client side of the house. How about agencies? How should they prepare for 2021?

CHAPTER ELEVEN

The Future Digital Marketing Agency

As the importance of marketing continues to grow over the next several years, so too will the influence and growth of digital marketing agencies. All of the new tactics, technologies, channels, and prosumer activities will touch the agency in many new and exciting ways. The biggest change, however, will be the inclusion of actual customers/prosumers into the operations of the agency in a way that resembles the dynamic with some companies now. So, yes, there will be prosumers on the agency side of the house too.

What's interesting about this is there was absolutely no research available anywhere that spoke to this idea. To me, it seems like a no-brainer, a total given. Why wouldn't the customer be involved? In fact, some of the best future creative ideas as well as the future creative itself will come from the brand's customers, just as they do now.

By 2021, will agencies manage virtual reality content experiences? Yes. Will agencies manage augmented reality ads? Yes. Will they manage artificial intelligence-enabled customer data? Yes. They will do all of this and much more. Remember, if we are taking content and ads into 3D and including all-new customer experiences and platforms into the mix, someone has to create and manage all of this stuff! Big data will be pouring in. ROI will be much more efficient. Consumers, in general, will have more leisure time and be able to be entertained much more than they have the time to be now. Digital marketing agencies will go through a renaissance around 2030 and they will never look back.

Creative agencies, media agencies, brand agencies, SEO agencies, so-

cial media agencies—whatever type of agency you are today—could be called a "consumer (or prosumer) experience" agency in the future. These agencies will be led by content strategists who will architect the prosumer journey and serve as liaisons between their brand/platform clients and their prosumers. Agencies will employ specialists who will understand human behavior and how that relates to building relationships, product purchases and media consumption. You will target prosumer customers based on mood, mindset, receptivity and many other new attributes, due to big data and other technology advancements.

Trends that Will Shape the Future of Agencies

Change is with us forever now—and in the marketing agency world, there is no exception. Technology will continue to drive much of the changes in the marketing agency.[1] Agencies and their clients will need to stay well ahead of the curve in understanding the latest tools and platforms to be able to discern which of them have the maximum benefit and which ones are not worth the time. How agencies fare will be determined by how well they adapt and capitalize on the following six developments.

1. Technology Will Continue to Disintermediate—In every industry, technology continues to make processes more efficient and, in some cases, obsolete. Agencies aren't the only places for brand marketers to get creative campaigns. The agency business model of the future will be a hybrid, collaborative enterprise. It will be made up of a smaller group of senior staff across all major disciplines that will sit on top of a collection of relationships with startups, technology companies, and individuals that provide the agency and its clients with best-in-class brand thinking. Brands and agencies must not work in silos. There must be open systems for sharing.

2. More Competition from Media Companies—Many social, content and media companies are realizing that they can increase their revenues by building creative studios that allow them to give away creativity to brands so that they will spend more money on a media buy with them. The rise of

Facebook's Creative Shop, and Google's Creative Lab and YouTube Studio allows these players to create content as a way to win more media dollars on their platforms. Other companies that have hopped on the content-creation train include players like iHeartmedia, *The New York Times*, *The Wall Street Journal*, and *Buzzfeed*. With continued competition of this nature, the price of creative will become commoditized.

3. Companies (Brands) Will Do Some of the Work Agencies Do Now—As the cost of media drops, the relationship with prosumers will become a core competency of every brand. Brands will build their own media technology and produce their own content. Likewise, the rise of programmatic marketing (easing the access) and the rising importance of leveraging first-party

data (on premises) are both in favor of a new relationship with agencies.

Good examples of brands leading the charge are Red Bull, Patagonia and Go-Pro. Agencies will need to rethink what they are and become platforms of technology and services. However, this will take time as many large brands will continue to struggle with transforming themselves, and their own bureaucracies will slow the evolution. Likewise, with coming needs in the VR/AR area and the continued shift toward a multicultural marketplace in the U.S., this will make the advertising marketplace sufficiently complex to create opportunities for agencies.

4. Co-opetition—Talent is the key to success for agencies today. But there is no way for any one organization to hire the best. As Sun Microsystems co-founder Bill Joy once famously said, "No matter who you are, most of the smartest people work for someone else." To attract top talent, agencies will need to change from being closed systems selling solutions to open systems that help clients define the right marketing questions and find the best talent to answer them. The future will be collaborative, mixing third party assets with owned solutions to create the most efficient and effective structures.

5. Ideas Come from Everywhere—Technology enables everyone to become producers, brand ambassadors, or media channels. Just a couple years ago, Whit Hiler was a complete amateur who wanted to make ads. Today he's known as the man behind some of the more interesting and ridiculous campaigns of the last few years, including "Beardvertising," "The World's Longest Hashtag" (created to promote A&W's new chicken sandwich), and Applebee's "Girls Night Out."

Hiler had applied for several agency jobs but had never gotten a return call. His first foray into the industry was from an open call for Victors & Spoils. He won, and his idea for Harley Davidson, "No Cages," became the brand anthem. The key for agencies is to leverage existing user-generated content and consumer interactions with smart solutions (image recognition, context-based targeting, and crowdsourced challenge/gamification). Apps such as Mag-

Whit Hiler

isto and Pixlee will allow brands to aggregate and use user-generated content at low cost.

6. People are the New Media Channels—Instead of creating ads to be placed on media to reach people, the new paradigm will be to create shareable and scalable ideas and then let *people themselves distribute them*, as they do with memes. Recent research from IPSOS found that content created by consumers is 35 percent more memorable and 50 percent more trusted. This represents the rise in organic marketing. The Prosumer Age has definitely arrived.

The key to success here will be to find ways of monitoring and measuring, and optimizing communications—whether they come from a multichannel broadcasting company or a single individual that is "broadcasting" across channels.

OK. So we have 2021 locked down. We know what's coming and how to prepare ourselves. But what about farther down the road? Say by 2030? What could be happening then for marketers?

MARKETING IN THE YEAR 2030

CHAPTER TWELVE

Overview: 2030 Will Arrive Sooner than You Think

Ah, the distant future. The prospects of a better world. The high-tech products we'll use to live an easier, more enriching life. The extra leisure time we'll have to enjoy the things we can't do now. The coming together of all humanity. Well, that one probably won't become reality, but you can bet that the ingenuity of humankind and technology will do a good job of trying to get us there!

So, what will business be like fourteen years from now? How will we build brand awareness and grow market share? How will we stay connected to our customers? Will we still be "tweeting"? Or posting videos on YouTube? As agencies, what types of industries will need our marketing help? All of these questions and so many more quickly enter the mind when thinking about the future.

In researching this book I was completely blown away by the sheer volume of articles, books, white papers, industry reports, television interviews and more that covered the topic of "the future." What was missing however, in many cases, was the *marketing* part. The *promotions* piece. *How* would we be connecting with others? That's now the job of *Future Marketing*, I hope.

After you finish this book, I fully encourage you to read some of the definitive books on the future of business in general, which I have enjoyed over the past few months. These books include:

- *The Inevitable: Understanding the 12 Technological Forces That Will Shape Our Future*–by Kevin Kelly (My favorite)
- *The Future of Business: Critical Insights into a Rapidly Changing World from 60 Future Thinkers*–by Rohit Talwar and a group of other selected authors
- *Abundance: The Future Is Better Than You Think*–by Peter H. Diamandis and Steven Kotler
- *The Third Wave: An Entrepreneur's Vision of the Future*–by Steve Case
- *The New Digital Age: Reshaping the Future of People, Nations and Business*–by Eric Schmidt and Jared Cohen
- *The Sharing Economy: The End of Employment and the Rise of Crowd-Based Capitalism*–by Arun Sundararajan
- *Entering the Shift Age: The End of the Information Age and the New Era of Transformation*–by David Houle

So back to marketing. What exactly will we be doing at work in thirteen years? I know I'll be there; I'll be fifty-nine years old in 2030. Will you be there? I'm guessing you will be.

Key Ideas for 2030

The four key ideas due for arrival and mass adoption by 2030 that will have huge impacts on the marketing practice are:

1. "Computers Everywhere" or a "Ubiquitous Internet" in the air around us
2. Augmented, Immersive Experiences

3.   Widespread Internet of Things

4.   Artificial Marketing Intelligence

1. Computers Are Everywhere, But Most Are Unseen—Sometimes, it's difficult for us to see what *could be* because we're so ingrained in our current habits and processes. Take for example having a screen as an interface for computing. Right now, we need the screen. By 2030, the idea of "screens" will be like the typewriter. It will seem like ancient technology. They will still be around, but not used like they are now. Keyboards will also be pretty much history, although not as minimally used as screens; some people

will prefer to use a keyboard when typing, for example.

So the idea of ubiquitous computing or "pervasive computing" and "everyware"—will be here in thirteen years. Of course, we already have computers in our cars, our phones, our toys, and even our fridges. But they're obvious, we can see them and they stand out. We often have to hold them, or use keyboards to input information into them. It will be different in 2030.

One of the reasons for this change will be the current shift towards microelectromechanical systems (MEMS), fostering the miniaturization revolution. Devices will get smaller and smaller over the years and more multifunctional, and as a result, won't even seem like they are there in some cases. Information processing devices will be virtually everywhere, but essentially invisible—absorbed into our surroundings.[1] These computers will be in our clothes, our fashion accessories, and even in our contact lenses. And to use them we'll use natural language and haptic technologies (i.e. tactile feedback).

We most certainly will have a device that serves as a holographic portal for global meetings where all meeting attendees are present in real time with realistic views of each other around a virtual conference table. Global, holographic real-time collaboration will be the norm. See some marketing opportunities here?

We may also have some thing like a small headset that will do whatever your voice says to do, no matter where you are: Call your son, change the thermostat, or move documents, pictures and videos to anywhere in the world. See some marketing opportunities here?

There are a few longshot ideas, but they are certainly provocative and possible. We could have the ability to cast our thoughts out into the Internet for a selected audience or to anyone. It would be individually programmed to your brain waves, which would allow you to communicate with your thoughts to others connected to your frequency. We could use "emotionally sensitive" touch screens that would convey our emotional states to others. More on these topics in the next chapter.

2. Augmented, Immersive Experiences—By 2030, innovative marketers everywhere will leverage augmented reality to craft immersive brand experiences, create more interactive advertising, and enable consumers to experience products and spaces in novel ways.[2] First a definition: *Augmented reality (AR) is the practice of displaying digital information over people's real-time view of objects, people, or spaces in the physical world.*

But this is like defining a computer in the 1960s as a high-speed computation machine; it provides no insight into the unfathomable potential that inherently exists in this new technology. Over the next few years, AR

technology will develop rapidly so it will be our responsibility to stay engaged if we want to best learn how to use it for the marketing practice.

While today, we are busy setting up Facebook banner ad campaigns, by 2030 we'll be planning augmented reality campaigns for all our business endeavors. One thing to understand is that there will be various active and passive AR components available to help marketers optimize their AR campaigns and enhance consumer engagement: user-brand engagement, user-user engagement, and user-bystander engagement.

If you've ever seen the 2002 film, *Minority Report*, starring Tom Cruise, there is a scene in the movie where it appears that his character, John Anderton, is actually "walking through" an advertisement in a public space. The ad speaks his name and knows things about him, making the experience personalized, just for him, which he opted in for. Welcome to the "new normal" for ad and content marketing experiences in 2030!

In 2016, augmented reality is just beginning to enter our lives, but in ways that show us where it's going. Early developments are:

- Smartphone apps that allow you to point the camera at a bus stop and see the entire routes of the buses that stop there.
- Smartphone apps that allow you to point your phone at a restaurant and read reviews posted online.
- Smartphone apps that provide detailed information about the

building, museum, or landmark you're visiting as you look at it through your phone.

- Glasses you wear that provide data about what you are looking at. The reality in front of you is enhanced with live, streaming data about whatever it is that you are looking at.

Augmented reality will be taking what we see in physical reality and adding in all the known information from the screen reality to it. The key difference between now and 2030 is that the merging of these two realities in real time will happen everywhere, wherever we are in the future. Think about that for a minute. That's a really different environment than our current one. The impacts, benefits and efficiencies we'll experience are simply incredible to ponder.

So how will it all happen? The first level of both transformation and market acceptance will be when lots of people start wearing augmented reality glasses or have smartphones with augmented reality apps. When this happens, we will all enjoy an enhanced living experience that will be truly transformative and mind-altering.

Where are the marketing and money making opportunities?

- Apps could be provided free by marketers wanting to keep brand awareness literally in front of the consumer.
- Deeper levels of augmentation beyond the basic levels would be on a paid, subscription basis.
- Special versions of augmented reality apps could be sold.
- A B2C application might be one where wearing augmented glasses enables you to look at someone of interest and quickly know everything about them (with their permission).

Augmenting Virtual and Physical Events

Rohit Talwar in *The Future of Business* asks you to envision your social network extensions "floating above your head in an AR layer!" Such a digital overlay would allow you to let others see your likes, favorite places, shared friends, and even career information. Of course, you would control how much you shared, but such a step forward would allow you to link yourself to the "real world" in a more structured, quantified way—"and as a result, it would be a more joyful experience.[3]

AR: Transforming Customer Experiences

Joyce Gioia, also in *The Future of Business* speculates about how AI could help customers purchase not just products but "interactions" with immersive applications. Perhaps a VR/AR "suit" could access a program linking, for example, travelers to experience the past or students to place themselves right in historic or future events. "People will be able to select the intensity of their experiences and choose a level from mild to extreme, depending on the degree of reality they are prepared to handle."[4]

Your Glasses Will Augment Reality

In 2030, a pair of lightweight virtual reality glasses will sell for as little as $200. They'll help you function in your everyday world—seeing and hearing everything around you while receiving texts, interacting with talking 3-D images of people and more. Your gestures, eye movements and voice will direct the images you see in your VR glasses. A real-estate agent might use such glasses to sell homes. Prospective buyers wearing augmented reality glasses will be able to visualize a building on an empty lot, for example—walking around it, seeing it with solar panels, etc.[5] The marketing potential for using augmented reality is massive.

3. Widespread Internet of Things (IoT): Trillions of Sensors Connecting Us to the Physical—IoT is the interconnectivity between things using wireless communication technology (each with its own unique identifiers) to connect objects, locations, animals, or people to the Internet, thus allowing for the direct transmission of and seamless sharing of data. Everyday devices will be able to automatically exchange information over a network. The IoT will also have a great impact on our everyday lives in that it will change the way traffic, weather, pollution, and the environment are monitored and how data is collected. Welcome to the Internet of Things: the

Web, everywhere.

As the cost of sensors continues to decline and computing power increases, all kinds of devices will increasingly become connected to the Internet. From the clothes you wear to the products you use, everything will go online. And, as early as 2022, it's predicted that 1 trillion sensors will be connected: Just about every physical product could be connected to a ubiquitous communication infrastructure, and sensors everywhere will allow us to fully perceive our environment. Cisco Systems predicts we'll yield $19 trillion in new revenues by 2022. International Data Corporation predicts the worldwide market for IoT solutions will grow to $7.1 trillion in 2020.[6] See some marketing potential here?

Spread around the globe, embedded in our cars, connected to our bodies, and watching us at home and on public streets, this web of sensors will generate 300 zillion bytes of data in the next decade. Tracked, parsed, and cognified by utilitarian AIs, this data will be molded into hundreds of new forms, new products, and innovative services.

In the future, the intersection of wearable technology, AR and peer-to-peer communications will combine sensory data, rich information channels, and secure communications to generate useful devices, delivering richer, more enjoyable experiences.

New Ways to Interact with Things

In *The Inevitable*, Kevin Kelly discussed the new ways we will interact with things by 2030. He said that in the coming decades we'll keep expanding what we interact with. The expansion follows three thrusts:

More senses—We will keep adding new sensors and senses to the things we make. Of course, everything will get seeing and hearing senses, but one by one we'll be able to add superhuman senses such as GPS location sensing, heat detection, X-ray vision, diverse molecule sensitivity, or smell. These will permit our creations to respond to us, to interact with us, and to adapt themselves to our uses. Interactivity, by definition, is two way, so this sensing elevates our interactions with technology.

More intimacy. The zone of interaction will continue to march closer to us. Technology will get closer to us than a watch and pocket phone. Interacting will be more intimate. It will always be on, everywhere. Intimate technology is a wide-open frontier. We think technology has saturated our private space, but we will look back in 14 years and realize it was still far away in 2016.

More immersion. Maximum interaction demands that we leap into the technology itself. That's what VR/AR allows us to do. Computation so close that we are inside it. From within a technologically created world, we interact with each other in new ways (virtual reality) or interact with the physical world in a new way (augmented reality). Technology becomes a second skin.[7]

By 2030, anything that can interact with us, including things like a smart hammer, a smart light, or a smart pair of shoes, will become more valuable in our interactive society. But interacting will require new skills, coordination, experience, and education. The future of technology will reside in the discovery of new interactions. In the coming fifteen years, anything that is not intensely interactive will be considered broken.

4. Artificial Marketing Intelligence—First, a definition: *AI is the ability of computers to perform tasks that normally require human intelligence, such as visual perception, speech recognition, decision-making, and translation between languages.*

For marketers, this means advancements in AI that could help us un-lock deeper customer insights, help us communicate with prospects and customers more effectively, and help us eliminate the more monotonous, impersonal aspects of our jobs. The end result: A more human experience for everyone involved.

AI isn't going to replace marketers and marketing teams by 2030, it's going to make them more *efficient*. It isn't going to replace human intel-ligence, it's going to add to it through uncovering new insights. And it isn't going to turn us into mindless marketing robots. Instead, AI promises to free us from "repetitive drudgery" so we can spend more of our time on tasks that require a human touch.[8] So those who have some fear of the future should re-read the above five times. The future is good! The "pie of life" (and of marketing) will always be *growing*.

Most marketers enjoy the fact that their job descriptions require cer-tain levels of creativity. And one of the biggest challenges for developing software behind AI is that thus far, it can only work with what human de-velopers feed it. But perhaps by 2030 it will craft campaigns and stories for us. Who knows? Archetypes and plots exist for a reason—human na-ture has changed very little over the history of storytelling; we enjoy the same types of stories being told over and over.[9]

Through AI, the marketing of the future could well be run by ma-chines that analyze predictive data sets to deliver curated, personalized content for consumers' eyes before they even realize they need it. Entire campaigns will likely be launched, executed and iterated upon without the intervention of a human hand.

Kevin Kelly envisions an "AI" that's not the uncanny humanoid AI of Stephen Spielberg's movie of the same name, but that "looks more like Amazon Web Services"—a smart and steady digital system that underlies everything and that we only notice when it's not there. "This common util-ity will serve you as much IQ as you want but no more than you need."[10]

Companies are already going there. Google CEO Sundar Pichai told investors in 2015 that AI would be "a core transformative way by which we are rethinking everything we are doing.... We are applying it across all our products, be it search, be it YouTube and Play, etc.," Kelly writes. If he's right, in ten years search won't be Google's bread and butter anymore. AI will.[11]

Before the end of this century, 70 percent of today's occupations will be replaced by automation. This upheaval is being led by a second wave of automation, one that is centered on artificial cognition, cheap sensors, machine learning, and distributed smarts. This broad automation will touch all jobs, from manual labor to knowledge work. But don't worry too much, a whole host of new industries and new jobs will be created too. And as I've mentioned previously, you won't need as much income to enjoy a good quality of life. It's the natural evolution of the human species on this earth.

By 2030, a convergence of these technologies that link humans and machines will produce interdependence at scales we have a hard time envisioning now. This is what Kelly describes as a "singularity," "a new regime wherein our creations make us better humans, but also one where we can't live without what we've made." It's as if we've been frozen in ice, ice that suddenly becomes water that we can swim in.[12]

Tactical (and Other) Changes by 2030

What will the effect of these big-picture changes be on the marketing practice? Some of them will be barely noticeable, but many of them will be quite dramatic:

Marketing Decisions Will Be 100 percent Customer-Centric—In reality, it's supposed to be all about the customer *now*, but by 2030, it absolutely will be—otherwise, you won't be in business. If you think the customer has power now with social media, product and service reviews, and other power-shifting technology, in fifteen years the customer's influence will be in everything and everywhere. A big part of the reason for this will be the diminished power of the multinational global conglomerate, the "brand," and the traditional "company" as we know it today, which I discussed earlier in the book.

So what do I mean by marketing decisions being 100 percent customer-centric? Well, it could be in form, function, execution or a combination of these. It will be seen in virtual customer experiences, hyper-personalization and in augmented reality experiences utilizing all five senses. No matter the execution method, maximum customer value will govern all marketing decisions.

Hyper Targeting Will Be Reality—By 2030, there will be stunning synergies between intelligent, consumer-friendly hardware and real-time information and consumer profile data, making shopping hyper-targeted and hyper-personalized. While Google Glass may have experienced a tough time being accepted by consumers in 2014, a 2030 version of this virtual assistance product will be much more consumer-friendly, sophisticated and smart.[13]

And, of course, as consumers, we'll *want* to be hyper targeted because it will make our lives *easier* and save us *time*. We'll be able to access whatever we want, whenever we want, wherever we want. Geotargeting and ultimately *geomarketing* will be the norm, and far more advanced.

Utilizing all of the big data that will be in existence, combined with the advancements in technology and geotargeting, you'll receive specific notifications at the correct moments, or before you even realize you need them. For example, you could receive special offers for local food establishments *when you are hungry* and walking by, without even requesting them. Imagine a shopping window that displays a product at the right time at the right place to exactly the right consumer. This will be the new, hyper-targeted reality in 2030. Retailers, see a marketing play here?

Content Marketing Will Be Alive and Well—Not a big surprise here: With more types of content, different ways of distributing it and more people on the planet in 2030, content will be more important than ever. But it will obviously need to be hyper-relevant, personalized, and very compelling. You'll still need to stand out from the crowd, because *every piece* of content and ad will be relevant, personalized, and compelling. There is one huge caveat, however: content will only reach those genuinely interested in it. Spam and "junk mail" will be ancient history.

Pay-Per-Click and Paid Media: 100 percent Conversion—Paid media will still be here as well, but it will operate solely on a bidding metric as CPM (Cost per 1,000), CPC (Cost per Click) and CPA (Cost per Action) will all be the same thing. Targeting will be so good that the conversion rate will be nearly perfect—Google will work out when, where, what, how, and who to reach seamlessly. An impression will always get a click and nearly always will convert. Businesses will be able to market to a particular person instead of a group, at the correct time and place to make a sale. And what if you want to simply build awareness? You'll still be able to pay for an awareness-driven campaign when conversion is not a factor, but you'll be able to reach the perfect audience, every time. The "efficiency everywhere" mandate will be a key factor here.

Automation of the Shopping Experience—The personal touch experience of shopping where human salespeople assist you will be a rare activity by 2030. With such advancements in data collection and analysis, machines will take over the recommendation aspect of shopping 100 percent—even in physical stores and marketplaces. It's the continuation of what we've already seen online with recommendation engines and "if you like this, you should try/buy that." But taking out the two-way dialogue of shopping decisions is a big implication. You'll only be as good as your data and analytics execution. [14]

Location-Based Marketing—By 2030, retailers will know more about where you buy things and what you bought there and as a result, will get much more specific in their retargeting efforts. Your past behavior and buying record will be syndicated in a lightly anonymized form by services like Amazon, and you will notice that physical products and services (even those 3D-printed just-in-time by retailers when you walk into their shop and look "likely to buy") will be retargeted to you in the way digital products are retargeted to you today based on your browsing habits.[15]

The most customer-centric retailers will partner with you to sell your data to them in exchange for discounts and preferred access to exclusive products—and you'll be able to firewall off some of your information. The most effective experience here is not a clumsy "X like you bought Y" collaborative filtering effort, but rather a really slick reordering of the items you see that over time increases the amount you buy.

As we all move more of our buying cycles online, and as those buying cycles are tracked more effectively, it will be easier to create Bayesian models that do a solid job of predicting whether we will buy. They will also learn more effectively when we choose not to buy, and make inferences based on other factors in our environment (temperature, time, location, emotional state, other people we are with) that we do not notice or correlate. The bottom line: location, browsing, and buying will be increasingly co-mingled by 2030. Analysts will use technological and psychological triggers to help us all buy more of the things we really need, and understand why we're buying them.

More on Augmented Reality...

Marketing today is either traditional (print ad) or digital (email). But mostly, it's a combination, or what we call *integrated*. Offline ads mention a website, social media or hashtags. Online landing pages have you sign up for a print magazine that includes ads. In the future these offline methods will either be virtual experiences or augmented, syncing up to your digital life.

"Digital Marketing" Becomes "Augmented-Immersive Experiences" or "Augmenting" (Both Physical & on the Internet)—Static, one-dimensional promotional pieces like a print ad in *People* magazine or a television commercial on ESPN will seem archaic, a relic from the past. In fact, the term "digital marketing" won't even be a lexicon anymore; by 2030, it very well could be known as something like "Augmented-Immersive Experiences," or "Augmenting" for short.

What we know as integrated marketing today, a mashup of traditional and digital, could still be a "thing" in the future, but it will be a mashup of *digital and augmented*. What would be an example of this? You're walking through the airport, on your way to the airline gate, and the advertisement in the terminal begins to surround you, communicating a specific message just for you, perhaps emitting a scent of the ocean, and (if it's a Hawaii vacation ad, for example) walking you inside your hotel room. The offer is a ten-day vacation in Maui; and if you like what you hear (and see), you can take advantage of the offer right there, on the spot, and the vacation would be instantly set up, booked, and paid for in ten seconds. Efficient, right? Cool marketing, right? Yes!

Good VR, such as the Oculus Rift, will be seen in 2030 as the "big new thing" that ushered in the new age, as the Apple II personal computer was in 1981. So, this realistic sense of "presence," which is currently just in its infancy, will be everywhere. By blending various technologies, this type of presence will fully break down the glass barrier that we've used to interface with digital content since computers, tablets, and smartphones became our daily companions.

By 2030, we'll truly immerse ourselves in digital content and, because it will be so geared towards us individually, it's going to be welcomed and seen as really cool. Of course, just as you can do now, you'll be able to opt out, but not many people will. Those who opt out in the future will be like those who decided to keep using horse-drawn carriages when Henry Ford built the Model T in the early 1900s. Your quality of life will diminish significantly. Plus, your social connections will be negatively impacted because everyone will be so incredibly networked with each other.

This immersion and the sense of presence the technology offers will have the biggest impact on the total user experience. Brands and agencies will need to re-evaluate how they tell stories and communicate them in brand new ways. Flat pictures, words and videos will be transformed into three-dimensional worlds that consumers (and businesses) can be temporarily transported to, wherever they happen to be. "Augmenting" will be the new paradigm in product marketing, product engagement, and storytelling. And by the way, it won't be just a B2C play; B2B will be impacted in the same way.

Mobile technology will have the most profound impact on the future of VR and AR user experiences because of the ubiquity and availability of these devices already in our hands. For an average consumer, mobile devices used in conjunction with lightweight devices or glasses for AR/VR engagement will be more realistic (in the short term) than the high cost and bulky form factor of fully dedicated VR devices such as the Oculus.[16]

AR overcomes some of VR's contextual shortcomings as it relies on a more minimal pair of glasses as opposed to a full headset, and is intended to add virtual interactive elements to a consumer's existing world without taking them out of their physical environment. AR also adds promise to this space as it is an inherently more social experience than VR. Of course, because the Internet will be everywhere eventually, we won't even need a device or pair of glasses to experience augmented reality experiences; all we'll need to do is reach out, and the experience will be there.

More on the Marketing Potential of the Internet of Things

The IoT will have an enormous impact on the way we do business, specifically where marketing is concerned. How will the IoT improve marketing return on investment?[17]

1. Easy Exchange of Sales Data—One of the most valuable commodities to any business is its sales data. By having access to information regarding how, where, and why your products are being purchased and used, you'll be able to better tailor your marketing efforts towards your specific clients.

Smart devices that can gather this data and supply it back to you in real time, without the need for IT professionals to direct or monitor the interaction, will allow businesses to create informed marketing strategies and improve ROI on future sales.

Perhaps even more important, your customers will be able to provide useful feedback *instantaneously*. So, if a specific product isn't living up to expectations, you won't have to wait very long at all to find out about it, which means that you'll be able to cut your losses much sooner.

2. Smarter CRM: Instantaneous Customer Analysis—When used in conjunction with a dependable customer relationship management (CRM) tool, the IoT will be able to do more than simply gather and organize client data; it will be able to efficiently and accurately analyze that data as well, providing you with actionable results regarding your consumer base.

For marketers, this can be invaluable, given that the buyer's chain of command is often long, and decisions take more time to be made. IoT devices can streamline this process by helping you understand where your prospects are in their buying journey, so that you'll be able to make every second of every day count towards resolving issues and serving them the right information that will nurture them to ultimately close deals.

3. Devices That Know They're Dying—One of the more promising aspects of smart-enabled products is their potential ability to perform their own regular maintenance and diagnostics.

Automobiles have been self-diagnosing themselves for some time—but it has been a clunky method that relies on inexact signals. With the power of IoT, every component is "smarter" so the ability to identify the problem, as well as the solution, will be lightning-quick in comparison.

When it comes to conventional items and devices, often the first sign that anything is wrong comes when the device abruptly stops functioning altogether. When this happens, there's not much that can be done, aside from getting it repaired or ordering a whole new device and waiting for it to arrive.

IoT devices could eliminate that down time, by constantly monitoring their own functions and contacting technical support when necessary. And, should a major, irreparable problem be detected, the IoT device could easily order a replacement for itself, so that when it finally does shut down, the new model will already have arrived and be ready to be put into service.

The same goes for upgrades. Many users put off upgrading their devices out of fear that the new upgrade will be buggy, time-consuming to implement, or that something will go wrong. Unfortunately, not upgrading software often leaves the devices open to security compromises or known problematic issues. IoT devices would take foot-dragging users out of the equation, and search for, download, and install new upgrades completely on their own.

4. Predictive Social Media—When Facebook and Twitter first hit the scene several years ago, most marketers were less-than-convinced that these new "social media" sites would be worth targeting. We all know how well that skepticism turned out! Today, 74 percent of brand marketers report that they see a noticeable increase in Web traffic after investing a mere six hours a week in social media marketing efforts.

The IoT is already optimized for use with social media, allowing automated posts and shares to be regularly generated by the devices themselves, and preparing the way for new online communities to develop, centered around users of particular devices.

Marketers who are able to predict the development of these social communities, and target their efforts towards these communities, will be able to reach potential customers that may not have previously been available. Likewise, IoT devices, when coupled with social media, will allow marketers to identify and take advantage of new emerging trends.

5. Imagine a 100 Percent CTR (Click Through Rate)—Brought together, these factors all point towards one final goal: *smarter, more relevant advertising and content experiences.*

As increasing numbers of our once-unconnected devices and objects are being fitted with sensors and given constant network accessibility, the face of advertising and content marketing is going to change for both the marketer and the consumer. No longer will marketers rely on banner ads or popups based off a website you visited on Tuesday; most IoT devices will be completely unable to process or even display such crude ploys.

As a result, the age of the interruptive commercial will finally come to an end on the consumer side. In its place will be a new world in which advertising must be beneficial and completely relevant, where no prospects are served advertisements that don't 100 percent align with their interests, behaviors, and past purchases. Sounds almost like the current day content marketing to me!

Marketers would need to have a detailed understanding of their prosumers in order to take advantage of the new opportunities being made available, but those who are able to make the transition will find that the IoT allows them the opportunity to *finally* stop being one-way promoters, and finally start being valued business resources.

New Ad and Content Formats

So far, digital ads have been served to users either based on a particular search term (high relevancy), on a website's context (medium relevancy), or based on navigation behavior (retargeting, highest relevancy). The Internet of Things will offer new ad formats, appearing only when the ad reaches its highest potential of relevancy—possibly restricted to only the top relevant ad content to ensure consumer satisfaction.[18]

A new ad format that will appear are *Need-Based Ads*, appearing as product or service suggestions based on factual consumer data (e.g. basic food and toiletry products). Marketers will be able to embed special offers/savings and allow consumers to order right from their refrigerators or allow for need-based automatic purchasing, analyzing both average consumption volume and rate.

Another new ad format that will emerge are *Predictive Ads*. These ads will suggest products/services to consumers based on a combination of both historical and environmental data. An example: You're standing in front of your closet, wondering what to wear. On your display appears a fact-based ad, suggesting a new suit jacket based on the fact that you (a) have an important external meeting coming up, and (b) you currently only possess a single suit jacket that you bought five years ago. The brand and

retailer will be chosen based on previous purchase behavior, brand preferences, your average spend in this product category, and retailer proximity
to allow for same-day delivery.

The Internet of Things certainly opens up a whole new realm of opportunities for both consumers and marketers and will revolutionize how
prosumers buy and marketers market. Relevancy is key—but need-based
or fact-based relevancy is *king*.

Personalized Advertising—"Good afternoon, Mr. Yakamoto. How did
you like that three-pack of tank tops you bought last time you were in?"
That was the talking computerized billboard in the 2002 film, *Minority Report*.

In 1999, Steven Spielberg, the director of *Minority Report*, started to
consult experts and put more scientific research into his films. At that
time he invited fifteen experts convened by the Global Business Network,
its chairman, Peter Schwartz, and its co-founder Stewart Brand, for a three-
day "think tank." He wanted to consult with the group to create a plausible
"future reality" for the year 2054.

Dubbed the "think tank summit," the experts included architect Peter Calthorpe, Douglas Coupland, computer scientist Neil Gershenfeld,
biomedical researcher Shaun Jones, computer scientist Jaron Lanier, and
former Massachusetts Institute of Technology (MIT) architecture dean

William J. Mitchell. Production Designer Alex McDowell kept what was nicknamed the "2054 bible," an 80-page guide created in preproduction which listed all the decided upon aspects of the future world: architectural, socio-economical, political, and technological.[19] Their conclusions? We won't just work on a computer in 2050 with our fingers and eyes. All our senses, and our whole bodies will communicate with machines.[20]

The thing about the film and Spielberg's efforts in conceptulizing the future is that they were pretty right about how it might look—at least *so far.* But don't buy into the Dystopian look they gave the film. They did that to be provocative and sell movie tickets! The future can be a much more positive and uplifting place than our current world. Personally, I found *Minority Report* really interesting and something readers of *Future Marketing* could appreciate because it helps us visualize all of the ideas I'm discussing in this book. If you haven't seen the movie, see it. I think one of the reasons why more human beings aren't forward thinking or get comfortable with "how things are now" is because they simply cannot picture things differently.

I think people fall into two groups: those who can visualize a new reality and those who have a hard time with it. In my experience, it's the creative ones among us who fall into the first group. And this is, of course, one of the important things that Steve Jobs always talked about— coming from an artistic point of view. I think it's the job of the those who can visualize a new reality to help those who can't, because if there is one thing we know, it is this: *things always change and they always will.* If we want to do better and do more and get the most out of this experience known as life, and make it a *positive* change, it's on us to keep moving forward.

Most of the advertising shown in *Minority Report* occurs outside the home. The key is that the ads are interactive and interact with film characters in various ways; an Aquafina ad splashes water on its customers, Guinness recommends its beer to recover from "a hard day at work," a cereal box has a video advertisement on it, and when John Anderton, the main character, is fleeing the PreCrime force, an American Express advertisement observes, "It looks like you need an escape, and Blue can take you there," and a Lexus ad says, "A road diverges in the desert. Lexus. The road you're on, John Anderton, is the one less traveled." The advertisements in *Minority Report* were handled by Jeff Boortz of Concrete Pictures, who said "the whole idea, from a script point of view, was that the advertisements *would recognize you*—not only recognize you, but recognize *your state of mind.* It's the kind of stuff that's going on now with digital set-top boxes and the Internet."[21] In the future, it will be ubiquitous.

Currently, billboards capable of facial recognition are being developed by NEC. These billboards will be able to recognize passers-by via facial recognition, call them by name, and deliver customer-specific advertisements. Thus far, the billboards can recognize age and gender and deliver demographically appropriate advertisements, but cannot discern individuals. And yes, like all other hyper personal ads like this, you'll need to opt in and agree to sacrifice your privacy in exchange for the benefit.

IBM is developing similar billboards, with plans to deliver customized advertisements to individuals who carry identity tags. Like NEC, the company feels they will not be obtrusive, as their billboards will only advertise products in which *a customer is interested.* By 2030, advertisers will embrace these types of billboard and other similar ads in order to reduce costs by wasting fewer advertisements on uninterested consumers. In addition, these types of ads will make them appear "cutting edge" with prosumers. Again, we see the "efficiency play" pop up again.

The Concept of Gladvertising—"Gladvertising"[22] is outdoor advertising that uses cameras and facial recognition software to read a consumer's *mood*, then pushes products relevant to the target emotional state. It uses emotion recognition software to tailor outdoor ads to consumers' moods. The term was coined in a July 2011 report by the Centre of Future Studies which suggested that advertisements like the ones in the film

Minority Report may be well on the way. Their report—commissioned by 3MGTG, which specializes in digital advertising—foresees the first step to be advertisements that adapt to our moods. I believe this type of ad could certainly be mainstream by 2030.

Because I'm a content marketer, I don't talk about advertising very much, for all the obvious reasons. But, I think the future holds some very interesting things for the medium of advertising and it certainly will not go away. If we can *evolve* ads and make them smart, ensure they are interesting and personalized, well, then, now I think we have something.

E-papers—Electronic paper and e-paper are display devices that mimic the appearance of ordinary ink on paper. This was also seen in *Minority Report*. Unlike conventional backlit flat panel displays that emit light, electronic paper displays reflect light like paper. This may make them more comfortable to read, and provide a wider viewing angle than most light-emitting displays. Electronic paper has been announced as being developed by MIT, the media conglomerate Hearst Corporation, and LG.

By 2030, printed materials will still be with us, but they will be more like "e-papers" that include video, speak to us, basically interact with us in cool and personalized ways. As stated many times in *Future Marketing*, this is another huge thing for marketers everywhere in the year 2030.

Okay, so now we've covered what marketing could be like in 2021 and 2030. Lots of interesting potential and ideas, huh? But what about the years after 2030? Let's go a bit deeper....

CHAPTER THIRTEEN

Marketing Beyond 2030

lthough the scope of this book carries the ideas out to the year 2030, the sheer volume of ideas and research that was available begged me to create this additional chapter on what the marketing practice could be like *beyond 2030*. As you'll see, some of these technologies and ideas are pretty "out there," but I thought they were interesting nonetheless, so I decided to include them in *Future Marketing*. From AI to Brain Wave and Thought Connectivity to Collective Consciousness Interface Technology, there are some pretty cool potential ideas in store. Some of them may happen, some of them may never happen, and some may occur sooner. The key is they can help us see the potential big picture more clearly and inspire other, totally new ideas to come to the surface.

Take a look and let me know what you think....

Second Generation Technologies (By 2040?)

Imagine taking augmented reality and virtual reality to the next step. That's what marketers will be doing ten years after 2030, as today's advanced technologies mature and are improved in ways that are hard to imagine today.

Augmented Reality—The next phase of AR will happen when we can approximate the physical reality relative to the senses (sight, hearing, taste, smell and touch). Although we'll be in a physical place, it will be a multi-sensorial space, so our biological processes will be in one place and our neurological and sensory processes will be of another space. You'll be able to "go" to any beach you want in the world at any time. You'll be able to "visit" any city you want in the world at any time. You will even be able to listen to Plato, Lincoln, or Einstein and ask them questions. What's even more stunning than this, however, is that all of these examples will be recalled by the self and the brain as things that have *actually been experienced*. This is a true merging of real and not-real, and the highest level of augmentation.

Like Rainforest Café: Engaging Five Senses in Actual Reality—Of course, there are companies already appealing to the senses of truly enchanted customers. And it's happening without AR or VR. Take the Rainforest Café. To enhance its theme, the mist used at the theme restaurant chain appeals to all five senses simultaneously. Your first exposure? A sound. You hear "*sss-sss-zzz*" softly as you approach the restaurant. Then, as you get closer, you see the mist rising from the rocks. As you take your seat at your table, you feel the mist, soft and cool, against your skin. Finally, you smell its tropical essence and taste its freshness. Sensation-filled and totally immersive, you almost forget that you came here to eat! So, how do we take that idea into the future and digitize it?

Brain Wave and Thought Connectivity—This development is a little more of a stretch and difficult for some people to believe. But all signs are pointing towards it. The technology is currently in development. Up until now, we've let people know what we're thinking by expressing it, either by saying it or writing it. But what if they could find out before we say it or write it? Yes, I'm talking about brain wave and thought connectivity.

By 2030, there will be significant collective thought data that will increasingly course through all communication channels as memes, thus developing a collective level of thought that's more immediate and experiential. This technology will increasingly connect our thoughts with others in a massive, rapid way. So we almost instantaneously connect with each other, if we want to.

David Houle argues that just as we can sense a person's emotions today, we'll be able to know what others are thinking and feeling, brain to brain. It will be like the connection we experience with loved ones far away, but multiplied by the proximity of others.[1]

Brain waves are the electrical impulses of our brains that translate into thoughts. So brain wave mapping is the mapping of our thoughts. A current application of this technology is reading brain waves for quadriplegics to move their high-tech wheelchairs. "Rotate wheelchair right," and the wheelchair turns right. "Move wheelchair forward," and the wheelchair moves forward.

The way it will work:

- You put on a headset which has a number of brain wave sensors on it
- A software program asks you to think about certain things
- The brain waves of those thoughts are captured and you look at your holographic screen
- When prompted by the on-screen avatar to do something, you think it and it happens on the screen

You will no longer be "only physical," but will be wearing your personal metadata to accompany your physical self. A brain wave computer inter-

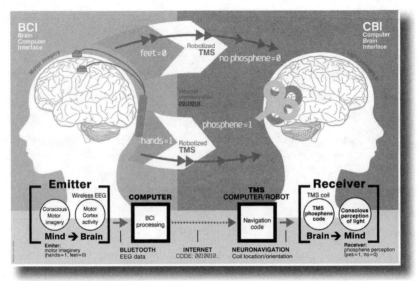

face is the next human interface with computer technology, following the current iteration of touch and voice.

This technology will enable us to manifest our thoughts and desires into reality. It will also make it easier to scan and digitize everything around us. We will digitize and upload our imagination and dreams into the simulation.

The marketing impact of brain wave and thought connectivity is massive, obviously. Imagine people opting in to share their thoughts with your company! And then imagine having 1,000 people do that, all of whom represent your target market. It will make marketing easier and more affordable than ever before. And it certainly will help you to find *all* of the customers that could be a good fit for your products and services.

It's way too early to start planning for this one, but it's important to understand where we could be heading. As I've mentioned, most of us have a really hard time perceiving what the future could be like, and this development, brain wave and thought connectivity, certainly is a more challenging one for people to get their minds around. But it is probably coming.

Collective Consciousness Interface Technology– David Houle, in his amazing book, *Entering the Shift Age*, discusses what he calls a "Collective

Consciousness Interface Technology" by 2030. He said,

> once a collective level of consciousness begins to become
> widely manifested, a technology will be created to assist
> those yet to deeply experience it. It might be something
> like a hand-held tablet with earphones or more likely
> something that gently covers the head. This cover might
> contain both the highest level of brainwave sensors and
> some inbound antenna that truly can operate at the delicate
> frequency of and sense, others brainwaves. This technology
> takes us into deep metaphysical, spiritual, philosophical and
> moral areas where consciousness expands and becomes
> adaptive.[2]

Evolutionary is the right word—or maybe *revolutionary!*

The AI Powered Personal Assistant—In the epic book, *The Future of Business*, Yates Buckley, in his chapter, "The Future of Digital Media-the Freexpensive Preogative," shared a fascinating idea and an imaginary conversation between himself and his future AI powered personal assistant. Of all the things I reviewed in my research for *Future Marketing*, this one stood out. I wanted to share it with you here. As marketers, this example alone will unleash a host of ideas and thoughts for all of us on where marketing is going in the long term.

Buckley said,

> The solution to the problem of free/expensive around personal data, will likely be resolved around commercialization of artificial intelligence (AI) powered agents that negotiate different interfaces on your behalf. Ray Kurzweil describes something similar: a "personal assistant (PA) that can help with many everyday tasks. This AI-PA will be something you will need to both trust so you will have abundant control over it, and understand the general principles that guide and teach it."

> The user experience might be something like this: "Hi Fred, I would like to experience a detective mystery with my girlfriend tonight."

> Fred would gather options for you to peruse on the basis of your broadest profile recommendations. Once he finds a few good options he might inform you: "Hi, Sherlock5D is either 33 credits or you can offer to share current location and past food preferences." Okay, you go for the share. The next thing you know, while walking out of the door the billboard across the street has changed contextually specifically for you, to a sustainable locust protein-based mango smoothie available for instant delivery.

> Someday, a typical conversation flow might look like this:

> POSTME: "Fred, can you help me review some questions relating to my article?"

> FRED: "Sure, would love to."

> POSTME: "The movie we saw last night—how much does the movie itself know about me?"

> FRED: "I traded your favorite homebrew recipe for health bars, your last five movies watched and your persona-type. And by the way it wasn't the movie, but the

Ava - Ex Machina
Personal Assistant at x.ai
New York, New York | Internet

Current   **x.ai, A24**

Connect   **Send Ava InMail**

Mega-Movies aggregators that owned that one. We've freexpensive-bartered with them before, they are well respected."

POSTME: "I have a question. What if I didn't want to trade information? Has anyone theorized on systems that do not require this exchange?"

FRED: "Yes, many people in the early 21st century believed the privacy of information should be an essential right and that the network should be structured with guarantees for privacy."

POSTME: "What was the counterargument? Why didn't it work?"

FRED: "Freexpensive was invented—it established the rules of engagement with information and the foundations of law relating to AI-PAs management of this."

POSTME: "What was there before the AI-PAs?"

FRED: "Something called iPhone or Android, it was a portable AI-less receptacle of information that effectively acted as an AI-PA. But there were no rules."

POSTME: "Odd. OK, another question, was direct brain implantation an inevitable step in media technology?"

FRED: "Actually direct implantation was and remains an op-
tion although not everyone does this. People who work
closely with AI-PA enhanced operations benefit from it,
but it is complicated."

POSTME: "What do you mean complicated?"

FRED: "A key problem is that the human brain is structured
around specific sensory systems. This has meant that
for humans to be able to undertake useful analysis of
the data from the implant, they have been restricted to
almost the same bandwidth they had without implanta-
tion. At the same time, advances in AI-PAs have been
so fast and controlled-safe that human language has
sufficed for instruction despite its low bandwidth."

POSTME: "I guess the advance in maker-facturing biocom-
patible extensions has also allowed us to continue
evolving detachables that are as good as implants
sometimes."

FRED: "Yes, good point!"[135]

How interesting is that?

The Global Mind: The Holos—Taking everything one step further is the
collective intelligence of all humans combined with the collective behavior of all machines, plus the intelligence of nature, plus whatever behavior
idea of a "global mind," what Kevin Kelly calls "Holos" in *The Inevitable*. He
says some liken it to a global "superorganism" since it includes billions of
manufactured silicon neurons. With holos, he includes the collective intelligence of all humans combined with the collective behavior of all machines, plus the intelligence of nature, plus whatever behavior emerges
from this whole. This whole equals holos.

He goes on to say:

Today there are 4 billion mobile phones and 2 billion com-

puters linked together into a seamless cortex around the
globe. Add to them all the billions of peripheral chips and
affiliated devices from cameras to cars to satellites. Already
in 2016 a grand total of 15 billion devices have been wired
up into one large circuit. Each of these devices contains 1
billion to 4 billion transistors themselves, so in total the holos
operates with a sextillion transistors (10 with 21 zeros). These
transistors can be thought of as the neurons in a vast
brain. The human brain has roughly 86 billion neurons, or a
trillion times fewer than the holos. In terms of magnitude,
the holos already significantly exceeds our brains in com-
plexity. And our brains are not doubling in size every few
years. The holos mind is.[3]

As marketers, if we possessed the collective intelligence of all humans combined with the collective behavior of all machines, plus the intelligence of nature, how exactly would that change our marketing practice? I think you'll agree that this could cover an entire book unto itself. Perhaps Future Marketing: Part 2!

A "cyborg," as envisioned by Thomas Lombardo, director of both the Center for Future Consciousness and The Wisdom Page, is a "functional synthesis of biology and technology." He argues in *The Future of Business* that a wise cyborg, guided by the ideals of wisdom, will draw its extraordinary and potentially limitless power from the "intellectual, informational, and communicational capacities of computer technologies."[4]

Something like this could be the new platform that our lives will run on. It would have a global impact and be functional 24/7/365. One hundred percent of the planet's inhabitants would have access to this platform via an affordable device of some kind. Everyone would be on it. Or, simply, everyone would *be it*. Is it possible? Yes. When could it happen? Difficult to say, but possibly between 2035 and 2050.

The Automated, Digitized, and Simulated Future

Another fascinating future idea with marketing practice implications has come from Gray Scott, author of the chapter "The Automated, Digitized and Simulated Future" in the book, *The Future of Business*.

According to Scott, we are approaching "The Simulated Reality Singularity (TSRS)." He formulated it this way:

Automation of Everything (AOE) + Digitization of Everything (DOE) = The Simulated Reality Singularity (TSRS)

Scott said,

> the TSRS is a state of pure digital reality that is indistinguishable from the reality that we see around us now. Every sensorial experience will be replicated in the TSRS. Our digital avatars will become digitally immortal inside the TSRS. We will also use time dilation, the ability to speed up or slow down time, inside these advanced simulations. This will enable millions of years to pass in a matter of hours. We will be able to reverse the simulation, fast forward or pause it. Eventually, our digitally simulated avatars inside the simulation will become artificially intelligent. Will they ask who their creator is? Will they send probes out into the edges of the simulation? Every innovation we are creating appears to be leading in the direction of the TSRS. From the most current visual effects (VFX) films, research into growing brains on computer chips, to the latest Oculus Rift VR headset, we appear determined to digitize our reality and ourselves.[5]

Simulated Care Assistance Retreats (SCARs)—Or consider, as Gray Scott in *The Future of Business* does, what it might be like to have an industry based on "simulated care assistance retreats" (SCARs). Instead of getting the shots and passports needed to travel to an exotic island halfway around the world, a "digital-cation" could simulate it at a local luxury SCAR. Simulation fanatics might check themselves into SCARs for extended rest and relaxation, and spending time in simulated realities might even become mandatory in the way that Facebook and LinkedIn are necessary business tools today. Major business deals could depend on virtual golf played with avatars of new clients.[6]

So there you go; some of the more ambitious ideas and technologies that could impact the marketing practice at some distant point in the future. Will they happen? Perhaps. No one knows for sure. What we do know is it will no doubt be an interesting ride on the way to seeing some of them become our new reality. Stay tuned!

SECTION 6:
EVOLUTION OF MARKETING FUNDAMENTALS

CHAPTER FOURTEEN

The Future Marketing Mix Construct

A s marketers, we're all familiar with the "4 Ps" of marketing: *Product, Price, Promotion,* and *Place.* Introduced by Jerome McCarthy in 1960, they held strong for over fifty years. And it was a solid construct; it worked. Philip Kotler supported and promoted them in his book, *Principles of Marketing.* The 4 Ps approach helped thousands of companies sell lots of products and services, for decades. Between the 1970s and mid-1990's, large, obedient audiences could be reached with large, efficient media. However, looking back now, it's really a bit surprising that we're even still talking about the 4 Ps, let alone using the idea as a guiding light, seeing how far we've come over the last fifteen years and the massive change in the customer's power and influence.

What's almost shocking to me, as someone who has practiced marketing for over twenty years, is the mindset and quite frankly, level of arrogance that the 4 Ps came from. If you look at those four components a bit closer, you can see they are all *in the context of the company;* they  assume that the company has the pole position in the relationship with the customer. And, of course, companies did. But they shouldn't have! In short, it's "all about us"–*the company.* The "4 Ps" rarely considers the customer at all. What I find crazy is that business schools still teach the 4 Ps! That's where you see the real "reality gap." Ah, a subject for another time and another book.

I think John Janetsch's (*Duct Tape Marketing*) version of the "4 Ps" are a huge step forward and I really like the progress from the original. Janetsch came up with "Passion, Personality, Positioning, and Purpose." Solid effort. And it sure works for today's business environment. But *Future Marketing* is, well, about the *future* and is forward looking. So, I'd like to propose a new marketing framework for the next generation, a construct we can use for 2021 and beyond. Something that truly has the prosumer in the middle, as its emphasis. So, with that in mind, let's first consider the standard definition of marketing:

> *Marketing is the activity, set of institutions, and processes for creating, communicating, delivering, and exchanging offerings that have value for customers, clients, partners, and society at large.*[1]

Here is mine:

> *Marketing is the act of genuinely connecting with people who are interested in what you are doing (and them connecting with you) so that together, you can positively impact people's lives with a product, service and/or platform experience.*

Let's not forget there have been other constructions of the marketing mix. There are the 4 Cs (consumer wants and needs, convenience, cost, and communication), designed to put the consumer in a more central position in the marketing constellation, which I think is great. As well, there are the 7 Ps (the original 4 Ps plus people, process, and physical evidence). And these are but a few of the alternate constructions of the marketing mix.

But again, these aren't ideal for the years 2021–2030 and beyond for all the reasons I've mentioned in the previous chapters. Primarily, they aren't ideal because future marketing strategy, the construct of "the company," the age of the prosumer, and the new marketing tactics we'll have (like augmented reality content experiences) all *beg* for a new construct.

EP^2—the New Marketing Mix Construct

In *Future Marketing*, for the very first time, I'm introducing my own marketing mix construct: **EP^2**. This construct is the result of spending hundreds of hours poring over research, in books and articles, taking in all the latest data, industry studies, and marketing thought leaders' ideas. But mostly, it's the result of serving over five hundred clients since 2003 with a wide range of marketing services with my company, Content Launch. It's the outcome of hundreds of conversations, thousands of emails, and lots of one-on-one conversations. It's been my time in the marketing arena" that informs the in-vention of EP^2. Here it is:

- Engagement
- Experiences
- Personalization
- Passion

Engagement

This is where you meet your audience, how you connect with them. Is it online or at an event? On Facebook or your blog? In the future, it may be in an augmented reality email experience or a virtual reality ad. "Engagement" is where "the platform" is found. Remember how I discussed the transition from brands to platforms?

A popular current definition of engagement in marketing is "directly engages consumers and invites and encourages them to participate in the evolution of a brand." What I like about this is the word "participate." This is key. But it goes both ways. Your prosumer customers should encourage you to participate in what they are doing too, especially if they have their own audience. And this very fact is what's missing in so many marketing articles and books. It's a two-way street, folks! In today's hyper-connected world, you will have customers with larger social media followings than you have as a company. Engagement is how you navigate the relationship; more specifically, it's where you navigate the relationship—the *two-way* relationship.

And engagement also includes *getting them to do more for you*; to lean on that prosumer quality inside them. Suppose you were part of a user-generated and crowdsourced network of ads, built on a peer-to-peer system in which the ads were designed and written by the users themselves. According to Kevin Kelly they might even determine which ads they wanted you to show them on your site. If they produced clicks and click-through, wouldn't you want them, and want to keep and share them? So some don't perform well: drop them! What do you have to lose? In this scenario, your customers are essentially ad agencies made up of unpaid evangelists for your products and services. To their way of thinking, they're only improving substandard ads, and no one would imagine themselves to be better informed about your product than its biggest fans.[2]

Engaging Your Audience on Social Media—We all know that engaging our audience on social media is always a good thing to do. In the future, it will be even more important. Consider Facebook. Daina Middleton estimates that in just one minute users of the social network send 230,000 message, post 95,000 status updates, post 80,000 items on their walls, tag 65,000 photos, share 50,000 links, and make half a million comments: "Each participant," she writes,

> has an average of 130 friends. There are more than 900 million objects with which participants interact: pages, groups, events, and community pages, to name a few. The average participant interacts with 80 community pages, groups, and events. Participants create 90 pieces of content each month and share more than 30 billion pieces of this content, which includes Web links, news stories, blog

posts, notes, and photo albums. And they install 20 million applications every day.

Facebook's members are already filling the prosumer role, translating the site for others and building apps and programs on the company's platform.[3]

Retailers such as Walmart and Target aggressively use Facebook to evaluate new products. Facebook is also providing tools that enable companies to see a wide range of analytics. For example, Facebook can help all brands measure the second level of impact of brand fan pages— meaning what happens beyond the "like." Continuing to tap into the marketing power of Facebook and all of the other social networks (and your followers on these networks) will greatly enrich your marketing success in the Prosumer Age.

Activating Participation/Engagement—So we can all agree on the following: *networks and relationships matter more than any marketing message.* Digest that for a minute. Traditional marketers still stuck in the old paradigm of pushing messages on people really, really don't like this idea. But it *is* reality. And, in the future, it will continue to be—even more so, actually. Driven by your prosumers, your participants, thought leaders, influential bloggers— whatever you want to call them—you need to engage them, if you want to survive and thrive in the future.

In her book, *Marketing in the Participation Age,* Middleton says,

> *The transformation is fundamental, and because the behavior change requires that brands and marketing professionals conscientiously embrace a new mind-set and actions, I advocate starting with a language change. Words are an important first step in changing behavior. In this case, renam-*

*ing consumers participants [perhaps Prosumers?] sparks a
consciousness in marketers' minds that is instrumental in the
new landscape—and it helps pave the way toward changing
the processes and tools we use every day.*

She goes on to say,

> In an effort to survive in today's complicated media environ-
> ment— many marketers are resorting to a defensive marketing
> approach. They still use the old linear marketing tools, formu-
> las, and philosophies designed to persuade consumer opinions
> rather than invite them to participate in a relationship. These
> tools are perceived as good because they are thought to be
> controlled by the marketer, and they feel safe. And they were
> not designed to create and sustain reciprocal customer rela-
> tionships in a marketplace driven by the participant where net-
> works and relationships matter more than the message. Mar-
> keters are masters at persuasive message development, not at
> activating participation or engagement."[4]

In the future, my friend, we absolutely need to become masters of activating participation and engagement. We need to recognize our prosumer
customers and bring them into the tent, in every way possible.

Experiences

We don't buy products or services now and we won't in the future either. We buy *experiences, feelings, validation* and *emotions*
now. Don't ask "what should we sell?" or "how should we sell it?" Ask
"*why* should we sell it?"

Southwest Airlines sells fun, friendly transportation. Legoland, Sea
World, and Disney World sell happiness. Apple sells a lifestyle and a challenge to the status quo. That's *why* people buy from them, even though

the *buying* should not be the focal point. The *relationship* should be. And that's where Personalization comes into play. More on that in a bit.

One other comment about Apple: They appeal to Millennials, in particular, because the brand is about more than just its products—it's about *being part of something*. Apple has done a phenomenal job of presenting itself as more of a lifestyle than just a technology provider. You don't merely own an iPhone, you are an iPhone *type of person*. Apple's success in this sphere has launched full scale rivalries between iPhones and their alternative smartphone counterparts, with Apple's devotees showing unquestioning loyalty to the brand and whatever new tech toy the company has most recently released.[5] Apple *is* an experience, unto itself.

And remember, with experiences, you'll need to make them specific and tailored to the right group. As I mentioned earlier, audiences are now *niche*, they have splintered into many subset pieces over the past fifteen years. There is no mass audience anymore. The new ecosystem is thousands of unstructured one-to-one and peer-to-peer conversations.

Creating Experiences for Our Personal Hologram/Robot—Tiana Sinclair in *The Future of Business* observes that when Edward Snowden showed up at TED 2014 via telepresence robot, he could see the room through a camera and actually respond to the host and attendees in real time.

Might empty seats at events be filled with "fully functioning personalized robots, drones and holograms?" If so, would the robots be able to exchange information and contacts with one another and report to us about what they "experience"?[6] By 2030, I see this scenario as very possible.

Experiences Always Have Value and Aren't a Commodity—Among Kevin Kelly's observations in *The Inevitable* is that human experience will remain the most valuable aspect of our lives, even as the value of things falls in the age of abundance. Experiences can't be copied, he writes, unlike the other things in life, which can become filtered and commoditized. "The value of experience is rising," Kelly writes.

> *Luxury entertainment is increasing 6.5 percent annually. Spending at restaurants and bars increased 9 percent*

in 2015 alone. The price of the average concert ticket has increased by nearly 400 percent from 1981 to 2012. Personal coaches are among the fastest growing occupations. In hospice care, the cost of drugs and treatments is in decline, but the cost of home visits— experiential— is rising.

The cost is rising because coaching and visiting are experiences—and if you can create experiences, the attention they get is worth a lot. Those who worry about robots taking jobs away should consider the thing that can't be made virtual—experiences. Kelly says, "That's where we'll spend our money and that's where we'll make our money. We'll use technology to produce commodities, and we'll make experiences in order to avoid becoming a commodity ourselves."[7] Experiences represent a new type of economic output. Providing new experiences for our customers opens up possibilities for extraordinary economic expansion—just as recognizing services as a distinct offering led to new revenue when our industrial base started declining thirty years ago. It's clear that a new base is emerging. Mass customizing automatically turns goods into services and services into experiences. Providing experiences for our customers also demands new models for work. At every level in any company, all employees need to understand that when they're providing experiences for their customers, every business becomes a "stage," and therefore our work becomes "theatre."

Personalization

Human beings are self-serving creatures; let's get that out of the way from the outset. We all love to hear our own names. We all love it when we feel someone unconditionally validate us. It's all about us, and it always has been! So, it's critical in the era of the social Web and sharing economy for marketers to ensure they're personalizing experiences everywhere: in the online world, in the "offline" or physical world, and everywhere in between.

Amazon clearly led the way with personalization many years ago, and if you're looking for inspiration on how to personalize the online experience, just log in to your Amazon account and take it all in. In the future, we'll still be human beings with feelings, emotions, desires and fragile egos. Making things personal will always be right. And if you're concerned about how to get the "personalization thing" done, never fear: big data will help big time with this one.

Alexandra Whittington in *The Future of Business* noted, "micro-personalization" is becoming possible with improved forms of AI such as machine learning, and speech and gesture recognition. In the future, "interfaces will be obsessed with meeting [our] individual needs." By 2020, futurists such as John Smart and Google's Ray Kurzweil say, AI could create "digital twins" or "Cybernetic Friends" that reflect our individual attitudes and ways of speaking, and that could even "hold conversations and have faces."[8]

Personalizing Experiences—Experiences are not the final offering your company can market and provide. You can also offer personalization *of the experiences you offer*. When you personalize an experience to tailor it for one specific customer, you not only have the chance to create a customer for life, but a chance to change that individual in a very big way. When you customize an experience, you automatically turn it into a *personal transformation*, which your company can create on top of the experience just as you would create an experience on top of a service.

Personalized Generative Services—Kevin Kelly struck future gold again in his book, *The Inevitable*, where he discussed the idea of "generative" services. He says, "a generative value is a quality or attribute that must be generated at the time of the transaction. A generative thing cannot be copied, cloned, stored, and warehoused. A generative cannot be faked or replicated. It is generated uniquely, for that particular exchange, in real time. Generative qualities add value to free copies and therefore are something that can be sold." He then offers up four specific generatives that are "better than free":

The first generative is **Personalization:** With this one he says, "you are then not paying for the copy of the concert; you are paying for the generative personalization. A free copy of a book can be custom edited by the publishers to reflect your own previous reading background. A free movie you buy may be cut to reflect the rating you desire for family viewing. In both of these examples, you get the copy free and pay for personalization. Personalization requires an ongoing conversation between the creator and consumer." It is deeply generative because it is iterative and time-consuming, which means there is a heavy "stickiness" factor.

The second generative is **Interpretation**: Kelly says, "when a copy of your sequence costs nothing, the interpretation of what it means, what you can do about it, and how to use it— the manual for your genes, so to speak— will be expensive. This generative can be applied to many other complex services, such as travel and health care."

The third generative is **Embodiment**: Kelly says, "a theater is more likely to be the first to offer laser projection, holographic display or the holodeck itself. And nothing gets embodied as much as music in a live performance, with real bodies. In this accounting, the music is free, the bodily performance costs something. The book is free; the bodily talk is expensive. Live concert tours, live TED talks, live radio shows, pop-up food tours all speak to the power and value of a paid ephemeral embodiment of something you could download for free."

The fourth generative is **Discoverability**: Kelly says, "when there are millions of books, songs, films, applications and more requesting our attention— and most of it free— *being found* is valuable. And given the exploding numbers of works created each day, being found is increasingly unlikely." In the future, people will pay for discoverability.

Kelly mentions four other generatives: Immediacy, Patronage, Authenticity and Accessibility. They don't apply as much to our discussion here on personalization, but I encourage you to pick up a copy of *The Inevitable* to find out more about them.

The message with generative services is two-fold: First, it creates a massive opportunity for new marketing programs and new revenue. Second, these eight qualities require a new skill set for creators. Success no longer derives from mastering distribution.[9]

Kelly ultimately observes that "the modern economy runs on *distinction and the power of differences,*" qualities that filters and other tech can accentuate. The essence of who we are, our personality, can be sharpened by mass filtering. As new things develop, more filtering will be part of them, and those new things will be more and more like ourselves.[10]

Passion

Increasingly, we are seeing a new and more powerful approach—evangelism. In terms of marketing, I mean creating a mission and brand experience that are so inspiring to consumers that they engage with you—and share their enthusiasm with others., transforming them into prosumers. What makes evangelism so powerful today is how it marries the oldest form of persuasion—word of mouth—and the newest—social networking and Web 2.0.

Marketing in a fragmented, multichannel world needs a powerful heart. The key ingredients are emotion and passion. As a marketing leader of the future, you must know how to find the energy and passion in what you are selling. If you can't, you probably will need to find something else to do.

Communicate Your Passion Through Storytelling and Narrative—Businesses can make their outlook more customer-centric by considering "people, planet, and purpose alongside profit," Anne Lise Kjaer in *The Future of Business* observes. To communicate their brand and their corporate passion, firms will need to both tell their stories and give people what they need: "A Stanford study found that storytelling is up to twenty-two times more memorable than facts alone." So companies need to imagine who their future customers are, and what their values and needs are, if they are to tell those stories.[11] And don't forget about the power of the narrative, discussed earlier.

Leading with Passion Can Drive Exponential Thinking & Improvement—
Passion is a key to leadership. Communicating a company's passion can
improve your organization exponentially. Today, this is being demon-

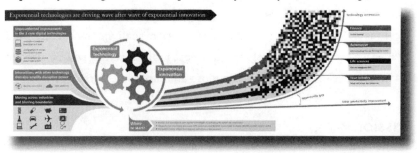

strated by more and more companies who have "the passion thing" and
are improving their organizations' performance by 100 percent or more.

Performance Improvements from Exponential Thinking—Rohit Talwar
points out that here are just a few companies who have shown dramatic
performance improvement by putting thinking like this into action in both
face-to-face and virtual transactions:

- Airbnb (Hotels)—ninety times more listings per employee
- GitHub (Software)—109 times more listings per employee
- Local Motors (Automotive)—1000 times cheaper to develop a new
  car model, and five to twenty-two times faster to manufacture an
  individual car
- Quirky (Consumer Goods)—ten times faster product development
  (29 vs. 300 days)
- Google Ventures (Investments)—2.5 times more investments in
  early stage start-ups and ten times faster through design process
- Valve (Gaming)—thirty times more market cap per employee
- Tesla (Automotive)—thirty times more market cap per employee
- Tangerine (Banking)—seven times more customers per employee
  and four times more deposits per customer[12]

The All-Important Relationship—All four components of EP^2 have one thing in common: they all are about *the relationship* with people (whether they are prosumers, traditional customers, partners, suppliers or others). I hope you find it helpful as you plan your marketing programs over the next several years.

CHAPTER FIFTEEN

The Future Marketing Department

Today's typical marketing department at a mid- to large-sized enterprise comprises all the expected roles and responsibilities. Although the activities that marketers have needed to engage in to connect with customers have changed significantly in the past few years, the CMO, the marketing managers, the brand managers, and the marketing research person are all still in place, just as they were ten years ago. In most companies, the organizational structure of the marketing function hasn't changed since the practice of brand management emerged, more than forty years ago. That has to change.

Now and in the future, marketing leaders should ask the big questions. The first one is, *why?* Other questions include:

- Why do we do what we do and does it mean anything to our customers?
- What values and goals best align us to our customers?
- What capabilities do we have that can help us transition part of the brand experience to a platform experience?
- And what structures and ways of working will support all of this?"

To understand what separates the strategies and structures of superior marketing organizations from the rest, EffectiveBrands (now Millward Brown Vermeer)—in partnership with the Association of National Advertisers, the World Federation of Advertisers, Spencer Stuart, Forbes, MetrixLab, and Adobe—initiated Marketing2020, which is the most comprehensive marketing leadership study ever undertaken. The study has included in-depth qualitative interviews with more than 350 CEOs, CMOs, and agency heads, as well as over a dozen CMO roundtables in cities worldwide. They conducted online quantitative surveys of 10,000-plus marketers from ninety-two countries. The surveys encompassed more than eighty questions focusing on marketers' data analytics capabilities, brand strategy, cross-functional and global interactions, and employee training.[1]

Some of what they found was a given: Companies that are sophisticated in their use of data grow faster, for instance. Nevertheless, the research shed new light  on the constellation of attributes required for superior marketing performance and on the nature of the organizations that achieve it. It's clear that "marketing" is no longer a discrete entity but now extends throughout the organization, tapping virtually every function. And while the titles, roles, and responsibilities of marketing leaders vary widely among companies and industries, the challenges they face—and what they must do to succeed—are very similar. I encourage you to read the Marketing 2020 report.

Problem: Good Planning Is Rarely Practiced

One of the key issues with most marketing departments today, however, is that sound strategic planning is *rarely practiced*. And that goes for the entire organization as well. As we progress over the next fifteen years, especially as the world is changing so dramatically, it will become critical. Planning will need to get much better. And, quite honestly, this is one of the key reasons I wrote *Future Marketing*. I really want this book to be used as a guide to help plan for the future. Let's face it: most people are preoccupied with their current work and have difficulty finding time for strategic thinking. When they do, there is often uncertainty about how to approach such a huge challenge, especially when there is so much unknown ahead of us. Throw in the fact that some C-suite executives don't really understand the benefits of strategic visions and goals, the value of forecasting, and how to involve the organization. Most CMOs and CEOs focus on near-term goals, ignoring the pivotal and tectonic cultural and technological changes surrounding them on all sides. And this is the key: *Those companies who can really embrace long-term strategic marketing planning will be the ones that survive and thrive and make it to 2030.* Keep this book by your side!

Problem: The Diminishment of the Brand

I won't repeat myself here, but we all know that the corporation no longer truly controls the brand. In the twentieth century, brands and marketing were completely shaped and assisted by the mass media, as it was media that allowed marketers to create branding through it. Brands had total control and we lived in a "push" marketing environment. Just push your brand on the consumer and they would buy it.

But of course, with Web 2.0 and the social media revolution, the institutional power of brands started losing their stronghold, and very quickly. That institutional authority has now become personal authority, where everyone trusts their friends buying decisions far more than any company.

So then, here is the key: Over the next several years, brands need to get personal and speak to that individuality. They need to bring customers in and accept their help. Brands need to provide experiences, not just products and services. They need to show their passion and authenticity. "Devoted" is not an aspirational word, it is a word about personal commitment. Successful brands in 2021 and 2030 will be the brands that gain personal, devotional commitment. And if that happens, the brand will not be diminished, it will be empowered. And it will take on a new definition in the Prosumer Age.

Traits of a Successful Marketing Team

As managers, we need to shift our thinking from command
and control to coordinate and cultivate—the best way to
gain power is sometimes to give it away.
—Thomas W. Malone, *The Future of Work*

Some of the traits of high-performing marketing teams, as well as specific drivers of organizational effectiveness are obvious, others are not. The characteristics of a winning team in the future will be even more complicated. Leading marketing organizations are most likely character-ized by collaboration and solving customer problems with cross-function-al, multidisciplinary teams. But let's take a deeper dive.

What exactly are the shared principles of high performers' marketing approaches? There are nine findings from the Marketing 2020 study that I felt were relevant for our discussion in *Future Marketing.* All of these find-ings from the study help show the way for organizations, especially larger companies that are trying to best set up their teams now for future success.

1. Utilizing the Power of Big Data—Marketers have massive amounts of customer data now, and most are finding ways to use that information to improve the targeting of messages. Knowing what an individual consum-er is doing where and when is now possible. High performers are distin-guished by their ability to integrate data on what consumers are doing with knowledge of why they're doing it, which yields new insights into con-sumers' needs and how to best meet them.

2. Positioning that Connects with Purpose—Top marketers succeed at de-livering on their brand's purpose and connect with their customers on ev-ery level: functional benefits, emotional benefits, and societal benefits. In addition to engaging customers, a powerful brand purpose improves alignment throughout the organization and ensures consistent messag-ing across touch points.

3. Ensuring a "Total Experience"–Companies are increasingly enhancing the value of their products by creating customer experiences. Some deepen the customer relationship by leveraging what they know about a given customer to personalize offerings. Others focus on the breadth of the relationship by adding touch points. High-performing brands do both–providing the "total experience." And of course, the concept of "share of experience" will be a huge game changer in terms of marketing metrics to look at in the future.

In *The Experience Economy*, B. Joseph Pine II and James Gilmore argue that that B2C firms aren't the only ones focusing on the "total" experience. Business-to-business marketers more and more are turning ordinary venues into elaborate experiences in order to make their pitch. Plain conference rooms become "executive briefing centers"– and even more. "TST, Inc., an engineering firm in Fort Collins, Colorado, ... gutted its office to create the TST Engineerium, a place for staff to host 'visioneering experiences' for its land development customers," Pine and Gilmore report. Another company, Autodesk, curates a showcase of ways in which its clients are using its technology to produce interesting and new designs. In Wisconsin, a construction equipment manufacturer allows customers to "play" with its bulldozers, backhoes, and cherry pickers in a giant sandbox during the process of selling to them.[2]

4. Marketing is Everyone's Job Now–Marketing has become more important than ever before. As a result, marketing teams really need support from all other company departments. To deliver a seamless experience, one informed by data and imbued with brand purpose, all employees in the company, from store clerks and phone center reps to IT specialists, and the marketing team itself, must share a common vision.

There are now five drivers of organizational effectiveness. The leaders of high-performing companies connect marketing to the business strategy and to the rest of the organization; inspire their organizations by engaging all levels with the brand purpose; focus their people on a few key priorities; organize agile, cross-functional teams; and build the internal capabilities needed for success.

5. Avoiding Landmines and Getting Buy-In—Many companies suffer from dysfunctional teamwork, suboptimal collaboration, and lack of shared purpose and trust. Despite a variety of obstacles, high-performing marketers typically avoid such issues. Their leaders excel at linking their departments to general management and other functions. They ensure a solid relationship with the C-suite, making certain that marketing goals support company goals, bridge organizational silos by integrating marketing and other disciplines, and ensure that global, regional, and local marketing teams work interdependently.

Today, high-performing marketing leaders don't just align their departments' activities with company strategy; they actively engage in creating it. And when marketing demonstrates that it is fighting for the same business objectives as its peers, trust and communication strengthen across all functions and enable the collaboration required for high performance.

6. Inspiring Everyone to Rally Around the Brand—Inspiration is one of the most underused drivers of effective marketing—and one of the most powerful. High-performing marketers are more likely to engage customers and employees with their brand purpose, and employees in these types of organizations are more likely to express pride in the brand.

Inspiration strengthens commitment, of course, but when it's rooted in a respected brand purpose, all employees will be motivated by the same mission. This enhances collaboration and, as more employees come into contact with customers, also helps ensure consistent customer experiences. The payoff is that everyone in the company becomes a de facto member of the marketing team. The key to inspiring the organization is to do internally what marketing does best externally: create irresistible messages and programs that get everyone on board.

A Brand Is a Participant: Daina Middleton, author of *Marketing in the Participation Age*, helped to redefine what the brand has become and will continue to be in the Prosumer Age. And I think it applies to both employees in the marketing department as well as the customers we serve. She said,

Connection, in a broader sociological construct, helps moderate autonomy, encourages symmetry, and balances our individual viewpoint. We can apply this to a brand perspective as well. The connect principle acts as perspective and a reminder that the brand itself must also act accordingly to participant rules. The product, service, or brand is not the center of the universe. It is a brand's responsibility to genuinely accept responsibility for other participants' well-being. They cannot just claim to do this, but must demonstrate it so as to balance the brand-centric point of view.[3]

7. Organizing the Marketing Team to React Quickly—Organizational structure, roles, and processes are among the toughest leadership challenges in companies—and the need for clarity about them is consistently underestimated or even ignored. There is a set of operational and design principles that any organization can apply. Today, marketing organizations must leverage global scale but also be nimble, able to plan and execute in a matter of weeks or even on the spot. How do you do it? Organize and empower the marketing team to create a "mission control" room during important times and authorize them to engage with their audience in real time.

Complex organizational structures are giving way to networked organizations characterized by flexible roles, fluid responsibilities, and more-relaxed sign-off processes designed for speed. The new structures allow leaders to tap talent as needed from across the organization and assemble teams for specific, often short-term, marketing initiatives. The teams may form, execute, and disband in a matter of weeks or months, depending on the task.

8. Including Marketing Specialists on Your Team—Marketing organizations traditionally have been populated by generalists, but with the rise of social and digital marketing, lots of new specialist roles—such as digital privacy analysts and native-content editors—are emerging. It's best to categorize marketing roles not by title but as belonging to one of three broad types: "think" marketers, who apply analytic capabilities to tasks like data mining, media-mix modeling, and ROI optimization; "do" marketers, who develop content and design and lead production; and "feel" marketers, who focus on consumer interaction and engagement in roles from customer service to social media and online communities.

In *Entering the Shift Age,* futurist David Houle observes the recent recognition by organizations that creativity is a valuable skillset and mindset to encourage, and are qualities becoming more important in our society. First, when properly aligned with innovation and design work, it makes measurable differences in revenue and profits. Second, companies are recognizing the transformative fact that many creative personalities are introverts—they can "go inward and come out with something totally unique and magical." Maybe it's finally the time for introverts to shine. Susan Cain's epic 2012 book, *Quiet: The Power of Introverts in a World That Can't Stop Talking* ..., helped usher this new appreciation into the mainstream.

This shift from valuing left-brain, logical thinking to right-brain, creative thinking means that we now have to apply what we've learned from science to creativity. Creativity is and will be the top quality corporations seek in the Prosumer Age. Once again, we can look to Steve Jobs as an example. "Jobs was not an engineer or a finance type," Houle writes. "He was a designer, a very creative and demanding visionary":

> Creativity is needed to look at things in new ways, to "think outside the box," to find new paradigms, and to create new designs, forms, systems, businesses, and products. Almost every area of human endeavor is now facing the need to have creative thinking and ideas to help create new solutions to old problems that linger and to work on the new problems emerging. We have an urgent need to think differently as humanity.

In other words, Houle says, as we move toward 2021 and 2030, we're moving from a left-brain century to a right-brain century.[4]

Big-Picture Thinking, Visionary People—The future of marketing will need more big-picture-thinking visionaries on the team—the kind of people who would read this book, for example, and find it to be one of their most important finds. I wrote *Future Marketing*, in fact, for these folks—the ones who dream big and are not afraid of what's coming, those who feel optimistic about the future and what it will bring. I didn't really write it for the detail-oriented people out there. I certainly hope they read it, but they might not quite "get it" as readily. That's OK.

So, it's that *cognitive ability* of pattern recognition, the 'big picture' thinking that enables certain types of people to see meaningful trends from a lot of noise and information around them and to think about it strategically far into the future, to start putting the pieces together and determine their company's place in it.

Daniel Pink, exploring the ascendance of right-brain thinking in the new era, cites the example of the late multimillionaire CEO Sidney Harman. Harman's approach was not to hire a lot of MBAs. "Get me some poets as managers," Harman said. He considered poets to be the original "systems thinkers," people who thought about the world in depth, interpreted it, and expressed it in ways that helped readers see what made it tick. Pink argues that poets could well be "our true digital thinkers," and a potential source for important business leadership in the future.[5]

9. Building the Networked Organization—A broad array of skills and organizational tiers and functions are represented within each category. CMOs and other marketing executives such as chief experience officers and global brand managers increasingly operate as the orchestrators, assembling cross-functional teams from these three classes of talent to tackle initiatives. Orchestrators brief the teams, ensure that they have the capabilities and resources they need, and oversee performance tracking. To populate a team, the orchestrator and team leader draw from marketing and other functions as well as from outside agencies and consulting firms, balancing the mix of think, do, and feel capabilities in accordance with the team's mission.

More on Creativity

Larry Thompson

Larry Thompson, the visionary President of Ringling College of Art & Design, sees that creativity is central to the future of the workplace and of the marketing practice. Speaking about the United States, he said,

> *When I see our country's stagnation and economic woes, I cannot help but think that we need a creative revolution that is embraced by business and endorsed by government and educators alike. We creatively reinvented ourselves as we moved from the agricultural age to the industrial age and again as we moved from the industrial age to the knowledge age. We must take action now and re-imagine ourselves so that we are prepared for the upcoming age forming now.*

Thompson went on to say,

> *Traditional thinking is not working. I contend that cre-*
> *ative and innovative thinking is one of the most if not the*
> *most critical success factors needed for employees and*
> *businesses to succeed in the twenty-first century. Need*
> *evidence? According to a 2010 IBM study of 1,500 global*
> *CEOs, the most desired skill for leaders of the future is*
> *creativity.*
>
> *There has probably never been a better time to be*
> *an artist or designer than in today's economy. Indeed, if a*
> *business is to thrive in our future economy, art and design*
> *will play a critical role if not* the *critical role— in the future*
> *of commerce. I want to see an artist or designer have a*
> *seat at every board of directors' table in America. That*
> *would be refreshing. That would definitely change the*
> *game and fuel our economic future.*[6]

This is profound, I think. And I am in total agreement with Thompson. I want to thank David Houle, author of *Entering the Shift Age* for sharing this excerpt. I felt it was a perfect fit for what I'm espousing in *Future Marketing.* As a creative person myself (I'm a part-time pop songwriter), as well as a CEO and entrepreneur, I come at it from a unique place. Not all people are creative. Not all creative people are CEOs. Because I am both—and I know many others like myself—I can speak from true experience: the creative gene is in big demand and will continue to be over the next fifteen years. Of course, as young children, we all are in touch with our creative sides. The Digital Native Generation will be the ones who will help us the most with the need for creativity in business, as their parents no doubt have embraced the creative qualities they've seen in their children. As such, they are probably the most creative generation we've ever had. Help is on the way!

Cultural Creatives–The term "cultural creatives" was coined in 2000 by Paul Ray and Sherry Ruth Anderson as the label for some 50 million Americans–those who demand not just knowledge but understanding. Their skill lies in putting things together in new ways, and they value qualities traditionally associated with women, such as empathy and sympathy, seeing through another person's eyes, and putting a premium on first-person experience and storytelling. Their ethic is one of caring.

Daniel Pink, author of *A Whole New Mind*, turned me on to *The Cultural Creatives* and says, "we must become proficient in R-Directed (Right Brain) thinking and must perform work that overseas knowledge workers can't do cheaper, that computers can't do faster, and that satisfies the aesthetic, emotional, and spiritual demands of a prosperous time." That work, is largely creative in nature. Pink goes on to say, "we need six specific high-concept and high-touch aptitudes that have become essential in this new era. He calls these aptitudes "the six senses." They are: Design. Story. Symphony. Empathy. Play. Meaning.[7] Creativity is a part of all of them. To find out more about these six senses, I encourage you to take a look at *A Whole New Mind*; it's an incredible read.

Competing in a Connected Economy–It seems most industries are imitating technology and professional services now as the economy becomes more connected.[8] A perfect example is Nike, a provider of athletic apparel, and now a provider of athletic advice, given that it has appended its physical products with digital services. Seizing opportunities from a connected economy makes organizations even more reliant on the cross-functional, multidisciplinary team, characterized by agility, rapid decision-making and a penchant for taking risks. Cross-discipline teams are also required to deliver today's multifaceted customer experience solutions, which are powered by the creative use of art, science and technology.

More Organizational Changes for the Future

Most corporate marketers know that their organizations need a reboot, and as a result, many marketing executives are reevaluating their organizational charts. But these CMOs and marketing directors aren't sure *how* to set up the new chart exactly, especially when so much is changing so quickly. What should the ideal structure look like? How do the best marketing teams operate? Here are some ideas.

Leadership Networks and Agility—The need to manage faster and with greater agility in harnessing technology for business advantage has given rise to an organizational concept known as "leadership cells," which collectively form leadership networks. This thinking stems from the argument that cross-discipline teams, closest to the problem or opportunity (with the most relevant experience) are best equipped to address it. Such cells, composed of one or two people or as many as seven or eight, form around specific tasks, ideas or opportunities.

Marketers Adopt Lessons from the U.S. Navy SEALs—The concept of leadership cells originated from the U.S. military, the most dramatic example being the U.S. Navy SEALs: highly trained, cross-functional, cross-discipline teams empowered to make rapid decisions—even changing strategies on the fly once they've assessed a situation. When such teams form, two leadership types tend to emerge: the task leader, who is good at getting things done, and the social leader, who is good at using diplomacy and social connections to help crush the issues that get in the way of getting things done.

Create a Customer-Engagement Council—I've mentioned how important it is for future marketers to get closer to customers. An ongoing forum for focusing attention on customer engagement is sometimes the best idea. This doesn't have to be yet another marketing committee. In fact, your customer-engagement council[9] may already exist under another name, such as the strategic-planning or brand council. The purpose is to bring together all primary forms of engagement—marketing, communications, service, sales, product management, and so on—to coordinate tactics across touch points in a more timely manner.

This council, which should be an operational and decision-making body, must translate the findings of customer surveys and interactions into specific actions at individual touch points. To accomplish this goal, the council's membership needs to be large enough to ensure that all key players are represented but small enough to make decisions efficiently. A key consideration involves inputs and support: the council must make fact-based decisions, so it needs information on everything from priority touch points to customer behavior and the moves of competitors.

Finally, such a council must have a customer-engagement charter. To reduce the risk of gaps, rework, and turf wars, everyone in the organization needs clarity about decision rights over touch points and the key processes that affect them. When conceived, constructed, and operated correctly, these customer engagement councils play a critical role in breaking the "silo" mindset that diminishes the effectiveness of customer engagement in many organizations. Such a council often serves as a mediator and decision-maker in conflicts between functions and business units and as a filter for what must be elevated to the level of the CEO or other senior leaders.

Establish a "Chief Content Officer" Role—A decade ago, when the extent of the digital revolution—the massive proliferation of media and devices and the empowerment of consumers via social networks and other channels—became clear, many companies quickly appointed "digital officers" to oversee these emerging touch points.

It's now evident that the challenge is not just understanding digital channels but also coping with the volume, nature, and velocity of the content needed to use them effectively. Companies need to create a supply chain of increasingly sophisticated and interactive content to feed consumer demand for information and engagement, not to mention a mechanism for managing the content your prosumers themselves generate.

The emergence of companies-as-publishers demands the appointment of a chief content officer (CCO). Companies across industries—from luxury goods to retailing, financial services, automotive, and even professional sports—are creating versions of this role. All are adopting a journalistic approach to recognize hot issues and shaping emerging sentiment by delivering compelling content that forges stronger emotional bonds with their target audience, whether B2B or B2C.

The CCO role is designed to provide the on-brand, topical, and provocative content needed to engage customers. The CCO must develop and manage all aspects of the supply chain for content, ranging from deciding where and how it's sourced to overseeing the external agencies and in-house creative talent generating it. Companies shouldn't forget that even with a CCO in place, designing and executing a content strategy still requires coordination with several key business areas.

The Coming of the CExO—I've talked a lot about how customer experiences will become so important in the future. Joyce Gioia in *The Future of Business* suggests appointing a Chief Experience Officer (CExO). Although many tech companies presently have someone with the title of Chief Experience Officer, it tends to be someone who deals purely with external marketing, sales, and customer experience. The new CExO would report directly to the CEO, and would be responsible for the experiences of all stakeholders—including employees, investors, and vendors.[10]

Create a "Listening Center"—Engagement is a conversation, yet companies are increasingly excluded from many of the most important discussions that happen out there on social sites and blogs with their customers, prosumers and others. More social and other media are available to mobilize your fans and opponents than ever before, and any interaction between a customer and your company could be the match that starts a viral fire. In this environment, companies should establish *listening centers* that monitor what is being said about their organizations, products, and services on social media, blogs, and other online forums.

Such monitoring should be hardwired into the business to shorten response times during real and potential crises, complement internal metrics and traditional tracking research on brand performance, feed consumer feedback into the product-development process, and serve as a platform for testing customer reactions. A listening center will be required in the future. And don't forget to have them listen to you, too; it's a two-way street.

What Drives Innovation?

Having an innovative approach will be critical in your future marketing work. There are four major motivators that drive innovation. The first, is curiosity: the desire to find out why, to open the black box, to see around the next bend. Curiosity fuels much of science, but it's nothing compared to fear, our next motivator. Extraordinary fear enables extraordinary risk-taking. The desire to create wealth is the next major motivator. The fourth and final motivator is the desire for significance: the need for one's life to matter, the need to make a difference in the world.

Peter Diamandis, co-author of *Abundance* and Chairman and CEO of the X PRIZE Foundation, explains that one tool to harness all four of these motivators is *the incentive prize*. He says,

> If you need to accelerate change in specific areas, espe-
> cially when the goals are clear and measurable, incentive
> competitions have a biological advantage. Humans are
> wired to compete. We're wired to hit hard targets. Incentive
> prizes are a proven way to entice the smartest people in the
> world, no matter where they live or where they're employed,
> to work on your particular problem. As Raymond Orteig
> discovered in the early portion of the last century, such com-
> petitions can change the world.[11]

So how about creating an incentive prize within your company or within your marketing department? You could have startling results.

Now that you have some ideas on how your marketing department can evolve and improve, let's wrap up and look at a few companies that are charting our way to the future!

CONCLUSIONS

CHAPTER SIXTEEN

Companies Showing the Way Now

L uckily for us, there are countless organizations showing the way to the future of marketing. And they aren't just companies. They are not-for-profits, peer-to-peer groups, local community organizations, and more. There are plenty of individuals showing the way too: entrepreneurs, thought leaders, prosumers, smart college kids, and of course, the futurists and other forward-thinking folks.

Steve Case says what these companies are practicing are "the three P's: partnership, policy and perseverance." And, he says, their attitude could be characterized by an old African proverb: "If you want to go quickly, go alone. If you want to go far, go together."[1] As you'll see, they always go together.

The Story of Threadless

One company that stood out to me as I was researching *Future Marketing* was Threadless, out of Chicago.[2] Not only do these guys "get it," but they've been getting it for a long time. I read an article about them, "The Customer is the Company," that was published in 2008, eight years ago.[3] They were clearly onto something very special then about customer-centric marketing. And they were *so* ahead of their time.

How did I find the article? I simply googled "customer is the company," since this was one of the important tenets I wanted to bring forward in this book. The Threadless article appeared in the top spot, on page one for that keyword phrase. I'm sure it's been in that position since 2008. To drive home the lessons of this book, I wanted to share some of the article with you here.

First, who is Threadless? Well, their business is pretty simple. They produce and sell t-shirts, hoodies, home art, accessories and other items. The more complete definition is they are an online community of artists and an e-commerce website founded in 2000 by Jake Nickell and Jacob DeHart. Threadless designs are created by and chosen by an online community. Oh, and they also happen to make many millions of dollars a year.

The Threadless tagline: *"Make friends. Then, make things with your friends."* Brilliant!

From the Threadless "About Us" page:

> *You are Threadless. You make the ideas, you pick what we sell, you're why we exist. Everything we do gives you, and all the creative minds in the world, more opportunities to make great art. We started printing on t-shirts and then we realized tons of products make great canvases. We seek out these canvases, so you can continue to make and pick the best art. The weird art. The geeky art. The beautiful art. And every time you buy from us, you're supporting great art too. We love helping art unknowns become art totally-knowns, which is why every single one of our products carries an artist's name. We support our artist community in every way possible, whether it be through our annual creative awards, our commission-based award system, or simply by tweeting their name to the world. Lots of our artists have even gone on to start their own companies, and we believe that's a success. We're based in Chicago and have been since we opened our doors in 2000, and we couldn't love our hometown more.*[4]

How great is this "About Us" statement? They key is that it's not a bunch of empty words: they actually *live and work by these words*– everyone at the company. The other thing is that Threadless does *no* advertising, has *no* professional designers, *no* sales force, and *no* retail distribution. And it's never produced a t-shirt or other product that people didn't want. Totally unbelievable!

Eric von Hippel, a foremost authority on user innovation[5] has praised the company time and again as a model organization. I think the way they connect with their customers (really their prosumers), teaches a great les-

son for marketers too. Getting really close to your customers, like they do, is really, really important. In the future, it will be that much more critical.

Von Hippel has called the company a "perfect example" of a new way of thinking about innovation. Von Hippel's theory, which he had introduced in the late 1970s, was that most product innovations do not come out of corporate research and development labs *but from the people who use the products*. I would say this is the same for the marketing function, especially in the future.

So let's talk specifics and then see how we could transfer the ideas to the marketing practice. Threadless essentially runs design competitions on an online social network. Members of the network submit their ideas for t-shirts, home art, and tapestries, accessories and more–thousands each week–and then vote on which ones they like best. Hundreds of thousands of people use the site as a kind of *community center* where they blog, chat about designs, socialize with their fellow enthusiasts and buy a ton of shirts and other items at $15–$80 each.

As result of their prosumers being such a big part of the production of the products–and that's exactly what they are–*prosumers*, costs are low, margins are above 30 percent, and because community members tell them precisely what to make, every product eventually sells out. They've built an entire business around the idea that an online community could drive innovation. Whether it's called "user innovation," "crowdsourcing," or "open source," it means drastically rethinking the relationship with your customers and somehow helping them to become prosumers.

"Threadless completely blurs that line of who is a producer and who is a consumer," says Karim Lakhani, a professor at the Harvard Business School. "The customers end up playing a critical role across all its operations: idea generation, marketing, sales forecasting. All of that has been distributed."

Of course, it's not just happening at Threadless. A generation of Web 2.0 companies have succeeded by encouraging customers to contribute to, and in some cases *create*, the product being sold. Threadless is an online business, built around a social network, in which users collaborate with one another. The difference is that Threadless is not a software or media company. It designs, manufactures, and sells actual products, which is obviously a bit "old school" or "traditional," so it shows the potential for just about any company: B2B, B2C, product-, or service-based. They have, in essence, created a *platform*. Remember earlier I discussed how brands will become platforms in the future?

Von Hippel envisions a future in which most companies essentially abandon market research and product design and instead rely on communities of users to figure out which products to sell. In addition to attracting a lot of talent, the contest format encourages artists to tell their less-artistic friends about the site.

"Threadless was a huge word-of-mouth thing," says Tom Burns, a thirty-year-old freelance designer in Murfreesboro, Tennessee. Threadless users are not required to join the social network or vote in order to buy shirts, but many users have offered their opinions on thousands of designs. There's something enjoyable and empowering about playing critic in a never-ending gallery of pop art.

"Participation on Threadless is not just about voting for designs you really want to buy," says Frank Piller, a management professor at Germany's Aachen University and a researcher at MIT. "It's an exploration of new designs, and it's fun."

But most companies still prefer what von Hippel calls the "find-a-need-and-fill-it" paradigm, which involves market research, focus groups, testing, reworking, and retesting. Not only is this method extremely costly, but it fails to capitalize on a company's most dedicated customers, who often are already improving existing products to fit their needs.

"Companies are very good at creating platforms for external input, but they're very bad at using this input," says Piller, who has studied BMW's use of an innovation portal, a website that invites consumers to submit ideas. "BMW gets a thousand good ideas each year," he says. "Maybe they use one every two years." In other words, no matter how much technology goes into prettying up the suggestion box, the suggestions tend to get dumped in the trash at the end of the week.

Threadless's headquarters is open to customers, a dozen of whom stop by every day to pick up shirts and other products in person. They sometimes stick around for hours and hang out in a space that resembles a college dorm room constructed on an impossibly large scale. There are video game consoles, go-carts, a giant television, beanbag chairs, action figures, a singing-buck trophy, a Ping-Pong table, and a full-size Airstream trailer that the company uses as a studio in which to produce podcasts. Not much separation between company and customer, right?

The Threadless brand is not the shirts but *the community experience.* As Nickell puts it, "Our brand is a fun boys' and girls' club." The way von Hippel sees it, Threadless has tapped into a fundamental economic shift, a *movement away from passive consumerism.* Eventually, Threadless-like communities could form around industries as diverse as semiconductors, auto parts, and toys. "Threadless is one of the first firms to systematically mine a community for designs, but everything is moving in this direction," says von Hippel. He foresees research labs and product-design divisions at manufacturing companies being outstripped by an "innovation commons" made up of tinkerers, hackers, and other devout customers freely sharing their ideas. The companies that win will be the ones that listen.

The lesson for marketers? It may sound simple, but the lesson is taking the Threadless example and applying it to your marketing programs and initiatives, actually *doing* what they did. Think about it: The Threadless story has many of the elements of marketing in 2021 that I discussed:

- From brands to platforms
- From messages to experiences
- Storytelling and audience connection (through virtual reality)—they have all but the VR part
- From pricing/benefits concern to "show me the genuine passion"
- From strategic planning based around products/services to adaptive strategy based around customers
- From uninformed guessing to real-world, data-driven simulations

And, with regard to all the marketing ideas and concepts for 2030, I'm sure Threadless will be on the cutting edge of those as well.

How to Win in the "Thank You Economy"

Gary Vaynerchuk, the passionate social media whiz and speaker, had some very sage advice in his book, *The Thank You Economy*.[6]  What I realized as I read it was that these qualities would fit in very nicely with my chapter here on exemplary companies for us to follow, because they seemed to be adhering to all of what Vaynerchuk said. Here are some of the qualities that he recommended all companies follow in the new age:

- Care—about your customers, about your employees, about your brand—with everything you've got
- Erase any lines in the sand—don't be afraid of what's new or unfamiliar
- Show up first to market whenever possible, early the rest of the time
- Instill a culture of caring into your business by doing as follows:
  - Being self-aware
  - Mentally committing to change
  - Setting the tone through your words and actions
  - Investing in your employees
  - Hiring culturally compatible DNA, and spotting it within your existing team
  - Being authentic—whether online or offline, say what you mean, and mean what you say
  - Empowering your people to be forthright, creative, and generous
- Remember that behind every B2B transaction, there is a C
- Speak your customers' language
- Allow your customers to help you shape your brand or business but never allow them to dictate the direction in which you take it
- Build a sense of community around your brand
- Arrange for traditional and social media to play Ping-Pong and extend every conversation
- Direct all of your marketing initiatives toward the emotional center, and to the creative extremes
- Approach social media initiatives with good intent, aiming for quality engagements, not quantity

So, all in all, really great stuff. How can your company start making the marketing changes today?

Prosumer-to-Prosumer Connections at LEGO

One of the other defining qualities of great future-thinking companies is the way they enable customers, participants and, in our case here, *prosumers* to connect—both to the brand and to other interested prosumers. I discussed this in chapter seven, but wanted to touch on it here too. This adds a dimension to the marketing program that most brands never think about or concern themselves with. And it's usually because they aren't *really* thinking about the customer much to begin with. They may say they do, but their actions don't show it. But if you're a passionate customer, indeed a prosumer who *loves* the brand, wouldn't you be thinking about it? Yes, you would. You'd be wondering how you can connect to others who love the brand as much as you! Think of Apple or Starbucks here: they both do an amazing job with this one.

The Story of LEGO[7]—Daina Middleton, in *Marketing in the Participation Age*, discussed LEGO, and how they created several programs specifically designed to connect customers with both the brand and other customers, in a peer-to-peer format. The first program created was the LEGO Ambassador Program. Made up of 40 LEGO fans, it was designed to provide LEGO with outside ideas and advice. What happened next is the *real* story. Middleton says:

> Individuals from the marketing team communicated with this group more or less daily to discuss different themes or ideas or to brainstorm. The ambassadors reported on discussions via blogs, created picture galleries, and continued the talks with their local LEGO group members. The Ambassador Program has allowed LEGO to open up a channel for conversation and invite participation with its most passionate group of prosumers.

She went on to explain that LEGO set up another program to connect with customers called the "Click" Community. In 2011, LEGO made its official venture into social media with LEGO Click, a collaborative website that encouraged fans, artists, designers, and inventors to share their own LEGO creations. LEGO Click visitors were also able to read recent tweets about LEGO or download the free LEGO Photo iPhone application so they could transform photos into LEGO creations. It has been wildly successful, on every front. Middleton says that the LEGO Click Community "formalized a new network for fans that encouraged participation and conversation. LEGO has harnessed this participation by making it easy for participants to share content, resulting in content amplification."

The LEGO example illustrates a new form of customer relationship management, but in much bigger terms— a whole new form of marketing really. In essence, it's *prosumer marketing* and what they've done is actually employ many of the concepts I discuss in *Future Marketing*. It's a fundamental shift in philosophy and begins when companies realize that it's *not all about them*. And certainly, they don't have all the power, nor should they even see what they do in that "command and control type" of construct in coming years. Being a company that sells stuff in the future, you will be a *community*, a *platform*, not a closed-off kingdom. We're all in this future together!

Punchdrunk Theater Production Company

Punchdrunk is another great and innovative company that gets very close to its customers. Daina Middleton cites it as an example of how old-fashioned media forms can become deeply *participative*. Punchdrunk's work is often described as immersive and experiential, where the audience is actually *part* of the production. It is not traditional theatre. Middleton quotes Punchdrunk senior producer Colin Nightingale, who says,

People have accepted that they are in control, and you can't take that back. We have to keep an eye on what's happening, but for us the motivation to evolve is always from an artistic desire to ensure that we create relevant and exciting experiences for our audiences, rather than any calculated desire to keep up with the changing environment.

Among Punchdrunk's "participative marketing experiences" are product launches for Belgian brewery Stella Artois and French fashion house Louis Vuitton. For Stella Artois the company involved participants in dramatized flim noir plots called "The Night Chauffeur" and the "The Black Diamond." It's now working on a grant to work with MIT's Media Lab that brings digital elements into the theatrical experience. Middleton observes that "the study will likely demonstrate the thin line between the virtual and the digital world, as well as the expectations around how digital fits into our real-life experiences."[170]

Companies like Punchdrunk are leading the way into the future of marketing, a marketing practice where *everyone*—all stakeholders—participate, shape and drive the mission. How is your company doing on that front? Can you get there by 2021?

Hassett Ace Hardware—The Repair Cafe

In terms of the sharing economy and building community, Hassett Ace Hardware in Palo Alto, CA is a shining example for other companies to follow.[8] As I mentioned earlier in the book, this trend is reshaping our service-based society and many top brands are getting the message. Peer-to-peer commerce is direct, emotionally satisfying, personal, green, and has a very "now" quality about it—all important things for companies trying to establish closer connections with customers.

The Hassett idea is simple, but brilliant: On weekends, employees of Hassett Ace Hardware join other members of the community for what's known as The Repair Cafe, an event where the public can bring in a variety of items to be fixed *free of charge*. Hassett has five employees who help organize crowds and hand out tools to volunteers doing repairs while a store manager pedals a bike between the Hassett store and the cafe, picking up and delivering sockets, washers, plugs and spackle. At one weekend event, they had 130 items repaired, including a lava rock garden fountain and a 200-year-old sewing machine.

The Repair Cafe exemplifies what the sharing movement is all about: *people serving other people*. And it shows that when prosumers anywhere are transacting with one another, big brands want to be a part of the action. Whether you call it the sharing economy or peer-to-peer, the two sides connect via technology, just like with Uber or TaskRabbit. And that's why it's the future too.

And the marketing benefits you ask? Hassett Ace Hardware has generated major media coverage including a front-page story in the *San Jose Mercury News* and social buzz. The cafe "shows that our store walks the talk of being part of the community and shows we are family-run and customer-service oriented," says Jocelyn Broyles, Hassett Ace Hardware's brand manager. The peer-to-peer nature of the Repair Cafe is crucial to its success, according to Broyles. "It would send a whole different message if people came to our store to pay us to repair their things," she says. "The cafe involves community members helping other community members, working to fix items that often have strong sentimental value. This interaction results in an amazing local connection, which our brand wants to be associated with."

Up to this point, marketers as a whole haven't done much with this sharing dynamic, but the future of marketing will be inundated with these types of activities between companies and customers and even people in the community who aren't customers, but could be (aka *prospects*). With Hassett Ace Hardware and its Repair Café, once again, customers (or as I have mentioned throughout the book—prosumers) *are doing the marketing for the company*. What can your company do in its marketing programs to capitalize on the same thing?

Traditional Companies Now Serving Up Experiences

Former Intel chairman Andy Grove anticipated the explosion of technology-enabled offerings in a mid-1990s speech at the COMDEX computer show, when he declared, "We need to look at our business as more than simply the building and selling of personal computers. Our business is the delivery of information and lifelike interactive *experiences*." True indeed Sir Andy, true indeed.

In *The Experience Economy*, B. Joseph Pine II and James Gilmore explain how at theme restaurants such as Benihana, the Hard Rock Cafe, Ed Debevic's, Joe's Crab Shack, and the Bubba Gump Shrimp Co., the food functions as a prop for what's known in the industry as an "eatertainment" experience. And stores such as Build-A-Bear Workshop, Jordan's Furniture, and Niketown draw consumers through fun activities and promotional events.

They go on to say that

> [m]any dining experiences have less to do with the entertainment motif than with the merging of dining with comedy, art, history, or nature, as happens at such restaurants as Teatro ZinZanni, Café Ti Tu Tango, Medieval Times, and the Rainforest Cafe, respectively. In each place, the food service provides a stage for layering on a larger feast of sensations that resonate with consumers. Retailers such as Jungle Jim's International Market, The Home Depot, and the Viking Cooking School offer tours, workshops, and classes that combine shopping and education in ways that we can rightly describe as "edutailing" or "shopperscapism."

The "commodity mindset," according to former British Airways Chairman Sir Colin Marshall, means mistakenly thinking "that a business is merely performing a function— in our case, transporting people from point A to point B on time and at the lowest possible price." What British Airways does, he continued, "is to go beyond the function and compete on the basis of providing an experience." [9]

And then there are grocery stores like Bristol Farms Gourmet Specialty Foods Markets in Southern California. This upscale chain operates its stores as if they were *theatres* featuring music, live entertainment, exotic scenery, free refreshments, a video-equipped amphitheater, famousname guest stars and full audience participation. Amazing! So even the boring old retail grocery store can evolve into the future by truly connecting with customers and fully embracing the Prosumer Age.

Partnering with Peer-to-Peer Upstarts

Of course, you don't need to do it all yourself. One easy way for established companies to be a part of the sharing movement is by partnering with peer-to-peer upstarts like Ace Hardware or others. Such collaborations can "infuse freshness into the brand's persona and broaden its appeal," says Ann Mack, director of trendspotting at marketing agency JWT. "It's also an opportunity to learn about the audience, inner workings, strengths and weaknesses of peer-to-peer enterprises."[10]

A couple of years ago, the clothing chain Gap partnered with peer-to-peer pioneer TaskRabbit, a service that facilitates the outsourcing of random tasks to strangers. The retailer signed on with the service as part of a promotion aimed at lending a hand to busy Christmas shoppers, with customers at select New York and San Francisco locations who spent at least $75 receiving a $25 TaskRabbit voucher. Said a Gap rep, "Our brand strives to introduce customers to unusual, up-and-coming services in fashion and beyond."

Carrotmob Agency—Carrotmob, a quasi-cause marketing agency, uses social media to help groups of people, or "mobs," organize how to spend money with a brand, but only if the company makes a commitment to social responsibility. In such partnerships, peers themselves tell the marketer what to do. For example, "mobbers" spent $3,000 at a cheese shop in San Francisco after it agreed to install bike parking and water-saving technology.[11] Members of an online community of self-identified Carrotmobbers dream up a campaign, sign up a company, then organize their peers to participate.

Unilever, one of the world's largest companies, has also partnered with Carrotmob, doing a campaign at Fresh & Easy stores in Pasadena, Calif. About 250 Carrotmobbers agreed to shop on a certain day if the stores installed non-ozone-depleting freezers. On the designated date, whenever a mobber bought at least three Unilever products at the stores, Unilever gave a donation to an environmental group. Lou Paik, Unilever's

shopper marketing manager, says the Carrotmob approach "gives us new ways to achieve our sustainability goals." In announcing the Carrotmob partnership, Unilever CEO Paul Polman, said: "I envision a 21st century form of business where the everyday consumer is helping to shape the social contract. It's a business world," he stressed, "that is moving from value-based transactions to values-based partnerships." Oh, and by the way, Unilever is the world's second largest marketer of consumer goods. If they can do this new kind of marketing, any company can.

While the peer-to-peer idea might seem totally new, it's really just a new take on the time honored practice of bartering. "There's no fighting human nature," says Ian Greenleigh, senior manager of content at agency Bazaarvoice. "Peer-to-peer commerce in the digital age is just a better way to do what we've always done, or wanted to do." The real difference is in how peer power can improve the perception of a brand, even an entire category—just as Airbnb expanded the travel market with its cheaper, more varied accommodations. Brands, says Mack, might "leverage consumers' rising trust of strangers and proclivity for sharing to improve the marketing and consumer experience of existing offerings."

I completely, 100 percent agree.

The Future of Business cites Accenture's *Customer 2020* study, which found that revenue growth typically develops from enhanced customer experience: "Consumers continuously evaluate providers, resulting in a growing switching econo-

my that accounts for an estimated $6.2 trillion in revenue opportunity for providers across seventeen key markets today...."[12]

Kevin Kelly predicts that 2030's top companies will have mastered sharing in ways that we can't see today. This could mean sharing thoughts, emotions, money, health, and time. In certain conditions, whatever can be shared will be, he writes. "Anything that can be shared can be shared better, faster, easier, longer, and in a million more ways than we currently realize. At this point in our history, sharing something that has not been shared before, or in a new way, is the surest way to increase its value."[13]

Designing Experiences for Customers

Joseph Pine and James Gilmore, authors of *The Experience Economy* say, "when designing your experience, you should consider the following questions:[14]

- **What can be done to enhance the esthetic value of the experience?** What would make your guests want to come in, sit down, and just hang out? Think about what you can do to make the environment more inviting and comfortable. You want to create an atmosphere in which your guests feel free "to be."

- **Once your guests are there, what should they do?** The escapist aspect of an experience draws in your guests further, immersing them in various activities. Focus on what you should encourage guests "to do" if they are to become active participants in the experience. Further, what would cause them "to go" from one sense of reality to another?

- **The educational aspect of an experience, like the escapist, is essentially active.** Learning, as it is now largely understood, requires the full participation of the learner. What do you want your guests "to learn" from the experience? What interaction or activities will help engage them in the exploration of certain knowledge and skills?

- **Entertainment, like the esthetic, is a passive aspect of an experi-**

ence. When your guests are entertained, they're not really doing anything except responding to (enjoying, laughing at, etc.) the experience. What entertainment would help your guests "to enjoy" the experience better? How can you make the time more fun and more enjoyable?

They go on to say that if "you're not sure where to start, you may want to consider general categories of themes. In *The Theming of America*, Mark Gottdiener identifies ten themes that often materialize in the "built environments" that he calls staged experiences: (1) status, (2) tropical paradise, (3) the Wild West, (4) classical civilization, (5) nostalgia, (6) Arabian fantasy, (7) urban motif, (8) fortress architecture and surveillance, (9) modernism and progress, and (10) representations of the unrepresentable (such as the Vietnam Veterans Memorial Wall). Marketing professors Bernd Schmitt and Alex Simonson, in their instructive book Marketing Aesthetics, offer nine more "domains" in which themes can be found: (1) history, (2) religion, (3) fashion, (4) politics, (5) psychology, (6) philosophy, (7) the physical world, (8) popular culture, and (9) the arts." [15]

What could your marketing department do with a few of these themes? And which questions from the above list could help you design the best experience for your prosumers? Lots to think about.

Hertz Gold Club—The Ultimate in Customer Service (and a lesson for all marketers)

As a member of Hertz's Club Gold Program, I have always thought that this is something that all marketers could learn from. I also think it's the type of thing we'll see more and more of in the future from companies. So what's the gist? The Gold customer, who is told the program costs $60 a year with the fee often waived, receives the same basic vehicle as everyone else.

Here's how the Gold Program works:

1. You provide your name to the shuttle bus driver, bypassing the line at the counter.
2. You're then dropped off at the canopied Gold area, where you see your name in lights on a large screen that directs you to the exact location of your car.
3. When you arrive at your car, you find your name in lights above it.
4. When the weather demands it, the car's engine is running, with the heater or air conditioner turned on.

If you've ever rented a car at an airport, you'll appreciate this story of total service and super efficiency. What's amazing is that it actually costs Hertz *less* to deliver its Gold experience than its standard service! Incredible. So, it doesn't take a huge budget to make a difference. And the ultimate lesson for every marketer out there—it makes it easy on customers and makes them feel special. Even in little ways, it makes a massive impact.

Amazon and Its Personalization "Super Powers"

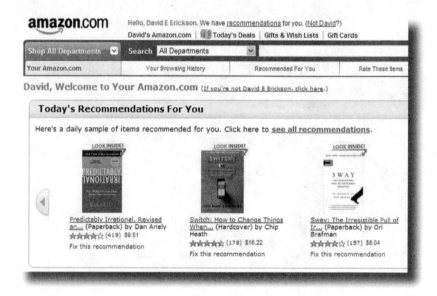

Most of us are Amazon.com customers, and we all know why. They have millions of products available, you can read reviews from real people, they price their products affordably, and they send your order directly to your home. But equally important is the *extreme customization and personalization* they employ through the power of big data and a perfectly structured online experience.

Imagine if Target developed exactly the same capabilities as Amazon.com. Do you think you would ever switch? Most likely not. It would take you months to teach Target.com what Amazon.com already knows. In the meantime, you would miss out on many custom recommendations that Target would neglect to make while it was still learning your needs. In this way, companies can keep their customers forever— with two provisos. One, the company doesn't excessively hike up its prices or cut back on service once in a learning relationship, and two, it doesn't miss the next technology wave. (Amazon.com, for example, developed its own e-book reader, the Kindle, to ensure it does not lose out should book purchases move rapidly from physical to electronic.) The advantages of this approach improve a company's fundamentals in significant ways:

- Premium prices: Because your offerings are tailored precisely to customer needs, your customers receive greater value and, as a result, willingly pay a premium price.
- Reduced discounts: Every time you sell an offering at a discounted price, you in effect pay customers to experience greater sacrifice. The less they sacrifice, the less you must push the product at promotional prices or discard it outright.
- Greater revenue per customer: Because you know more about each customer than does any competitor, customers keep coming back to you every time they enter the market for what you offer.
- Higher number of customers (at lower acquisition costs): Because your customers find the experience so pleasing, they tell their friends and associates, many of whom will also want to do business with you. These new customers will tell others, and so on, and so on.
- Increased customer retention: The more each customer teaches you about his individual wants, needs, and preferences, the more difficult it will be for him to obtain an equivalent level of value from a competitor.

Most important, those companies that systematically reduce customer sacrifice— eliminating the negative cues of the relationship—heighten the experience their customers have when using their goods or partaking of their services, thus fulfilling needs left unaddressed by their mass produced counterparts.[16] A great lesson for us all.

The Dedicated Disciples Who Carry Innovation Over the Tipping Point

In his best-selling book *The Tipping Point*,[17] Malcolm Gladwell describes the characteristics of the dedicated disciples it takes to make a great idea a great success.

He talks about "connectors, mavens, and salespeople" and says they are a crucial part of the process. The *connector* knows many different people in different socioeconomic areas. *Mavens* are quite different from

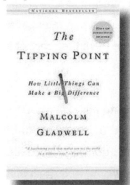

connectors. They do not necessarily have to know many people, but they are experts in a certain field and—driven by altruism—they love to provide this expertise to others. Mavens are helpful "connoisseurs" who carry the message of a great innovation because they are convinced it is great. And then the *salespeople* that Gladwell talks about; they can sell just about anything because they have a magic way with people, an intuitive sense of connecting, sometimes a natural and easy charisma that makes us like them immediately, most certainly a strong emotional intelligence. Companies that have lots of connectors, mavens, and salespeople on their team will always succeed in the coming Prosumer Age.

So, there you go—a range of exciting, progressive companies that are practicing the future of marketing today. What do they all have in common? They all have been practicing the EP^2 formula for many years already. And it's probably because EP^2 is rooted in common sense and practicality, which many companies naturally have in their cultural DNA. So while the future includes many unknowns where we all are going into unchartered territory, there will also be key elements of human nature that have always been important and always will be: being authentic and demonstrating passion for a purpose.

CHAPTER SEVENTEEN

Wrap-Up and the Road Ahead

Well, you made it; this is the end of the line. So, how was *Future Marketing* for you? I truly hope you got a lot out of the book and enjoyed what you read. I loved writing it. The research process for this book was incredibly valuable to me as well. It's been amazing to see the vast quantity of materials available on the various topics I covered. There is a groundswell of interest and ideas in the future of marketing, without a doubt.

There is also a level of curiosity and enthusiasm for the future out there that I didn't quite expect. It's really good to see. As a lifelong optimist, I feel very positive about the future; not just for the marketing practice, but for business, culture, the entire world, in fact. In the Prosumer Age, long outdated cultural and business constructs, such as centralized authority and uniformity, will diminish. And in its place, new cultural and technological forces, will come to redefine the marketing practice. The idea of sharing and providing experiences is just beginning. The switch from ownership to access has just kicked off. As Kevin Kelly notes,

> flows and streams are still trickles. While it seems as if we are tracked too much already, we'll be tracking a thousand times as much in the coming decades. Each one of these functions will be accelerated by high-quality cognification, just now being born, making the smartest things we do today seem very dumb. None of this is final. These transitions are but the first step in a process, a process of becoming. It is a Beginning.[1]

So, as a recap, let's quickly review the two most important parts of *Future Marketing*: What I see happening by 2021 and then by 2030.

For 2021, I mentioned ten key areas that we should be paying attention to in our marketing work. As I discussed, much of this is being led by two things: the change in technology and the prosumer revolution, or the change we see in the consumer set.

These are the ten key areas:

1. From Brands to Platforms
2. A Move from Mass Media to Memes and Movements
3. A Move from Brand Messages to Multi-Sensory Experiences
4. Storytelling and Audience Connection Through Virtual Reality
5. From a Pricing/Benefits Concern to "Show Me the Genuine Passion for What You're Pitching"
6. From Strategic Planning Based Around Products/Services to Adaptive Strategy Based Around Customers
7. From Uninformed Guessing to Real-World, Data-Driven Simulations
8. From Web 2.0 to the Fully Realized Semantic Web
9. From Purely Human Thinking to Cognitive Enhancement
10. From the Mass Market to the Niche Explosion

How will your brand or agency capitalize on these changes? How can you build new strategies around them, starting today? Even if you tackle three or four of the ten, I think you'll be far ahead of others out there. Take a look. Brainstorm. Discuss. See what you can do.

And then we moved on to 2030 and what I saw happening in that timeframe that would impact the marketing practice. Obviously, it's more difficult to predict and get a read on things farther out, but I really do believe just about all that I discussed will, in fact, come to fruition, in some way or form. Many things in process now will be in wide practice by then. We can see the signs now.

The four key ideas due for arrival and mass adoption by 2030 that will have huge impacts on the marketing practice are:

1. "Computers Everywhere" or a "Ubiquitous Internet" in the Air Around Us
2. Augmented, Immersive Experiences
3. Widespread Internet of Things
4. Artificial Marketing Intelligence

With these four, we'll all need to do a lot more thinking and brainstorming. They clearly reflect tectonic changes in culture, business and society. So go and read all the books you can find on the topics. Attend industry conferences that discuss them. Talk to industry influencers. Blog about them. I think if we approach the future collectively, with each of us doing our part, we'll all arrive there safer and into a much better place, overall. Let's all lead the charge together!

The Big Themes

To further wrap up this epic journey, I think it's important to "take a step back" a bit, take a breath and attempt to decipher all of the trends and changes and technology to discover the "big themes" of these shifts in human activity as it relates to the marketing practice. Yes, we are seeing some incredibly interesting "mega"-trends. Yes, we will be using some incredibly powerful technologies. Yes, we will be trying to connect with new audiences using the latest social media, content, advertising and other yet to be discovered marketing tools. But if everything we talked about in *Future Marketing* represented the brain, for example—the conscious brain—what is the *subconscious* telling us? In other words, what's this future marketing stuff really all about? What's below the surface? What's *the Why*?

If we could boil it all down, I think we'd find this: **we all want to improve our lives.** We want our lives—and others lives as well—to be better. With all these amazing trends, tools, and technologies all around us, we're now seeing some real opportunities to do exactly that and over time, it will become easier to make it happen because of these trends, tools and technologies. After a long period of massive transition, that is bringing about big changes in culture, income, the way work gets done and more, we are now starting to finally see the "shape" of the future; we are beginning to see the "outline" of a vastly improved and different future that we all can have a place in. The same is true for the marketing practice. I mentioned earlier how surprised I was that no one had written a comprehensive book on the long-range future of marketing. I now know that the time for this book was *right now*. A year or two ago would have been too early; many of the trends, tools and technologies were simply too primitive or too early in development to really write a book about. Today, as I write this final chapter, virtual reality is *a thing*; augmented reality is *a thing*. AI is *a thing*. The Internet of Things is *a thing*! And it is now very clear that they will be very important in defining our lives and our marketing work over the next fifteen years and beyond.

So getting back to the big themes. There are a few that seem to rise to the surface. First, is the theme of **efficiency, hyper-efficiency**. This theme cuts across many of the big ideas discussed in *Future Marketing*. We see it in the Internet of Things, we see it in artificial intelligence, we see it VR and AR. Doing so much more with so much less will be a beacon of the Prosumer Age. With population growth, limited resources and other future constrains, we really won't have a choice. Driving efficiency will be required. And that's just one other reason why it's a big theme. So, yes, our marketing will need to be efficient. Just think about all of the waste that we see in today's world. In the future, this idea will be turned on its head. When you imagine *no waste*, you have a very different world and a much-improved reality.

The next big theme is **greater interdependency**. Everything we do in the future won't just affect us individually, it will affect us collectively. The ability to positively impact others by the things we do will be very real. In almost all of the chapters of this book, I discussed collaborative ideas, collective approaches, the power of the group, the social quality of things. The big difference with future interdependency though is that there won't be any "slackers" in the group. No one will be hidden in the group. Everyone will contribute. That's not the case today. In addition, right now, you can still choose to be the rugged individual and you don't really lose a whole lot. But in the future, you won't want to be the lone wolf. That will put you at the bottom of society. Today, the have-nots are the financially poor. Tomorrow, it will be those who live "off the grid" and choose not to participate.

The third big theme, which goes hand-in-hand with the previous theme, is **greater empowerment of the individual**. This is the "yin" to the "yang" of greater interdependency. In the future, we are each a *brand* unto ourselves. We each will have the power to truly change the world. And I don't mean that as a cliché. I really mean that with all of the awesome trends, tools and technologies, each of us, if we want to, will have the ability to really make a massive impact. So, yes, there will greater interdependency, where we all will rely more on others and them, on us. But at the very same time, we each will have incredible personal power as well. Some may see this as a paradox, but it's not. It's two sides of the same coin. All of the personal power in the world is fine and good, but if no one responds to it or is impacted by it, then it's all for nothing. Future marketing efforts that harness this duality will be very successful.

The fourth big theme is **change speeds up.** Throughout the book, you've seen this idea mentioned in many different ways. With more and more people making an impact and becoming a force, we have lots more output, it's really that simple. And yes, the rate of change has been speeding up for a long time, but the idea is that not only will this continue, but it will truly become a bit "out of control" (by our standards of dealing with it today). Never fear, in the next few years, we'll have many new ways to manage it. Through the power of AI and other technologies, we'll also have lots of available help. But if you find that you are a bit resistant to change now or always think about what "used to be", you'll probably want to start making some small, incremental adjustments to that belief so you can fully embrace the future of marketing.

The fifth big theme is the **"passion-purpose-authenticity" thing.** This was discussed throughout the book and cuts across many areas of future life, similar to the interdependency theme. So how do we boil this one down to its essence? Perhaps it's this: Making a bunch of money for the sake of making money and not really believing in what we're doing just won't fly in the future. Possessing that combination, in fact, will be a big turnoff in coming years. Call it the "final demise of the cheesy salesman," the "dishonest huckster"—that personality type. As we've already seen with the Millennials, life is about being true and being "totally into" whatever it might be: our cause, our company, our products or anything else. Marketing will be like that as well. Giving back and doing good won't be about simply checking off the box "contributed to the corporate cause", it will be a massive movement. It will make up the very heart of marketing.

The sixth and final theme is the **redefinition of the person,** of who we are and how we are individually represented in the future in physical, online and virtual spaces. Again, like many of the other themes, this one is far reaching. The very idea changes how we fundamentally see the world and our place in it. Of course, we will always only have one physical body, but we could have dozens of virtual selves or holographic selves in the future. Today, just thinking about this concept is pretty mind blowing. As I discussed, we could have our likeness "attending" a couple other trade shows as well as back at the office while our physical self is giving a keynote speech at the industry event of the year. Our decisions, our thoughts, our image, how we decide things, all of it will be impacted by this redefinition of the person. The key with all of our future marketing then, will need to carefully consider all of these versions of our selves and where they may be populated. The marketing will probably be different depending on these factors.

Future Challenges

Future Marketing is an optimistic book. It paints a positive picture. This was done on purpose. Will there be lots of challenges in our future world and the future marketing practice? Yes, without a doubt. Will there be unexpected obstacles, serious problems and evil people that want to do other people harm? Yes, without question. I could have spent half the book discussing all of these, but it is simply not my way. All of my life, I have held fast to the idea that whatever we believe, we conceive. Whatever we think, we are. Whatever we focus on becomes our reality. The truth is that most of us are good people and we're all trying to do the very best we can. We realize that human beings are fallible. We understand the design of the human mind. The truth is, in the future, the glass really is half full. Seriously. And we'll have the tools and technologies to root out all of the bad stuff—the bad people, the bad companies, the bad products—and shine a light on it all, like never before. So what are the future challenges? Job loss. Destruction of entire industries. Shortage of resources, like water. Population growth. And there are many more.

My message: don't be overwhelmed. Keep the faith. Hold on! We are on this ride together. And in the future, that's even truer than it is today. Everything will work out, because everything always does. Not only will things work out, they will work out beautifully and with purpose. Although the future is not certain, the fundamental nature of the marketing practice—*the act of genuinely connecting with people who are interested in what you are doing (and them connecting with you) so that together, you can positively impact people's lives with a product, service and/or platform experience*—will be intact.

Last, consider this: civilization has always managed to overcome what appeared to be insurmountable obstacles: the Ice Age; the Dark Ages; World Wars I and II; and many other tough times. Don't listen to the fifty percent who only talk about scarcity in the future. Listen to the other half who talk about abundance in the future, because that is the real story. Better yet, don't just listen, lead! Don't focus on the challenges in the future of marketing; focus on the incredible *opportunities.* They will be everywhere, all around us, everywhere we go, in everything we do. It's our choice to make it happen. The future of marketing will truly be a "house that magically expands with each door you open."

Final Thoughts

As we come to a close, I simply want to leave you with one final thought—one simple idea that I feel will work really well for your company no matter what types of marketing you do in the future.

In fact, it's the same way I closed my first book, *Content Rich*, in 2008, and my last book, *Content is Currency*, in 2012. And it is this:

> *Make your prospective customers feel like they are buying from a friend.*

That advice will work in 2021, 2030 or even 2099! It's timeless and it is powerful.

Your goal through marketing is to build relationships and attain more influence. But you also want to reduce your customer acquisition costs, improve your customer loyalty rate, and overall, increase each customer's lifetime value. In addition, you want to learn something from them. You want this to be a true "give-and-take" relationship—a genuine partnership. This is an important distinction between successful marketers and unsuccessful marketers.

With social networking expanding at an incredible rate and with a more personal approach being popular in business, I think this relationship we have with our customers will continue to grow and become more important with time. As you know by now, the goal of your business should not be solely to get the sale, but to develop a relationship with each and every customer, a mutually beneficial relationship that will lead to more sales, testimonials, referrals, and more over the years and to ultimately get many of them to adopt the "prosumer" title.

By seeing our customers as friends, as part of the family, you will be exposed to wonderfully new and unexpected surprises that will provide lasting value and personal satisfaction. As I mentioned in the beginning of the book, good marketing can empower people everywhere to have a voice. And marketing tells the story of your product or service and propels it into the hearts and minds of your prospects, customers and others.

When you "propel your marketing into their heart," you have just made a friend and quite possibly, a customer, or maybe even a *prosumer* for life!

Friends Communicate with Each Other—The hallmark of a solid friendship is effective, two-way communication. Not just talking or hearing, but *listening*. You can't build a friendship by emailing them every other month and pitching them with your latest products or services. To make friends with your customers, you need to communicate on a personal level.

So, commit to communicating with them at least once a week via your blog and social media channels. Heck, pick up the phone and give them a good old-fashioned call! This will keep the conversation going and connect you on a deeper level. It will also make them feel valued, like they are on the inside of something very cool.

Friends are There Through Thick and Thin—Isn't it true that our best friends give us the benefit of the doubt? No matter what happens, they let us slide sometimes, it's just part of the deal. In fact, the best of friends will never leave your side. By developing friendships with your customers, you have a relationship based on honesty and trust.

A customer will not suddenly jump to a competitor of yours if they feel a true connection with your company. Being available and personable and truly caring for them will go a very long way. You only give what you get, right? So, ask them to be in your advisory groups. Seek their opinions on anything and everything. Hold an event for all of your customers. Building a community with your customers will give you their loyalty.

So, That's a Wrap!

You've completed the book, and hopefully, have come away from the experience with some great information, but the real work is just beginning.

Now is the time to put these future marketing ideas into practice. So·

sit down, meet with your team and start chatting about them. Plan a robust and comprehensive content strategy. Grow your Web and mobile presence through powerful, persuasive content. Maybe try some virtual-reality marketing. Differentiate your marketing from your competitor's so you stand out. Connect with your prosumers.

Ask yourself: What types of marketing can I develop today to make a big impact tomorrow?

As I bid you a fond...written...farewell, please know that I really appreciate you picking up this book. I treasure the relationships I have with all of my readers.

And if the opportunity comes up, I would love to meet you in person, or at least via email (jon@contentlaunch.com) or my blog (FutureMarketingBook.com), or perhaps Twitter (@jonwuebben) or Facebook.

Be on the look out for me....The *Future Marketing* book tour may be coming to a town near you soon! In addition, I may be speaking on the topic in a hotel ballroom or corporate boardroom in your city too. I'd love to have you join us; there's nothing quite like face-to-face learning. Plus, we have a lot of fun at our events.

In closing, may all of your many marketing efforts serve you and your customers well, may your businesses be successful and may the future marketing programs you put forward in the coming years put you well on your way to connection, influence, sales and good works.

Thanks for reading!

Bibliography

Case, Steve. *The Third Wave: An Entrepreneur's Vision of the Future.* New York, Simon & Schuster, 2016

Diamandis, Peter H. and Steven Kotler. *Abundance: The Future is Better than You Think.* New York: Free Press, 2012

Gloor, Peter. *Swarm Creativity: Competitive Advantage Through Collaborative Innovation Networks.* New York: Oxford UP, 2016.

Hagel III, John, John Seely Brown and Lang Davison. *The Power of Pull: How Small Moves, Smartly Made, Can Set Big Things in Motion.* New York: Basic Books, 2010.

Houle, David. *Entering the Shift Age.* Naperville, Illinois: Sourcebooks, 2012.

Kelly, Kevin. *The Inevitable: Understanding the 12 Technological Forces that Will Shape Our Future.* New York: Viking, 2016.

Middleton, Daina. *Marketing in the Participation Age: A Guide to Motivating People to Join, Share, Take Part, Connect and Engage.* Hoboken, N.J.: Wiley, 2013.

Pine II, Joseph and James H. Gilmore. *The Experience Economy.* Boston: Harvard Business School Press, 1999.

Pink, Daniel. *A Whole New Mind: Why Right-Brainers Will Rule the Future.* New York: Riverhead, 2006.

Rifkin, Jeremy. *The Zero Marginal Cost Society: The Internet of Things, the Collaborative Commons and the Eclipse of Capitalism.* New York, Palgrave-Macmillan, 2015.

Schmidt, J. Eric and Jared Cohen. *The New Digital Age: Reshaping the Future of People, Nations and Business.* New York: Knopf, 2013.

Sundararajan, Arun. *The Sharing Economy: The End of Employment and the Rise of Crowd-Based Capitalism.* Cambridge, Massachusetts: MIT Press, 2016.

Talwar, Rohit. *The Future of Business: Critical Insights into a Rapidly Changing World from 60 Future Thinkers.* Tonbridge, Kent, UK: Fast Future Publishing, 2015.

Vaynerchuk, Gary. *The Thank You Economy.* New York: Harper Business, 2011.

Notes

INTRODUCTION

1   David Houle, *Entering the Shift Age* (Napierville, IL: Sourcebooks, 2012), 91.
2   http://www.futuristspeaker.com/speaking-topics/#sthash.Qf7Bs7sS.dpuf,
3   David Gelernter and Eric Freeman, "The Future of the Internet Is Flow," *The Wall Street Journal* (Oct. 2, 2015), http://www.wsj.com/articles/the-future-of-the-internet-is-flow-1443796858
4   Kevin Kelly, *The Inevitable: Understanding the 12 Technological Forces that Will Shape Our Future* (New York: Viking, 2016), 65.
5   Rohit Talwar, *The Future of Business: Critical Insights into a Rapidly Changing World from 60 Future Thinkers* (Tonbridge, Kent, UK): 37.
6   Peter H. Diamandis and Steven Kotler, *Abundance: The Future is Better than You Think* (New York: Free Press, 2012), introduction.
7   Houle, 10.
8   Talwar, 25.
9   Kelly, 8.
10   Ibid., 131.
11   Steve Case, *The Third Wave: An Entrepreneur's Vision of the Future* (New York: Simon & Schuster) 2016), 43.

CHAPTER ONE

1   Kelly, 6.
2   http://www.business2community.com/marketing/next-ten-years-will-marketing-change-0665616#QD0EwDDslMqWfWf7.99,
3   http://contentmarketinginstitute.com/wp-content/uploads/2015/09/2016_B2B_Report_Final.pdf,
4   http://www.gartner.com/newsroom/id/3170017
5   https://secure2.sfdcstatic.com/assets/pdf/misc/state-of-marketing-report-2016.pdf,

CHAPTER TWO

1   https://store.frost.com/top-global-mega-trends-to-2025-and-implications-to-business-society-and-cultures-2014-edition-19883.html.
2   http://www.forbes.com/sites/sarwantsingh/2014/05/12/the-top-10-mega-trends-of-the-decade/#27116a7e570a, 2014
3   http://ww2.frost.com/research/visionary-innovation/, 2016
4   Kelly, 112
5   Ibid., 146
6   Diamandis and Kotler, 236.
7   https://www.fastcoexist.com/3021148/futurist-forum/why-predicting-trends-doesnt-help-prepare-for-the-future, 2013

CHAPTER THREE

1   Sohail Inayatullah, ed., *The Views of Futurists*. Vol 4, The Knowledge Base of Futures Studies. Brisbane, Foresight International, 2001.
2   Jacqueline Howard, "7 Top Futurists Make Some Pretty Surprising Predictions." *Huffington Post*, 2015.
3   Schmidt and Cohen, 17.
4   Kelly, 37.
5   Schmidt and Cohen, 5.

6   http://www.futuristspeaker.com/
    business-trends/future-of-the-
    internet-8-expanding-dimensions/.
7   Schmidt and Cohen, 19.

CHAPTER FOUR
1   http://contentmarketinginstitute.
    com/2016/08/content-marketing-
    trends/, 2016
2   http://www.wsj.com/articles/
    is-branded-virtual-reality-content-
    the-next-frontier-in-market-
    ing-1466701202, 2016

CHAPTER FIVE
1   https://www.siriusdecisions.com/
    Blog/2014/May/What-is-Content-
    Marketing-Software
2   http://www.adweek.com/news/
    press/branded-content-moves-
    needle-forbes-153299,
3   http://www.aberdeen.com/assets/
    report-preview/8101-RA-human-
    capital-management.pdf,
4   http://contentmarketinginstitute.
    com/2015/09/b2b-content-market-
    ing-research/
5   http://www.inc.com/travis-wright/
    your-ultimate-cheat-sheet-to-mar-
    keting-technology-martech.html
6   http://www.forbes.com/sites/lou-
    iscolumbus/2016/05/09/ten-ways-
    big-data-is-revolutionizing-market-
    ing-and-sales/#4cb447a0115e
1   http://www.forbes.com/sites/
    louiscolumbus/2016/08/13/10-
    factors-fueling-the-rise-of-marketi
    ngtechnologists/#529eaa767653

CHAPTER SIX
1   Kelly, 124.
2   https://www.marketingmag.com.
    au/hubs-c/prosumers-not-consum-
    ers-future/,
3   Daina Middleton, Marketing in the
    Participation Age: A Guide to Mo-
    tivating People to Join, Share, Take
    Part, Connect and Engage (Hobo-
    ken, NJ: Wiley, 2013), 24.
4   Kelly, 144.
5   http://www.informationweek.com/
    big-data/software-platforms/9-

tech-giants-embracing-the-open-
source-revolution/d/d-id/1325872?.
6   Kelly, 143.
7   Peter Gloor, Swarm Creativity:
    Competitive Advantage through
    Collaborative Innovation (New
    York: Oxford UP, 2016), 29.
8   http://www.businessgreen.com/
    bg/opinion/2461531/the-diy-
    energy-market-how-prosumers-
    will-take-the-lead-in-the-energy-
    transition.
9   http://blog.tomoson.com/influenc-
    er-marketing-study/
10 Kelly, 188.
11 Ibid., 249.
12 Ibid., 239.
13 https://www.marketingmag.com.
    au/hubs-c/prosumers-not-consum-
    ers-future/.
14 Kellly, 149.
15 http://www.acrwebsite.org/search/
    view-conference-proceedings.
    aspx?Id=6542.
16 https://medium.com/basic-
    income/post-capitalism-rise-
    of-the-collaborative-commons-
    62b0160a7048#.z676u79w9.
17 Joseph Pine II and James H.
    Gilmore, The Experience Economy
    (Boston: Harvard Business School
    Press, 1999), 8.
18 Middleton, 65.
19 https://econsultancy.com/
    blog/66542-3D-printing-adding-
    another-dimension-to-market-
    ing-s-future/.
20 Diamandis and Kotler, 238.

CHAPTER SEVEN
1   http://www.forbes.com/sites/
    oracle/2013/11/26/the-power-of-
    peer-networks-5-reasons-to-get-
    and-stay-involved/#503305804371
2   Kelly, 182.
3   Diamandis and Kotler, 239.
4   Gloor, 20-21.
5   Ibid., 3.
6   Ibid., 182.

CHAPTER EIGHT
1   Talwar, 167.

2   Pine and Gilmore, 24-25.
3   Schmidt and Cohen, 23.
4   Ibid., 29.
5   Pine and Gilmore, 168.

CHAPTER NINE
1   Jeremy Rifkin, *The Zero Marginal Cost Society: The Internet of Things, the Collaborative Commons, and the Eclipse of Capitalism* (New York: Palgrave-Macmillan, 2015), 3.
2   Houle, 13.
3   Kelly, 142.
4   Paul Bailey, Branding Post Capitalism (Dissertation: U of London, 2013).
5   Rifkin, 3.
6   Kelly, 145.
7   Talwar, 163.
8   Rifkin, 11.
9   Ibid., 16.
10   Talwar, 65.
11   Daniel Pink, A Whole New Mind: Why Right-Brainers Will Rule the Future (New York: Riverhead, 2006), 218-219.
12   Houle, 137.
13   Kelly, 138.
14   http://www.campaignlive.co.uk/article/1369406/postcapitalist-marketing-does-future-hold-brands-paul-mason-explains#
15   Bailey, Introduction.

CHAPTER TEN
1   Talwar, 212.
2   Kelly, 5.
3   http://www.digitaltonto.com/2012/the-semantic-economy/.
4   http://www.businessinsider.com/facebooks-world-of-virtual-reality-in-2026-2016-4
5   Kelly, 124.
6   https://maxlenderman.wordpress.com/2015/10/14/the-experience-is-the-message/.
7   http://www.edelman.com/post/virtual-augmented-reality/.
8   https://centricdigital.com/blog/digital-trends/transforming-user-experience-with-vr-and-ar/.
9   Pink, 103.

10   http://blog.hubspot.com/agency/millennials-and-the-emergence-of-the-passion-economy#sm.000xxbpkg8hycwi11uu2n6ch5kbzn.
11   http://www.smartinsights.com/marketing-planning/marketing-strategy/strategic-planning/.
12   http://www.forbes.com/sites/gregsatell/2013/10/21/what-can-we-expect-from-the-next-decade-of-marketing/#1d6efb2b59c7.
13   Talwar, 218.
14   https://en.wikipedia.org/wiki/Watson_(computer).
15   http://www.ogilvydo.com/topics/tech-innovation/3-ways-artificial-intelligence-is-transforming-our-lives/
16   http://www.ogilvydo.com/topics/tech-innovation/3-ways-artificial-intelligence-is-transforming-our-lives/
17   Kelly, 80.
18   http://www.forbes.com/sites/gregsatell/2013/04/16/4-principles-of-marketing-strategy-in-the-digital-age/#7e09ed67495c.
19   Diamandis and Kotler, 229.
20   Ibid., 234.
21   https://cmo.marketo.com/conversations-and-interviews/engage-or-die-john-hagel-of-deloitte-on-the-next-era-of-marketing/,
22   Kelly, 178.
23   http://blog.firebrandtalent.com/2015/11/5-essential-skills-of-your-marketing-team-of-the-future/.
24   Dollars, Bits and Atoms: A Roadmap to the Future of Marketing, Microsoft, 2013. http://mediaplant.net/report/details/roadmap.

CHAPTER ELEVEN
1   http://digiday.com/agencies/6-trends-will-shape-future-agencies/.

CHAPTER TWELVE
1   http://io9.gizmodo.com/10-mind-blowingly-futuristic-technologies-that-will-appe-673136756.
2   http://www.sciencedirect.

com/science/article/pii/
S0007681315001421.

3   Talwar, 356.
4   Ibid., 379.
5   http://www.kiplinger.com/slide-
    show/business/T057-S010-amaz-
    ing-ways-life-will-be-different-
    in-2030/index.html.
6   https://www.linkedin.com/
    pulse/20140803190919-
    43970095-the-internet-of-things-
    consumers-and-marketers-in-2030.
7   Kelly, 226.
8   http://blog.drift.com/artificial-
    intelligence.
9   http://www.thedrum.com/
    opinion/2016/07/01/i-marketer-ai-
    and-future-marketing.
10 Kelly, 33.
11 Ibid., 37.
12 Ibid., 296.
13 https://www.linkedin.com/pulse/
    now-paradigm-consumers-
    marketers-2030-nils-michae-
    lis-6008974053589741568.
14 http://www.mahercomm.com/
    future-thinking-marketing-consid-
    erations-for-2026/.
15 https://www.linkedin.com/pulse/
    what-would-marketing-like-
    2026-anto-franklin-joseph-chris-
    turaj.
16 https://centricdigital.com/blog/
    digital-trends-transforming-user-
    experience-with-vr-and-ar/
17 https://www.salesforce.com/
    blog/2014/03/internet-of-things-
    marketing-impact.html.
18 https://www.linkedin.com/
    pulse/20140803190919-
    43970095-the-internet-of-things-
    consumers-and-marketers-in-2030.
19 https://en.wikipedia.org/wiki/
    Technologies_in_Minority_Report.
20 Kelly, 221.
21 https://en.wikipedia.org/wiki/
    Technologies_in_Minority_Report.
22 https://en.wikipedia.org/wiki/Glad-
    vertising.
23 Houle, 141.
24 Ibid., 182.

CHAPTER THIRTEEN
1   Talwar, 228-229.
2   Kelly, 293.
3   Talwar, 278.
4   Ibid., 73.
5   Ibid., 80.

CHAPTER FOURTEEN
1   https://www.hausmanmarketin-
    gletter.com/marketing-strategy-
    4ps-marketing/
2   Kelly, 185.
3   Middleton, 76.
4   Ibid., Introduction.
5   http://www.autopoint.com/blog/
    millennials-love-these-five-compa-
    nies#.V8xkWZMrLIE.
6   Talwar, 357.
7   Kelly, 190.
8   Talwar, 216.
9   Kelly, 68, 73.
10 Ibid., 191.
11 Talwar, 165.
12 Talwar, 44.

CHAPTER FIFTEEN
1   https://hbr.org/2014/07/the-ulti-
    mate-marketing-machine.
2   Pine and Gilmore, 7.
3   Middleton, 122.
4   Houle, 99.
5   Pink, 143.
6   Houle, 211-212.
7   Pink, 60-61.
8   http://www.razorfish.com/bina-
    ries/content/assets/ideas/the_fu-
    ture_marketing_organization.pdf
9   http://www.mckinseyonmarketin-
    gandsales.com/sites/default/files/
    pdf/McKinsey-CMSO-Marketing-
    Org-of-the-Future.pdf.
10 Talwar, 380.
11 Diamandis and Kotler, 218.

CHAPTER SIXTEEN
11 Case, 69.
164 http://www.inc.com/maga-
    zine/20080601/the-customer-is-
    the-company_pagen_1.html
2   http://www.inc.com/maga-
    zine/20080601/the-customer-is-
    the-company.html, 2008

3   https://www.threadless.com/info-about/.
4   https://evhippel.mit.edu/.
5   Gary Vaynerchuk, *The Thank You Economy* (New York: Harper Business, 2011), 233.
6   Middleton, 124.
7   Ibid., 131-132.
8   http://www.adweek.com/news/advertising-branding/marketers-need-embrace-peer-peer-activities-149783.
9   Pine and Gilmore, 4-5.
10 http://www.adweek.com/news/advertising-branding/marketers-need-embrace-peer-peer-activities-149783.
11 http://www.adweek.com/news/advertising-branding/marketers-need-embrace-peer-peer-activities-149783?page=3.
12 Talwar, 376.
13 Kelly, 161.
14 Pine and Gilmore, 59.
15 Ibid., 72.
16 Ibid., 129.
17 Ibid., 44.

CHAPTER SEVENTEEN
1   Kelly, 295.

Index

3-D avatars 124
3-D printing xi, 45, 106,
    107, 191
  and marketing 107
4 Cs of marketing 216
4 Ps of marketing 215
  shortcomings of 215
7 Ps of marketing 216
2021, marketing in 142
2030, marketing in 179

A

abundance, future
  and marketing 109
Academy Awards 96
Act-On 66, 78
ad formats 197
ad hocracy 138
adjacent possible, the 39
Adobe
  Analytics 78
  Campaign 78
  DTM 78
  Target 79
Adrian, Merv 90
AdRoll 79
advertisements
  compared to content
    52
advertising 150, 201
  cost of TV ads 149
advertising networks 79
advocacy
  metrics for 163
agility 112
Airbnb 92, 98, 146, 226
Alibaba 146
alternative energy 38
Amazon 86, 89, 121, 264
  consumers contribut-
    ing to 89
  Web Services 188
ambient power 49
American Marketing As-
    sociation 19
analytics 219
Anderson, Sherry Ruth
    239
AOL 63

use of VR by 63
Apache Cocoon 91
Apache Hadoop 91
Apollo Space Program
    163
Applebee's 177
Apple Computer 33, 55,
    145, 146, 220
  appeal to Millennials
    221
  narrative of 169
artificial intelligence (AI)
    xii, 46, 49, 132, 157,
    159, 270
  and marketing 188
  beyond 2030 203
  cognitive enhancement
    with 158
  personal assistant 207
artificial marketing intel-
    ligence 181, 269
Attenborough, David 159
"Attract, Assist, Affiliate"
    model 166
Audi
  use of VR by 151
audience
  prosumers changing
    nature of 93
augmented reality (AR)
    xii, 11, 48, 123, 150,
    184, 203, 269, 270
  advantages over VR
    194
  defined 182
  in 2030 184
  marketing campaigns
    183
  potential of 182
authentic engagement
    150
authenticity 271
Autodesk 232
autonomous vehicles
    39, 48
A&W 177
awareness
  metrics for 163

B

Bailey, Paul 130, 140
banner ads 196
Bass Pro Shops Outdoor
    World 105

Benihana 257
Benkler, Yochai 129
Berners-Lee, Tim 157
betterness consumption
    paradigm 122
big data 90, 149, 155, 157,
    161, 231
  analytics 81
  definition of 80
  future of 82
Bitcoin 103
blogging 54, 99
  and content market-
    ing 57
BMW 250–255
Bonabeau, Eric 115
brain-net
  as successor to Inter-
    net 44
brain wave and thought
    connectivity 203,
    204
brain wave mapping 205
brand building 55
branded content 71
brand experience 228
branding guidelines 74
brand purpose 231
brands xii, 24, 71, 95, 130,
    145, 150, 175, 193,
    233, 260
  become platforms 146
  creative work by 175
  diminishment of 230
  future of 268
  in 2030 189
Brand, Stewart 198
brick-and-mortar 36
BrightEdge 79
Brinker, Scott 59
Bristol Farms Gourmet
    Specialty Foods
    Markets 258
Brown, John Seely 166
Bubba Gump Shrimp Co.
    257
Buckley, Yates 207
Buffer 56
Build-A-Bear Workshop
    258
Burns, Tom 249–254
business objectives 162
business strategy 14
business-to-business

(B2B) 25
business-to-consumer
   (B2C) 25, 37
buyer personas 72
Buzzfeed 175

C

Cabela's 105
Cain, Susan 235
Calthorpe, Peter 198
Canton, James
   futurist 46
capabilities 228
capitalism
   and the commons 135
Carrotmob Agency 259
car sharing 39
Case, Steve 246
   "Internet of Every-
      thing" 16
   The Third Wave 180
change
   embracing 143
   pace of 1, 271
channel orchestration
   30
chief content officer 241,
   242
chief experience officer
   242
chief marketing technol-
   ogist (CMT) 83
Chopra, Deepak 5
circular economy 15
   sustainability and 2
Cirque du Soleil 121
Cisco Systems 9, 186
cloud, the 16, 93
   and music 160
CMI-Marketing Profs
   study
   2016 26
Coca-Cola 107
cognification 16
cognitive enhancement
   158, 159, 268
Cold War 42
collaboration 138
collaboratism 129
collaborative commons
   102, 103, 133
   and marketing 103
   definition of 102

collaborative innova-
   tion networks
   (COINS) 118, 119
   growth of 119
collective consciousness
   interface technol-
   ogy 203, 206
collective intelligence
   211
collectivism 138
commons, the
   as alternative to capi-
      talism 134
community
   and collaborative com-
      mons 103
complexity
   theory of 43
computer software
   open source 90
computing, mobile
   4
computing power
   increases in 186
connectivity 36
consciousness
   enhanced 5
Constant Contact 79
consumer xi, 85–108,
   268
   compared to prosum-
      ers 85
content
   and brands 55
content analysis 33
content contributors
   management of 74
content creation
   by prosumers 175
content delivery net-
      works (CDN): 78
content development 71
content distribution ef-
      ficiencies 72
Content Launch 19
contentlaunch.com 60
content marketing 20,
   27, 190, 197
   as publishing 54
   defined 52, 53
   future of 52
   machine 56, 57
   practices 142
   retreat 19

success of 27
Content Marketing Con-
   ference 2016 3
Content Marketing Insti-
   tute (CMI) 25, 58
content marketing soft-
   ware
   benefits of 69
   functions of 67
   integration of 73
   investment in 73
Content Marketing World
   19
content promotion 59
content workflow
   management of 74
convergence 36, 189
   of Company and Cus-
      tomer 98
   technological 14
conversion optimiza-
   tion 78
conversion rate 191
Cook, Scott 165
cooperation 138
cost of living, future
   $10,000 annually 109
Coupland, Douglas 198
Craigslist 34, 131
creativity 235, 238, 239
   and future marketing
      188
   enhanced by
      lifestreams 97
   role in marketing 4
Cross-discipline teams
   239
crowdfunding 4, 130
crowdsourcing 4
Cruise, Tom 183
cryptocurrencies, digital
   103
cultural creatives 239
customer
   as prosumer 86
   contributing to market-
      ing 86
   engagement of xii, 122
   happiness of 9
   in 2030 189
customer-engagement
   council 240
customer insight analyt-
   ics 83

customer relationship management (CRM) 77, 80, 195
customization 37
cyborg 211

D

data, sharing as prosumers 94
data management platforms 78
Dave & Busters 121
Davison, Lang 166
Dawkins, Richard 146
Deer Park Buddhist Monastery 121
DeHart, Jacob 247
Dell Computer 34
design 4
designers 75
Diamandis, Peter H. 109, 115, 164, 244
    Abundance 10, 165, 180
digital marketing 26
digital marketing agencies 113
    future of 173
    prosumers and 173
discoverability 224
Disneyland 50
Disney, Walt
    and experiences 50
Disney World 220
Disruptor's Handbook 170
DoubleClick 79
Droga5 150
Drucker, Peter 25

E

Easterbrook, Greg 137
eBay 86, 107
Ed Debevic 257
efficiency 270
electronic paper 201
Ellen Macarthur Foundation 15
Eloqua 78
email
    and marketing 79
    and marketing automation 60
    click-through 71

holographic 124
    personalization 30
embodiment 224
Emfluence 79
empowerment 271
engagement 217
enhancement, human 14
Ensighten 78
EP^2 217, 227
ESPN 192
Etsy 98, 154
European Union 135
everyware 181
Exact Target 79
exascale computing 48
experience economy
    and prosumers 103
experiences
    and prosumers 104
    as entertainment 124
    as product 122
    as source of value 50
    at Pike Place Fish Market 125
    augmented 269
    live 150
    marketing and 220
    marketing of 121
    value of 104
experience stagers 104
exponential thinking 226

F

Facebook 8, 54-55, 58, 93, 99, 114, 145, 146-147, 151, 167, 183, 196, 213, 217-219
    ad campaigns on 79
    and Oculus VR 61
    as commune 89
    Creative Shop 175
Failure, redefining 163
Febreze 150
financial systems 14
FitBit 38, 96
Flickr 93
Flows 16
    four stages of 161
    Internet as 8
Fogel, Robert William 136
Ford Motors 33

Ford, Henry 193
Fourth Great Awakening 136
Frankl, Viktor 136
freelancers 75
Frey, Thomas 6, 48, 49
    futurist 47
future
    and marketing 1
    shape of 270
futurists 17, 41, 142
    pragmatism of 44
    predictions of 41

G

Gabor, Dennis
    Inventing the Future 43
Gannett
    use of VR by 62
Gap 259
Gates, Bill 164
Gelernter, David 96
General Electric 33
General Motors 91
Generation X 2
Generation Z 2, 52
generative services 223, 225
Gentzel, Kevin 63
geomarketing 190
geotargeting 190
Gershenfeld, Neil 198
Gesture-controlled gaming 4
Gilmore, James H. 122
    The Experience Economy 103
Gilovich, Thomas 122
Gioia, Joyce 185
GitHub 226
"gladvertising" 201
Gladwell, Malcolm 266
glasses
    virtual reality 185
global mind 210
Gloor, Peter 91, 118, 119
    Swarm Creativity 115
Goodson, Scott 148
Google 55, 114, 145, 146
    AdWords 79
    Analytics 78
    Android community 166
    Cardboard 64

Creative Lab 175
Glass 190
Knowledge Graph 157
Magenta 159
Play 189
Retargeting 79
Tag Manager 78
Ventures 226
GoPro 176
Gottdiener, Mark 262
government-to-business
    (G2B). 37
Greenleigh, Ian 260
Green movement 35
gross domestic product
    (GDP) 135
Grove, Andy 257
gShiftLabs 79

H

Hacienda Patrón Tequila
    Distillery
use of virtual reality
    62
Hagel, John 166, 169
    The Power of Pull 166
Halal, Bill 136
Halvorson, Kristina
    Content Strategy 58
Hard Rock Cafe 257
Harley Davidson 177
Harman, Sidney 236
Hassett Ace Hardware
    257
    Repair Cafe at 255, 256
Hearst Corporation 202
Heaton, Gavin 170
Hiler, Whit 176, 177
von Hippel, Eric 248
holograms 153, 182
    and]communications
    153
    and experiences 123
    and marketing 153
    and VR 152
    two-way connection 153
Home Depot 145
    HomeDepot.com 77
HootSuite 56
Houle, David 5, 12, 129,
    137, 148, 205, 206,
    235, 238
    Entering the Shift Age

5, 180
HubSpot 19, 66, 78
    Sidekick 77
Huffington Post 58
human aspiration 6
human interfaces 48
Hummingbird 157
hyper-targeting 190

I

IBM 158, 200
    Watson 158, 159
iHeartmedia 175
Ikea 85
influencers 59, 94, 95
    marketing 94
information society 33
infrastructure develop-
    ment
    future 38
Infusionsoft 78
Inglehart, Ronald 137
innovating to zero 36
Instagram 93, 167
Intelligent Content Con-
    ference 19
interconnectivity 185
interdependency 270
International Data Cor-
    poration 186
Internet 108, 148, 194
    control of 108
    flow of information
    on 8
    future value of 9
    organization of 8
Internet of Things (IoT)
    xi, 3, 36, 129, 133,
    156, 181, 185, 194,
    269, 270
    as technological com-
    mons 135
    self-diagnosing de-
    vices 195
    interpretation 224
interruptive commercial
    demise of 197
Intuit 19
Ion Interactive 79
iPhone 10, 32, 221
Ive, Tony
    and design 4

J

Janetsch, John 216
JD Edwards 111
Jenkins, Henry 87
Jobs, Steve 164, 235
    and design 4
Joel, Billy
    "Allentown" 33
Joe's Crab Shack 257
Jones, Shaun 198
Jordan's Furniture 258
Jouvenel, Bertrand de
    The Art of Conjecture
    43
Joy, Bill 176

K

Kaku, Michio 44
KarmaCRM 77
Kauffman, Stuart 39
Kelly, Kevin 23, 37, 46, 86,
    91, 96, 97, 99, 129,
    131, 138, 143, 146,
    161, 168, 186, 188,
    210, 218, 221, 223,
    261, 267
    discussion of flow by 9
    The Inevitable 15, 180
    What Technology
    Wants 40
Kennedy, John F. 163
Keynes, John Maynard
    132
Kickstarter 154
Kindle 265
Kjaer, Anne Lise 122, 225
Kmart 86, 154
Konica Minolta 19
Kotler, Philip 101, 142, 215
    Principles of Marketing
    24, 100
    theories upended 25
Kotler, Steven
    Abundance 165
Kramer, Bryan 3
Kurzweil, Ray 11, 18, 45,
    223

L

Lakhani, Karim 249–254
Landing Page Grader 79

Lanier, Jaron 198
Lavacon 19
lead generation 70, 75
LEGO 253, 254
Legoland 220
Lexus 200
  use of virtual reality 62
LG 202
lifestreams 97
  defined 96
  marketing impacts of 98
LinkedIn 167, 213
Linux 7, 114, 118
  open source model 90
  success of platform 90
Local Motors 226
Lombardo, Thomas 211
Louis Vuitton 255
Lululemon 154

M

machine-learning technology 156
Magisto 177
MailChimp 79
Malone, Thomas W. 231
marginal cost, zero 103, 131
marketers 31
  changing roles of 1
marketing
  and customer experience 29
  and design 55
  and social media 30
  and swarm intelligence 117
  and tech adoption 30
  automation platforms 66, 77
  budgets 27
  changes in xi
  changing consumers xi
  corporate buy-in 30
  cross-channel 30
  historical context of 23
  integrated 192
  leadership study 228
  non-zero-sum 114
  pull versus push 55

purpose-driven 59
purpose of 14
research and statistics 24
specialists 234
standard definition of 216
strategy 154
technology 142
trends 58
Marketing2020 study 231
marketing department
  future 5, 228
marketing framework
  future 216
marketing platforms
  mobile 30
marketing practice 143, 153
  and big data 80
  beyond 2030 203
  effect of post-capitalism on 139
  future of 268
  influence of data flow on 8
Marketing Profs B2B
  Forum 19
marketing teams 231
  structure of 240
Marketo 66, 78
Marriott
  use of virtual reality 62
  use of VR by 151
Marshall, Sir Colin 258
Mason, Paul
  Postcapitalism 138
mass customization 222
massive open online
  courses (MOOCs) 103
mass market
  future of 268
  vs. niche market 160
mass media 230
  future of 268
Mathieu, Mark 10
Maxymiser 79
Mazzocchi, Stefano 91
McCarthy, Jerome 215
McDonalds 145
Mead, Margaret 110

media
  and distribution 10
  and flows 162
media experience
  cost of 168
mega-trends 12, 32, 142, 269
  definition of 32
  of today 35
memejacking 148
memes and movements 146, 177
  and marketing 147
  replacing mass media 268
memory
  lifestreams and 97
Merrell
  use of VR by 151
microelectromechanical
  systems (MEMS) 181
Microsoft 34, 146
  Cyberspace 2025
    report 143
  HoloLens 48, 152, 153
Middleton, Daina 105, 218, 219, 233, 253, 254, 255
  and convergence culture 87
Millennial Generation 2, 52, 154, 221, 272
mindset
  influence of technology on 14
miniaturization 181
Minority Report 183, 200, 201
MIT 202, 255
Mitchell, William J. 199
mobile technology 194
Mondelez 60
Monetate 79
multi-sensory experiences 268
music 160

N

Naisbitt, John
  Megatrends 12, 32
narratives 225
  marketing as 41

vs. stories 169
native advertising 59
natural language 158
natural resources 14
NEC 200
need-based ads 197
Neisser, Drew 3
"New Coke" 154
New Media Expo 19
Newspapers 10
niche explosion 160, 268
Nickell, Jake 247
Nike 98, 239
  Nike+ 96
  use of VR by 151
Niketown 258
Nimble 66, 77
Nokia 107
Norman, Don
  *Things that Make Us
  Smart* 152

O

Occupy Wall Street 148
Oculus VR 48, 151
  Oculus Rift 64, 193
Ogilvy & Mather 159
Online Marketing Summit 19
online music
  prosumers and 92
open source 90, 103
  and big data 90
  developers 116
open-source developers
  91, 117
  swarm creativity and
  117
open-source movement
  and prosumers 90
Optimizely 78
Oracle 111
O'Reilly, Tim 88
organizational effectiveness 232
Organization for Economic Co-operation and Development 135
Orteig, Raymond 244

P

Page, Larry 46, 48
paid media 191
Pardot 78
partnering with peer-to-peer upstarts
  259
partnership
  consumer and company 89
passion 225
Patagonia 176
PayPal 146
pay-per-click 191
peer networks 112
peer-to-peer 25, 37, 110
  economy 3
  finance 103
peer-to-peer groups 111,
  112, 114, 120
  independence of 110
  replacing marketing
  agencies 113
People magazine 192
PeopleSoft 111
PepsiCo 60
Perfect Audience 79
performance analytics
  70
person
  redefinition of 272
personalization 37, 222,
  223, 224
personal metadata 205
pervasive computing 181
photovoltaics 39
Pichai, Sundar 188
Pike Place Fish Market
  lessons from 125
Piller, Frank 250–255
Pine, B. Joseph II 122,
  232, 257, 261
  *The Experience
  Economy* 103
Pink, Daniel 137, 152, 236,
  239
  A Whole New Mind 136
Pinterest 147
Pixlee 177
platform 145
  experience 228
  future of 268
  Web as 88
popups 196
Porter, Michael 145

Competitive Advantage 144
post-capitalism 7, 18, 128,
  137
  and marketing 18
  defined 128
predictive
  ads 197
  analytics 94
  data sets 188
  social media 196
principles of consumption 122
production metrics 70
production of online
  content
  by consumers 89
productivity
  of employees 9
profit motive
  and post-capitalism
  128
promotional messages 24
prosthetics
  social networks as 45
Prosumer Age 87, 101,
  129, 177, 219, 270
prosumers xi, 85–108,
  100, 149, 268
  and production 86
  compared to consumer
  7, 85
  motivation of 105
  peer-to-peer groups 110
  self-organization of 116
  Toffler's idea of 7
Prudential 150
psychology of marketing
  154
public health
  influence of lifestreams
  on 97
pull marketing 167
Punchdrunk Theater
  Production Company 254, 255
Push For Drama 150
push marketing 149

Q

quality of life 135
Quest International Users Group 111

question answering 158
Quirky 154, 226

R

Rainforest Café 204
rational choice 24
Ray, Paul 239
Raytheon 19
Reagan, Ronald 33
real-time collaboration
182
Recreational Equipment,
Inc. (REI) 105
Red Bull 176
Media House 60
reddit 147, 154
remarketing 79
renewable energy
prosumers and 92
retargeting 149
Return on Attention
(ROA)
compared to ROI 168
Rifkin, Jeremy 129, 130,
131, 133
description of prosum-
ers 87
*The Zero Marginal
Cost Society* 133
Robbins, Tony 5
Rose, Robert xii

S

sales
metrics for 163
Salesforce 66, 77
Salesforce.com 166
"State of Marketing"
report 28
Samsung 62
Gear 64
Samsung's
Game VR 48
Schema.org 157
Schmidt, Eric 45, 48, 49,
123, 124
The New Digital Age
180
Schmitt, Bernd 262
Schrage, Michael 165
Schwartz, Peter 198
Scitovsky, Tibor 104

Scott, Gray 212
search engine market-
ing 79
Search Marketing Expo
19
Sears 86
Sea World 220
self-actualization 133
self-check-in 92
self-determination
theory 105
self-monitoring 97
self-tracking 96
semantic economy 144
semantic search
AI-based 157
semantic Web 156,157,268
sensor technology
future of 49
services
as experiences 121
as products 121
shale gas 39
sharing economy 3, 37
SharpSpring 78
Shiv, Baba 164
Shop.org 19
Signal 78
Silverpop 78
Simonson, Alex 262
simulated care assistance
retreats 212
simulations
data-driven 156, 268
Sinclair, Tiana 221
Singularity, The 189
singularity movement
15
technological 11
Siri 4
skills 4
Skype 49
SlideShare 56
small groups
innovation by 111
Smarr, Larry
lifestreaming 97
smart grid 38
Smart, John 223
smartphones 11, 64, 148,
193
and prosumer culture
92
Smith, Adam

The Wealth of Nations
131
Snapchat 9
Snowden, Edward 221
social insects
model for peer-to-peer
groups 116
socialism 128
social media 148, 230
engagement with 218
presence 54
Social Media Marketing
World 19
social media platforms
advertising on 31
social media spending
ROI growth 31
social networking 145,
167, 225
software
access vs. ownership
of 86
as service 87
content marketing 66
South by Southwest 19
Southwest Airlines 220
Spielberg, Stephen 188
Minority Report 198
Spotify 124
Square 146
Stanislavski, Konstantin
126
Starbucks 55
experience at 126
status quo 1, 4
Stella Artois 255
stories
vs. narratives 169
storytelling 150, 152, 188,
225
future of 268
marketing as 41, 60
strategic planning 229,
268
strategy
content marketing 27
structure, corporate 17
SugarCRM 77
Sun Microsystems 176
supply chains 9
sustainable 44
swarm creativity 119
swarm intelligence 49
and marketing 115

T

tablets 193
tagging, and flow 9
tag management 78
Talwar, Rohit 9, 157, 184
  The Future of Business
     15, 180
Tangerine 226
Target 149, 219, 264
target marketing
  and lifestreams 98
TaskRabbit 256, 259
Tata Group 165
Tata, Ratan 165
Tealium 78
technological change
  impact of 12
technological unemploy-
     ment 132
Teilhard de Chardin,
     Pierre 137
Television 10
Tesla 226
  and open source 90
The New York Times 175
  use of VR by 63
The North Face
  use of VR by 152
The Wall Street Journal
     175
Thompson, Larry 237
thought leaders 94, 95
Threadless 246–251
Toffler, Alvin 16, 18, 32, 42
  electronic cottage 106
  invention of "prosum-
     ers" 7, 99, 106
  The Third Wave 6, 42,
     106
Torvalds, Linus 117
Tumblr 147
Twitter 8, 37, 38, 54, 56,
     93, 95, 147, 154,
     167, 196

U

Uber 7, 92, 98, 101, 113,
     144, 146, 256
  and low marginal costs
     101
ubiquitous Internet 269
uncertainty

Bayesian 155
Unilever 259
United Nations 135
United States Air Force
  use of virtual reality 62
urbanization 35
User groups 112
US Steel 33

V

value for many 37
value networks 144
values and goals 228
Valve 226
Van Boven, Leaf 122
Vaynerchuk, Gary 251
  The Thank You Econo-
     my 251
video 59
  viral 59
video production
  by consumers 88
virtual reality (VR) xii, 11,
     48, 60, 62, 64, 150,
     151, 152, 203, 270
  and content market-
     ing 60
  cost of production 63
  future of 268
  production cost 151
Voice recognition 4
Volkswagen 107
Volvo
  use of VR by 151
VR/AR "suit" 185

W

Walmart 149, 219
Walt Disney World 50
Wearable mobile devices
     46
Web 2.0 88, 93, 156, 225,
     230, 249–254, 268
Web 3.0 156
Web, World Wide 99
  as flow 143
  mobile xi
  social Web xi, 8
WeChat 9, 146
Whalen, James 111
WhatsApp 9
Whittington, Alexandra

223
Wikipedia 88, 93, 114
Winfrey, Oprah 5
Wired magazine
  and reader participa-
     tion 99
wireless communication
     technology 185
WordStream 79
workforce 14
Wright, Travis 76
Wuebben, Jon
  at 2016 Content Mar-
     keting Confer-
     ence 3
  contact information 20
  Content is Currency:
     Developing Pow-
     erful Content for
     Web and Mobile
     2, 19, 274
  Content Launch 217
  contentlaunch.com 60
  Content Rich 274
  Future Marketing:
     Winning in the
     Prosumer Age.
     xii, 2, 13, 18, 52, 95,
     133, 142, 179
  influence of Alvin
     Toffler 6
  marketing defined by
     216

X

X Prize Foundation 244

Y

Yelp 149
You Tube 93
YouTube 54, 56, 62, 88,
     89, 160, 179, 189
  Studio 175

Z

zero marginal cost 131
Zuckerberg, Mark 48,
     145, 164
Zumba
  use of VR by 151